FRONT ROW SEAT
AT THE CIRCUS

One journalist's journey through two presidential elections

www.mascotbooks.com

Front Row Seat at the Circus

For more information, please contact:
Mascot Books
560 Herndon Parkway #120
Herndon, VA 20170
info@mascotbooks.com

Library of Congress Control Number: 2015915273

CPSIA Code: PBANG1015A
ISBN-13: 978-1-63177-332-7

Printed in the United States

TABLE OF CONTENTS

DEDICATION

My parents Rol and Doris Heath gave me a tape recorder and movie camera at the age of five and encouraged my love of presidential history and television news from the beginning.

I miss you, Pop. And this is for you, Mom.

Acknowledgements

Thank you to the presidential candidates—and their staffs—for agreeing to the interviews, making this book possible.

Personal thanks to Tom Griesdorn, Elbert Tucker, Greg Fisher, Paul Heebink, Bruce Kirk, Billy Huggins and Victoria Spechko for giving me the opportunity to work in television, and thanks to all of my colleagues who I had the honor of working with in Ohio, South Carolina, and Arizona.

Many kudos to my publisher Mascot Books and CEO Naren Aryal who loved the concept of this book from the start. It was a pleasure collaborating with you, Meghan Reynolds, Christin Perry, and the entire Mascot team!

Thanks as well to my personal editor Pat Holt, along with Brad Dean, CEO and President of the Myrtle Beach Area Convention and Visitors Bureau, for their incredible support and friendship through the years.

Thanks Mom for being incredibly supportive and for providing me the space (the desk with piles of old scripts, tapes, newspapers—and that view of the lake!) to finish this book.

Also thanks to my brothers Mick and Bill and sister Marianne who helped fine-tune my interview skills over many years by taking part in the hundreds of Heath Family News tapes we recorded while growing up.

Special recognition to my fellow statehouse reporters across the land who work long hours every day to shine light on what our taxpayer-funded officials are doing. A big shout-out to all of those involved in the political arena—on the right and the left and in the center—willing to battle it out election after election for their ideals. If that debate ever ends, our Republic ceases to exist.

And, finally, hats off to the founders of this nation, who put into place a delicate but wonderful balance between politicians and the press.

"Our liberty depends on the freedom of the press, and that cannot be limited without being lost." -Thomas Jefferson.

It fascinates me that it manages to still work.

PROLOGUE

At noon on Wednesday February 13, 1861, a crushing crowd of about 60,000 greeted the former one-term congressman at the train depot in Columbus, Ohio. A thirty-four gun salute announced that Abraham Lincoln, who had just grown a beard for the first time after a young admirer encouraged him to do so, was near.

Lincoln exited the train and the crowd roared its approval. He then smiled and bowed his head, acknowledging the reception. With exceptional weather for a winter day, the streets of Columbus were packed as Lincoln made his way to the Ohio Statehouse welcomed by lawmakers and Governor William Dennison.

Perhaps tired after a full day of shaking hands at stops across Ohio, Lincoln shocked nearly everyone by offering overly optimistic remarks— "It is a good thing that there is no more anxiety, for there is nothing going wrong."—even as the winds of civil war stirred.

Lincoln was handed a telegram around 4:30 that afternoon while standing in the stateroom in the governor's office. He read it, quietly folded it and placed it in his pocket. He then smiled and remarked, "What a beautiful building you have here, Governor Dennison."

History learned that the telegram had informed Lincoln the Electoral College had certified his election and he was now officially the President-elect of the United States.

Now, 150 years later, I was seated in that very room at the Ohio statehouse where Lincoln had stood. I was about to interview famed presidential historian Doris Kearns Goodwin, who had written *Team of Rivals: The Political Genius of Abraham Lincoln;* arguably, the best Lincoln book of all time.

With three cameras rolling we discussed presidential leadership and what made Honest Abe so exceptional:

"If Lincoln had allowed the South to go, then the framers' whole experiment would have been undone," she said. "The idea that ordinary people can govern themselves, that's what the framers counted on. This was an era of monarchs and dictators and the idea that you could just let people govern themselves seemed very strange and it's what's so great about America. Lincoln made it possible, and he knew that's what he was fighting for. Lincoln saves the Union, wins the war, and ends slavery forever."

Twenty minutes to discuss Lincoln and various other presidents was not enough. I was wearing a tie that featured all their faces from Washington to Obama and there was no way to get to them all.

My love of presidential history started over forty years earlier at my Grandma Heath's house in Van Wert, Ohio.

In the late 1960s she had spent months collecting a set of miniature U.S. presidents from the local Kroger grocery store, which had been releasing a new one each week. She hand-numbered them, and when I was just two, she let me play with them alongside the little green plastic soldiers and dinosaurs in the bathtub. Thanks to those statues, my mom likes to tell everyone I learned the names of the presidents before I learned the alphabet.

When we left Ohio and moved to Arizona, my Grandma gave me the set of presidents to take along. As a kid I would stage mock debates— think Andrew Jackson versus Abraham Lincoln, (how awesome would that be?)—and used the presidents as newscasters on the "news sets" I made out of my Lego blocks (Jefferson was great on weather because his arm stretched out as if pointing to a map.)

The figurines—made by the Marx toy company—still sit proudly on my refrigerator at home to this day. Occasionally they make a special appearance on my Facebook page.

Weird, I know.

But from then until now, there is nothing I enjoy more than studying and debating presidential history.

There was a point during my interview with Kearns Goodwin that it hit me: I've been face-to-face with all the modern-day Americans who want to be president! From the first-in-the-south primary state of South Carolina in 2008, to the biggest and most historically important general election battleground state of Ohio in 2012.

A flood of memories about those experiences came into my head and I asked myself, "How many Americans have looked these leaders in the eye and asked them about the future of our country?" And then I thought, you should put all these memories and experiences in a book.

So here we are.

In the coming pages I'll take you on a behind-the-scenes look at my sit-down interviews with everybody from Obama to Romney to McCain to Clinton to Rubio to Biden and more.

We'll explore why Ohio is THE battleground state each presidential election year, and why South Carolina matters so much in the early primary process.

I'll also offer some insight into the television news business, and weigh in on the often-debated issue of media bias.

Truth be told, I'm a journalist who loves politics and covering the politicians. With rare exception (and I'll name names later), I have respected and liked the many public officials I've covered.

From the campaign rallies, to the interviews, to the national conventions, to election nights, here is my inside look at two national elections, from two pivotal states, from one television journalist's perspective: My Front Row Seat At The Circus.

PART ONE:
PALMETTO STATE

FROM BLUE TO RED

There is nothing in life quite as beautiful as looking up and staring at a palmetto tree slightly swaying in the breeze with a bright crescent moon behind it in the sky. There's a reason why that scene is featured prominently on the South Carolina state flag—the best designed flag in the country in my view.

Those palmetto trees are strong too, withstanding the brutal impact of British cannonballs during the Revolutionary War. And they've stood tall while hundreds of presidential candidates have journeyed around the state hoping a primary win will propel them to the White House.

It's an absolutely perfect place for political junkies and journalists to be situated heading into any presidential election year. Why? It sure beats the weather in January up North. Think blue sky and palmetto trees versus black ice and deep snow. While my fellow political reporters in early 2004 and 2008 were chasing around the presidential candidates in Iowa and New Hampshire wearing their wool coats, scarfs, and winter boots, I was enjoying life living on the beach.

Literally.

My place in Myrtle Beach was only a block away from the Atlantic Ocean with access to some of the finest beaches in the United States. My job was to show up at 3 p.m. each day to anchor the nightly 6, 7, and 11 p.m. news. That left a whole lot of time, even with covering presidential candidates all over the state, for some quality beach time each morning.

It was a tough life but somebody had to do it.

Myrtle Beach Days! We'll have some fun in the waves, I don't care what the West Coast says, But I love those Myrtle Beach, love those Myrtle Beach Days!

This song by the Fantastic Shakers captures the spirit of the Grand Strand perfectly! Southern hospitality is no joke. People are always smiling, they welcome you into their home or business, and drivers don't ride right on your bumper the way they do in those big northern cities like

New York and Chicago. And the sweet tea? Sweet, sweet perfection. Just don't plan on losing any weight.

What I witnessed during my six years in South Carolina between two presidential cycles was the rapid growth of seriousness with which Palmetto State voters take their role in the presidential primary nominating process. Since 1980, South Carolina has been the first-in-the-south primary for Republicans—Democrats since 1988—following the Iowa Caucus and New Hampshire primary on the presidential campaign calendar.

Home to about five million people, the Palmetto State is divided into four media markets. The heavily populated and politically ultra-conservative upstate (Greenville-Spartanburg), the more moderate Midlands (Columbia), the fast-growing "outsiders" population of the Grand Strand (Myrtle Beach), and the libertarian-leaning Lowcountry (Charleston).

When you add those four regions up politically, you have a state that has become dependable in recent years for GOP presidential candidates by about a 55 to 45 percent margin.

But here's the fascinating thing: For nearly 150 years, if I had stood and said there was a Republican advantage in South Carolina, I would have been laughed and/or booed right off the stage. It would have been completely inaccurate.

That is what makes the history of this early primary state so interesting for politicos to study today.

A long time ago in a galaxy far, far away...

South Carolina was a dependable "blue" state. For over 100 years—starting in 1829 with the first Democratic presidential candidate Andrew Jackson, who was born in the Waxhaw region of the Carolinas—Democrats could almost always count on its electoral votes.

South Carolinians through the decades backed a variety of losing Democratic presidential candidates such as Stephen A. Douglas, who lost to the first Republican president Abraham Lincoln. William J. Bryan, who lost twice to William McKinley and once to William Howard Taft. Alton

Parker who lost to Theodore Roosevelt. Alfred E. Smith who won just a handful of states against Herbert Hoover. And South Carolina never liked Ike, choosing instead Adlai Stevenson twice in 1952 and 1956.

Voters also backed winning Democratic candidate Woodrow Wilson twice, John F. Kennedy in 1960, and Jimmy Carter in 1976. What is really mind blowing is that South Carolina backed the liberal icon of the last century—Franklin D. Roosevelt—not once, not twice, not three times, but all four times he was on the ballot.

Now that is a long and loyal tradition of voting for Democratic presidential nominees.

So what happened?

Two words: Strom Thurmond.

Okay, it may be impossible to put regional political realignment on one person. But let me present the case that Thurmond had more to do with the South going from solidly blue to solidly red—in record-breaking speed I may add—than any other politician in America.

The battle over civil rights legislation reached its crescendo in 1964 when President Lyndon Johnson, a southerner from Texas, put his signature on the Civil Rights Act. When he was finished he remarked to his press secretary Bill Moyers: "I think we just delivered the South to the Republican Party for a long time to come."

That is exactly what happened.

In reaction to LBJ's backing of civil rights, Thurmond dramatically abandoned the Democratic party and re-registered as a Republican. Then the next crop of southern leaders, and voters, grew up in the GOP. As a result, South Carolina—and the other southern states—has not backed a Democratic candidate for president in decades.

So, who was Strom Thurmond? His political influence still casts a very big shadow over generations of South Carolinians. He was a U.S. senator from 1954 until his retirement in 2003. Before that, he was the governor of South Carolina for four years. Turn back the clock before 1950 and he was a county attorney for eight years followed by five years in the state legislature. Add to that his military service in World War II—which resulted in eighteen decorations, medals, and awards—and you have one of the lengthiest public service resumes in American history.

In 2003, when he died at the age of 100, South Carolina came to a halt. My station interrupted ABC's afternoon programming to broadcast Thurmond's funeral live. My co-anchor Allyson Floyd and I were on the set in our studio in Myrtle Beach with our reporter stationed in Columbia where the funeral was being held. We spent nearly three hours on the air non-stop discussing his life and legacy.

Incidentally, there were a couple of things explained to me, after I arrived from Arizona, about being a news anchor in the South. First, we would never forget to cover and mention Confederate Memorial Day, celebrated each year in South Carolina on May 10th. It's a day set aside to honor those who died fighting for the "Confederate States of America" during the "War between the States." That leads to the second thing, where I was warned to be careful not to call our nation's bloodiest conflict the "Civil War," a term to which many southerners still take offense. I was always respectful of southern heritage, but it did not stop me from mentioning often that, in my view, Abraham Lincoln was the greatest American who ever walked the face of the Earth.

Thurmond remains a beloved figure in South Carolina because just about everyone has a personal story or photograph with him. For decades he shook hands, and stopped and posed for pictures with families and school children all across the state and on Capitol Hill. Perhaps most importantly, he brought back home a lot of money. Thanks to Thurmond, South Carolina received more discretionary federal funds than any other state—think up to $10 return for every $1 paid. Talk about bringing home the bacon.

But besides the posing for pictures, shaking hands, and the federal funds—it's clear Strom Thurmond affected not just one state or one region, but the entire nation as he forever changed presidential campaign strategy.

Part of his legacy was the recruitment of a new generation of Republican operatives—often tutored personally by Thurmond—including South

Carolina's Lee Atwater who perfected the GOP's new "southern strategy" in the 1980s. His tactics, while controversial and often accused of having racial overtones, were remarkably effective. In 1981, after working on Ronald Reagan's landslide against southerner Jimmy Carter, Atwater acknowledged in an interview that the theme of GOP campaigns in the recent past had hurt African Americans:

"You start out in 1954 by saying, 'Nigger, nigger, nigger.' By 1968 you can't say 'nigger' — that hurts you, backfires. So you say stuff like forced busing, states' rights, and all that stuff, and you're getting so abstract. Now, you're talking about cutting taxes, and all these things you're talking about are totally economic things and a byproduct of them is, blacks get hurt worse than whites. And subconsciously maybe that is part of it. I'm not saying that, but I'm saying that if it is getting that abstract, and that coded, that we are doing away with the racial problem one way or the other. You follow me — because obviously sitting around saying, 'We want to cut this' is much more abstract than even the busing thing, and a hell of a lot more abstract than 'Nigger, nigger.'"

Seven years later, Atwater put his theory to work as the mastermind behind Vice President George H. W. Bush's campaign. During the summer of 1988, when Democratic nominee Michael Dukakis jumped up seventeen points over Bush in polls, Atwater created one of the most negative presidential campaigns in history. The Bush team linked Dukakis to a black convicted murderer who had escaped from a Massachusetts prison while on a weekend furlough and then raped a white woman and stabbed her husband. Pay no attention to the fact that the Reagan administration had its own furlough horror stories in the federal prison system. For whatever reason, Dukakis refused to respond and Willie Horton became the subject of now infamous pro-Bush TV ads that doomed his candidacy. Atwater said of Dukakis at the time he would "strip the bark off the little bastard" and "make Willie Horton his running mate."

In 1991, the forty-year-old Atwater, now chairman of the Republican National Committee, who had done so much to modernize the GOP "southern strategy," was at home dying from brain cancer. Reflecting on his campaign tactics he publicly apologized to Dukakis: "I am sorry for both statements: the first for its naked cruelty, the second because it makes me sound racist, which I am not."

Dukakis accepted the apology but it did not erase the historical fact that the Horton tactic worked and Bush crushed Dukakis in the popular and electoral votes by such huge margins that they have not been surpassed in any subsequent presidential elections.

But to fully understand what Thurmond pulled off in the South you must roll back the clock decades and study the entire record.

In 1948, Democratic president Harry Truman of Missouri, who used the "n" word in speeches and was not exactly known for racial sensitivity, became outraged at the murder and assaults on dozens of African-American veterans of World War II. As a result—and with an eye on the black votes he needed from northern cities in the coming election—he formed a Civil Rights Commission. Over time, he ordered the end of economic discrimination, racial discrimination in the Army, the end of state poll taxes, and he pushed for new federal anti-lynching laws.

Thurmond, then the Democratic governor of South Carolina, was outraged. When the pro-civil rights language was included in the party platform that summer, he led a walkout at the Democratic National Convention and announced the creation of the "Dixiecrats" party.

Just imagine that scene for a second. A group of delegates and elected officials tell the incumbent president—and leader of their party—to stick it over race issues, and walk out of the national convention to form an alternative party. In today's instant media world, the chaos from such an action would almost certainly spell instant doom for that president and party.

But Thurmond did it.

The "States' Rights Democratic Party", which he led, wanted white supremacy to continue and Jim Crow laws to remain. The Dixiecrats' platform backed racism: "We stand for the segregation of the races and the racial integrity of each race..." while promoting anti-Federal Government themes still familiar today: "We favor home-rule, local self-government, and a minimum interference with individual rights."

Thurmond, using the Confederate battle flag as a symbol of his new party, failed to qualify for the ballot in enough states to have a realistic chance at winning. Still, he earned over a million votes nationwide by spewing remarkably racist rhetoric:

"I wanna tell you, ladies and gentlemen, that there's not enough troops in the army to force the southern people to break down segregation and admit the Nigra race into our theaters, into our swimming pools, into our homes, and into our churches."

In an upset win, Truman managed to hold on and beat Republican nominee Thomas Dewey in the election despite Thurmond carrying four states in the South—Louisiana, Alabama, Mississippi, and South Carolina—and thirty-nine electoral votes. The election was so close that had Dewey carried Ohio and Illinois—he lost each by less than 1 percent of the vote—it would have forced the election to the House of Representatives. There, the Dixiecrats believed they could broker a deal to eliminate all of the civil rights gains.

Thurmond was "thisclose" to dictating drastic changes and perhaps setting the racial equality debate back decades. The 1948 election was the first signal that the Democratic stronghold on the South was cracking and Thurmond was in front doing the hammering.

Nearly a decade later Thurmond, now a U.S. senator and back in the Democratic Party, stood on the Senate floor and delivered the longest filibuster in American history—twenty-four hours and eighteen minutes—in opposition to the Civil Rights Act of 1957. His filibuster failed. The legislation was ultimately approved 72 to 18 in the Senate and signed into law by President Eisenhower.

Seven years later, when President Lyndon Johnson signed the Civil Rights Act of 1964, Thurmond had stomached all the legislation about race he could stand. Once and for all, he renounced his membership in the Democratic Party and became a Republican. He then endorsed Senator Barry Goldwater for president and while Johnson won that year in a landslide, Goldwater—who had voted against the act—managed to carry five states in the Deep South, the first Republican to do so since Reconstruction.

That feat gave pause to leaders of both parties and left Thurmond,

America's newest Republican senator, smiling.

A quick side note here about Barry Goldwater. As a college student at the age of twenty I emceed the final appreciation dinner for Goldwater, held in Lake Havasu City, Arizona, before he retired from public life. The 1964 Republican presidential nominee had become an icon in Arizona and around the nation.

During the dinner, seated next to him, I asked about his vote on the 1964 Civil Rights Act and whether he regretted voting against it. Goldwater, who led the integration of the Arizona Air National Guard and was a member of the NAACP, pointed out that he had supported earlier civil rights bills, including the one in 1957 which Thurmond had filibustered, and other previous bills his opponent Lyndon Johnson had not, but by 1964 he felt, if left up to the basic intelligence of the American people, racism would be eliminated without further legislation. He did not believe smart business owners would turn away commerce or economic opportunity because of one's skin color. He then shook his head and said perhaps he had been overly optimistic.

Goldwater, unlike Thurmond, did not oppose the 1964 Civil Rights bill on racial grounds. He was a libertarian at heart on issues of race and religion and on this one he made a principled mistake in my view.

By 1968, Goldwater was putting distance between himself and Thurmond, declining to write a foreword for Thurmond's book, *The Faith We Have Not Kept*. Goldwater specifically cited Thurmond's continuing hostility to the Brown v. Board of Education decision.

In later years, perhaps in a way to make up for the civil rights vote, Goldwater embraced gay rights—one of the first Republicans or Democrats to do so—and also supported a woman's right to choose an abortion and backed the legalization of medical marijuana.

Goldwater didn't care about polls, or what the extreme elements in his own party would say about him. He just did what he felt was right. Of all the public servants I've been around and covered through many years, Barry Goldwater remains the finest statesman I've ever met.

Back to Thurmond, whose influence in his new party continued to grow. In 1968, Richard Nixon was the frontrunner for the GOP presidential nomination and found himself in Miami at the Republican National Convention a handful of delegates short of securing the nomination on the first ballot. That was critical because he feared a second round of voting would favor California governor Ronald Reagan.

Under pressure, needing those last few delegates, Nixon met with Thurmond and made several promises. First, he would appoint "strict constructionists" to the federal judiciary. He also promised he would name a southerner to the Supreme Court (in fact as president he would nominate two southern judges, Clement Furman Haynsworth, Jr. of South Carolina and George Harrold Carswell of Georgia, for the seat of Justice Abe Fortas, but neither were confirmed by the Senate. Later, Judge Lewis Powell of Virginia was confirmed for another vacancy.) Next, Nixon assured Thurmond he would oppose court-ordered busing. Finally, he agreed to choose from a list of five people (Spiro T. Agnew was on the list and was chosen) to be his running mate.

With a deal in hand, Nixon's nomination was secured, and he received 264 of 356 southern delegates.

Four years after switching from a Democrat to a Republican, Strom Thurmond was clearly running the show.

Lifelong Republicans like Jackie Robinson, the first African American ballplayer in the major leagues who had supported Richard Nixon in 1960 calling him "a champion of civil rights" refused to do so eight years later. He claimed Nixon had "sold out" to Thurmond and "really prostituted himself to get the southern vote." Nixon had received 32 percent of the black vote nationally in 1960, but that dropped to only 12 percent in 1968 according to Gallup. Meanwhile, his support from southern states increased from 49 percent in 1960 to 71 percent by 1972.

Over the next two decades, support for southern Democratic candidates at the local level deteriorated substantially and a new generation of candidates started running as Republicans. This remarkable political realignment is striking when you visually compare the 1860 election map, and the states won by the first Republican presidential candidate Abraham Lincoln, with the 2012 map and those states won by Republican Mitt Romney. They are completely opposite. Or take a look at the states won by Democrat John F. Kennedy in 1960 and those won by Democrat Barack Obama in 2012. Again, almost completely opposite (Florida, the non-southern southern state, did its own thing in both elections).

You don't have to tell former vice president Al Gore, a southerner, any of this. Had he carried his home state of Tennessee and its eleven electoral votes in 2000—a state he and his father had represented in the U.S. Senate for decades—he would have garnered over 270 electoral votes and been elected president regardless of any recount in Florida.

"I know I'll spend time in Tennessee and mend some fences, literally and figuratively," Gore said on the night he conceded the race to George W. Bush.

President Ronald Reagan said many times, "I didn't leave the Democratic Party, the Democratic Party left me." In many ways the South could say the same thing. As the Democratic Party became more liberal on civil rights issues—once trumpeted by Lincoln and Republicans—the conservative South rebelled. That rebellion, led by Thurmond, flipped the modern political landscape upside down.

Abe Lincoln, the first Republican presidential winner, would never have dreamed of carrying a southern state. Today, a Republican presidential candidate wouldn't dream of a strategy to 270 electoral votes without winning all of them.

Thurmond, who continued to serve as a GOP senator for nearly forty years, never said he regretted his views on racial segregation but, perhaps ironically, his family confirmed after his death that he had impregnated a sixteen-year-old black girl when he was twenty-two. Despite his decades of opposition to race equality, he was secretly making payments to his black daughter who went on to earn a master's degree and become a public school teacher.

War hero, backer of Jim Crow laws, "family values" conservative who fathered an illegitimate black daughter, Democrat, Republican, lifelong taxpayer-funded politician who bemoaned big government, Thurmond was a fascinating political dichotomy if there ever was one.

The national Republican Party today remains perplexed by the Thurmond legacy. Senate GOP leader Trent Lott was forced to resign his post in 2002 after he said the nation "wouldn't have had all these problems over all these years" had Thurmond beat Truman and won on that Dixie-crat platform in 1948. That created a huge firestorm and renewed debate among Republicans on how to address race and minority voters.

In 2005 the chairman of the Republican National Committee publicly acknowledged the Democrats had offered "something real" to the black community in 1964 and the GOP had used the political shift in the South based on race for their electoral advantage. Ken Mehlman offered this apology to members of the NAACP:

"Some Republicans gave up on winning the African-American vote, looking the other way or trying to benefit politically from racial polar-ization. I am here today as the Republican chairman to tell you we were wrong."

None of this means all southern white voters today who back the GOP do so only because of race. It would be silly and incorrect to generalize it like that. As new generations come along, debate over racial equality becomes less intense as rights for all people become reality. In addition, the philosophical battle between those who favor more power for the Federal Government and those who favor more rights for states is as old as our nation itself. It should also be noted that the governor of South Carolina today, Nikki Haley, is of Indian American descent, while one of the state's two U.S. Senators, Tim Scott, is African American. Both are Republican.

But the South today in the post-Thurmond era still remains the most religious and evangelical region in the nation. Cultural issues—from race, to same-sex marriage, to continued debate on the meaning of sym-bols like the Confederate flag—will continue to pull GOP presidential candidates to the right in order to secure the nomination.

Considering the Republican Party's origin is rooted deeply in racial equality—and in its first president Abraham Lincoln—one has to wonder if the GOP can find a way back to appealing to minority voters in the South and elsewhere as their numbers increase and become critical to winning national elections in the decades ahead.

Titans in the Arena

Despite the fact South Carolina is not competitive in the general election, the state remains key for both parties early in the year. Its first-in-the-south primary can give a significant boost to the winning candidates while sending home many of the losers.

Election year 2008, which I covered in South Carolina, was unique because not since 1952 had there not been either a presidential or vice-presidential incumbent from either party on the ballot. That meant both parties were about to engage in a political free-for-all to determine their nominee.

There was a lot on the line for South Carolina Republicans who, since 1980, had correctly picked the eventual GOP nominee. Newt Gingrich would put a stop to that winning streak in 2012—as we will discuss later—but for 2008 it was still a coveted prize.

For presidential candidates, the year leading up to the first caucus and primaries is filled with many hours of fundraising and endless trips to Iowa, New Hampshire, and South Carolina. Those three states—one Midwest, one Northern, and one Southern—hold the power to weed out most of the candidates.

Too bad Iowa is first on that list.

Yes, I just said that. Having grown up a political geek I've always been less than impressed with a caucus. It's not a real election but rather a time-consuming circus of wheeling and dealing dominated by political activists.

Having watched the Iowa caucus process on C-SPAN since my teenage years, let me explain it as quickly as I can:

Inside an elementary school gym (or some other public building) participants head off to corners of the room to publicly show their support for a candidate. Undecided voters form their own group and stand in their own corner. Then speeches are given by supporters of all the candidates in an attempt to move the undecided to their camp (and make sure their own supporters don't bolt to a different candidate), much like herding cats. When a vote is taken and a candidate does not receive 15 percent of the vote (this applies to Democrats only) they are removed, but their supporters can then join another group. After several hours of wooing and voting, a final vote is taken and the group with the most people still in the room wins.

I am not making this up.

Prior to 1972, most national convention delegates were chosen by the caucus system but over time, voters realized the process was not fair and demanded change. By 2008 only 10 percent of Democratic delegates and 15 percent of Republicans were chosen by a caucus.

So why in the world is the Iowa caucus still leading our presidential selection process?

I once asked that question to former Iowa governor Tom Vilsack on my television show *Capitol Square*. The topic turned into a ten-minute debate on the merits of the caucus system. I rarely engage guests this way but, as you can tell, this whole Iowa thing has had me worked up since my little presidential statues started debating it when I was ten.

Vilsack, who was also our Agriculture Secretary, politely argued the caucus system goes back to the beginning of our nation. It allows unknown candidates to come from nowhere with strong organizational and people skills. Without Iowa, he pointed out, Democrats may not have had Barack Obama as the nominee in 2008.

That may or may not be true. What is certain is that the Iowa caucus is not a one-person one-vote system. Fewer voters participate because the process takes hours to complete. I mean hours and hours on a weeknight! So party activists (I'd use "hacks" but don't really care for that word) are in large part doing the voting and deciding.

In my view, Iowa, which is making millions of dollars from the candidates and the worldwide attention it receives, should lead the process only if it switches to a primary. Otherwise, New Hampshire should go first.

Vilsak smiled at that suggestion and said no. We agreed to disagree and the debate about the Iowa caucus goes on.

New Hampshire, by the way, has been a great start to our presidential selection process. What political junkie has not stayed up until midnight on Election Day to watch the first returns come in from Hart's Location or Dixville Notch? Doing so every four years is a bit of Americana.

I'm always reminded of New Hampshire when I hear the voice of Martin Gabel as he begins to narrate *The Making of the President 1960* the famous documentary based on the classic book of the same name by political journalist Theodore H White:

"It was invisible as always. High in the hills of New Hampshire as the clock passed midnight, the citizens of Hart's Location gathered to fit together the first fragments of the mystery. Before the clock came around again, sixty-eight million other Americans would join these first twelve voters to give the answer."

The Granite State forces presidential candidates to interact for months—sometimes years—with real voters. And on primary election day citizens weigh in, not in some convoluted caucus system, but by casting a single vote for a single candidate.

New Hampshire leaders haven't been overly pleased with the comparison to Iowa and its caucus either. Former governor John Sununu once said, "The people of Iowa pick corn, the people of New Hampshire pick presidents."

Sure, it is true New Hampshire has not been a perfect barometer in how the primary fight will end. Democrats, as an example, picked Hillary Clinton in 2008 (Barack Obama would go on to win the nomination) and Republicans chose Pat Buchanan over eventual nominee Bob Dole in 1996.

"Now I know why they call this the Granite State, because it's so hard to crack," a frustrated Dole told supporters after losing the New Hampshire primary for a third time.

Yet it is in the way New Hampshirites take the process so seriously that impresses me most. And in political terms you could not ask for a better statewide split among registered Independents, Democrats, and Republicans.

There is the reality, however, that New Hampshire—94 percent white—lacks diversity, especially as our Hispanic and Latino population grows nationwide. That will lead to debate soon on whether several primaries—

perhaps regional—should be held on Opening Day of primary season.

My own view is that New Hampshire should serve as the future model if and when changes are made. We need voters from smaller states who meet candidates personally over months or years to lead the way. Big states—where a campaign is driven by millions of dollars of thirty second TV spots—should not be the way we begin a selection for president.

For those in big states that are about to argue with me, I say be patient. Your state and its electoral votes will take center stage come November.

The 2008 election brought forward a group of candidates I'll call "modern political titans." These were incredibly well-qualified, well-known, and well-financed presidential candidates.

On the Republican side, the frontrunner was the maverick senator from Arizona, John McCain. War hero, elected to the Senate four times, he had sought the GOP presidential nomination in 2000, losing after a bruising and nasty primary struggle to George W. Bush.

There was also former New York City mayor Rudy Giuliani, who had become famous in the aftermath of September 11th. His executive experience—leading the nation's largest city—seemed particularly appealing as the war continued and the economy slowed.

Mitt Romney was the former one-term governor of very blue Massachusetts. He burst onto the national political radar when he helped save the 2002 Winter Olympics in Salt Lake City. His vast wealth—estimated at around a half billion dollars—made him a serious contender from the start.

Other candidates with a shot at the nomination included former Arkansas governor Mike Huckabee, former senator and actor Fred Thompson who entered the race late, and former Libertarian presidential nominee Ron Paul, who was building a diverse coalition across the country.

Hardly noticed and soon forgotten were Senator Sam Brownback, Virginia governor Jim Gilmore, former congressman Duncan Hunter, Congressman Tom Tancredo, and former governor Tommy Thompson.

For Democrats, the "modern political titans" included two-term New York senator and former first lady Hillary Clinton. Experienced, well-known, and able to raise a lot of money, for most of 2007 her nomination seemed inevitable.

There was also the popular up-and-comer first term senator from Illinois, Barack Obama, who had delivered such an effective speech four years earlier at the Democratic National Convention.

Former senator John Edwards was the 2004 Democratic vice presidential nominee and seemed next in line for the presidential nomination. He was also counting on his southern roots to help him win in South Carolina.

Back in the pack were Senator Joe Biden, Senator Chris Dodd, Governor Bill Richardson, former senator Mike Gravel, and Congressman Dennis Kucinich.

At the start of 2007, as most candidates officially began their campaigns, incumbent president George W. Bush was sitting on a 37 percent approval rating—a number that would drop down to 25 percent by election day 2008. Bush and his vice president Dick Cheney were so unpopular they would not attend the Republican National Convention (only two sitting presidents in my lifetime have skipped their party's big show—Bush and Lyndon Johnson).

The question in 2007 for the Republican candidates wasn't how close they'd campaign with Bush, but how far away from him they'd run.

Democrats sensed that after eight years, the country was ready to change parties. After all, only once in recent memory (George Bush in 1988) had a party been able to win three consecutive presidential elections in a row.

My job during the 2008 primary fight was to anchor four live weeknight newscasts on the ABC affiliate in Myrtle Beach. Covering the presidential candidates all around the state for over a year was self-volunteered—let's call it my hobby.

The resulting experiences were fulfilling, and my memories of them helped lead to the stories I'll share with you in this book.

READY FOR PRIME TIME

If you've followed politics you've probably heard of the "stump speech." The phrase originated back in 1876 when Democratic candidates would stand on tree stumps to give speeches at Galivants Ferry, South Carolina. For over 130 years the biannual event had been happening in western Horry County, also home to the ever-growing Myrtle Beach.

In 2006 the event, with candidates now speaking from the back porch of an old general store, featured U.S. senator Fritz Hollings. The state's senior senator was retiring after a whopping thirty-eight years, the eighth longest-serving senator in history.

When I was in high school, Hollings was seeking the Democratic nomination for president. I remember watching a debate on television and being impressed with his comments on controlling the huge budget deficit. Sitting beside Walter Mondale, John Glenn, Jesse Jackson, George McGovern, Reubin Askew, Alan Cranston, and Gary Hart, he was quite a contrast with his snow-white hair and deep Charleston drawl.

Hollings received next to zero votes in Iowa and less than 4 percent in New Hampshire in those early 1984 contests. But he did manage to get in a fairly memorable dig at his political nemesis John Glenn, the U.S. senator from Ohio. During one debate, Hollings looked at the former astronaut and said he was "still being all confused in that 'capsooool' of his."

Hollings offered many biting remarks during his career—he called Walter Mondale "a good lap dog, he'll give them everything they want, he'll lick every hand." He also called his colleague Howard Metzenbaum, another Ohioan, "the senator from B'nai B'rith." He said GOP congressman Bob Inglis was a "goddamn skunk." And he called the leaders of evangelical Bob Jones University "jackasses." At one point he said his fellow Democrat Bill Clinton was "as popular as AIDS" in South Carolina, and equated his impeachment trial in the U.S. Senate to "passing a kidney stone." The zingers always seemed to sting even more because of that deep drawl. NBC News anchor Tom Brokaw called his accent "more

27

southern than a bowl of grits."

Hollings once said to me during an answer to a question about the Iraq war, "we don't neeeeeed anymore diiiive bomberssss." I played that clip over and over again in the editing bay and chuckled each time.

In fact, it was so fun to listen to that I made it the ringtone on my phone for a while.

On this particular day, Hollings and I were set to go live right at 6 o'clock. My co-anchor would be starting the show and then toss out to me at the event. With about five minutes until airtime I grabbed Hollings who was on the other side of the crowd—about 1,000 strong—and got him into place.

A few seconds later I heard our news open in my IFB (interruptible fold-back, or more to the point, the thing in a newscaster's ear that lets them hear what's going on) and I told Hollings we were coming up soon.

As the national anthem wrapped up in the background I adjusted my tie, got my thoughts in place and heard Allyson say: "Let's go out live now to Jim Heath who is with Senator Fritz Hollings. Jim?"

At this exact moment—as if the broadcasting gods were having a good time at my expense—I heard the announcer over the speaker system say the three words dreaded most by live television reporters:

LET US PRAY.

The blood drained from my head.

I'm never especially nervous on live shots, especially political ones, but I instinctively knew this was headed for trouble.

As I said good evening, Hollings dropped his head and closed his eyes. Along with the hushed crowd, he listened as the preacher behind us beckoned for the Lord to bless the proceedings.

What is the protocol here? I frantically tried to answer in my mind.

I remembered Tom Brokaw speaking through a prayer during live political convention coverage, but he was anchoring from a booth, not down on the floor. Each second that ticked by, my indecision felt like a million years. My IFB was dead silent which meant my producer was obviously leaving it to me to figure out.

I whispered a question to Hollings about Democratic chances this year, and he attempted a whispered reply about how great they were, but this was ridiculous. Now I was convinced viewers would soon be calling in asking why in the hell I was badgering Fritz Hollings during a prayer.

I stopped and—in a career first—apologized for the situation and tossed it back to the studio. Allyson then tossed to a commercial break and the prayer ended.

Hollings chuckled and in that deep Charleston drawl said:

"That wasss unnnnusual."

A few minutes later, we went back on the air and the interview went on without a hitch.

It is interesting to note that Hollings supported Strom Thurmond for president in 1948 and the "Dixiecrats" platform. He admits that in the early part of his career he shared Thurmond's segregationist views. But in 1952, arguing in favor of school segregation before the Supreme Court, a lawyer for the other side asked Hollings how he could support blacks serving on the front lines in Europe but riding in the back of the bus when they came home. As a veteran, Hollings says he instantly realized it wasn't right, and returned home to slowly begin the work of integration into state universities without violence.

Over the following decades, Hollings and Thurmond would come to symbolize two very different southern roads traveled on the issue of civil rights.

Hollings retired from the Senate in 2006 and was replaced by Republican Jim DeMint, who would go on to head the well-known conservative Heritage Foundation. Talk about a contrast in personality and ideology.

Once, while interviewing DeMint, he told me that he would rather serve with thirty like-minded conservatives in the Senate agreeing on everything than a majority of fifty-one which included what he called the "John McCain types" who broke from the ranks occasionally.

I was astonished. Where was the Ronald Reagan philosophy of winning a majority in order to govern? Where was the well-established Reagan philosophy of the art of political compromise as he wrote about in his autobiography:

"When I began entering into the give and take of legislative bargaining in Sacramento, a lot of the most radical conservatives who had supported me during the election didn't like it. 'Compromise' was a dirty word to them and they wouldn't face the fact that we couldn't get all of what we wanted today. They wanted all or nothing and they wanted it all at once. If you don't get it all, some said, don't take anything. I'd learned while negotiating union contracts that you seldom got everything you asked for. And I agreed with FDR, who said in 1933: 'I have no expectations of making a hit every time I come to bat. What I seek is the highest possible batting average.' If you got seventy-five or eighty percent of what you were asking for, I say, you take it and fight for the rest later, and that's what I told these radical conservatives who never got used to it."

During his White House years, Reagan became frustrated with his fellow conservatives who refused any deal with Democrats on taxes and the budget. "He is in fact unreasonable," Reagan wrote in his diary about congressman Jack Kemp at one point. "The tax increase is the price we have to pay to get the budget cuts."

He also wrote, "A compromise is never to anyone's liking; it's just the best you can get and contains enough of what you want to justify what you gave up."

So this "radical conservative" DeMint philosophy of narrow agreement on all issues and no compromise—ever—seemed opposite of the Republican Party I had known growing up during the Reagan era.

A quick side story: In 2006 I moderated the final live televised debate for the US Senate between DeMint and his Democratic challenger Inez Tenenbaum.

With literally sixty seconds to go until airtime—with the debate being shown live in all television markets across the state and nationally on C-SPAN, DeMint refused to walk onstage because Tenenbaum, who was much shorter than he was, was standing on a wood crate behind her lectern.

I am not making this up.

My producer Diane Smith told me in my IFB that I needed to be prepared to start the live debate without him.

WHAT?!

I was already mic'd up, standing on stage in front of hundreds of people, about to go live, and felt helpless. What do I say, how do I explain this? I thought to myself. *Do I just talk to Tenenbaum like it's an interview and hope he eventually walks on stage?*

This had the potential of making all of us look ridiculous. (Don't believe me? Google "fangate" from the 2014 Florida gubernatorial election and see for yourself.)

As the audience started to whisper with a candidate AWOL, I noticed off to my side, behind the stage curtain, campaign staffers and Coastal Carolina University officials scrambling. With the debate opening theme song now playing in my IFB, a wood crate was found and rushed out and DeMint walked onstage to applause and stood on it.

Considering my role as moderator included twenty-five minutes of one-on-one time with the two candidates, my brain (as evidenced by the sweat hidden on my back) had been slightly rattled. But it turned out okay.

I was told later DeMint had grown tired of Tenenbaum attempting to look taller on television during previous debates and he had decided that night to do something about it.

Thanks to some fast-thinking stagehands, a political disaster was averted.

Back to Galivants Ferry where this stump meeting fell very early in the 2008 primary process, but it was nonetheless important because, as I mentioned earlier, there would be no presidential or vice-presidential incumbent from either party on the ballot. That had not happened in our country since 1952.

That meant both parties were about to engage in a political free-for-all to determine their nominee. While always expecting a lively battle among Republicans in the South Carolina primary, 2008 promised to deliver the Democrats to our doorstep too.

The headline speaker at the 2006 stump meeting was U.S. Senator Joe Biden from Delaware. Biden, a good public speaker with a dramatic life story (his wife and one-year-old daughter were killed in a car accident just weeks after his first election to the Senate), had sought the Democratic presidential nomination in 1988.

For a time in 1987 he was considered a frontrunner. That is until the Michael Dukakis campaign leaked to the press videotapes showing him plagiarizing speeches of British labor leader Neil Kinnock. When it also was discovered Biden had plagiarized some of his law school papers, his campaign quickly folded.

Nearly twenty years had passed since that debacle, and Biden was eyeing the 2008 race closely. From the start, it was clear he would be outmatched in fundraising by Senator Hillary Clinton, Senator Barack Obama, and Senator John Edwards. "Smiling Joe," as local Democrats called him, was popular with the grassroots but not many considered him to be on the upper-tier of candidates.

That week, gas prices were hovering around a historically high $3.00 a gallon in many parts of the country. As the Bush administration got hammered by Americans looking to fix blame, many Democrats were timid to blame the Big Oil companies. That fascinated me because rarely is an industry so big that it intimidates both major political parties. I wanted Biden's perspective on that but was told by his senate staff that he would not be taking any press questions.

No press questions? At the famous Galivants Ferry stump?

That was not acceptable to me, so I told our news photographer to tuck in behind as we pushed our way to Biden, parting a sea of Democratic activists along the way.

A C-SPAN cameraman whispered to me as I approached Biden in the middle of the crowd whether it would be okay to air my questions on their cable network later that night. "Of course," I said as I reached Biden and leaned in and asked him, "talk to me quickly about Big Oil. Why haven't Democrats been more vocal taking on the monopoly of Big Oil?"

Biden didn't seem fazed, smiled, and offered a brutally honest assessment:

"The truth is, it's hard to get traction."

That about summed up the reality of how big money works in Washington. During the Bush-Cheney years—both former oil executives by the way—the oil and gas industry spent $393.2 million on lobbying the Federal Government according to the non-partisan Center for Responsive Politics.

Just a staggering number.

To challenge the oil and gas industry is too tough and not worth the effort for most politicians—and that goes whether you are a Republican or Democrat. But Biden had tried, asking energy industry executives during a senate hearing whether any of them still thought they needed $2.8 billion in taxpayer subsidies while they were reaping record profits. No one responded.

"I'm the guy that got the Big Oil companies to agree that they didn't need the tax break the energy bill gave them," Biden told me. "I made them agree to repeal it, the chairman of the board of ExxonMobil (Rex Tillerson). I went to the floor of the United States Senate and Republicans wouldn't even let me get a vote on it. So you have to have a forum, and that's why it's important this year we win back either the House or the Senate."

"Are consumers angry enough about gas prices to fuel Democratic chances in the fall?" I asked.

"I think so, but they're still looking for us to step up to the plate. They've given up on the other team and they want to know whether we're ready for prime time..."

"Are you ready for prime time?" I interrupted.

"We are ready for prime time. We are ready," he replied.

The voters agreed, and in November, a majority of Democrats were elected to majorities in both the House and Senate.

As we stood there in mid-2006, the last question I had for Biden was whether he was ready for another national campaign, especially with polls showing him already way behind Hillary Clinton.

"Look, there's nothing I can do about any other candidate in the race. I can just be the best Biden I can be. The problem is everyone knows who I am and I'm not changing. If I lose I'll lose on my own terms and say what I think. And I think the American people are where I am. If I'm wrong I'll get a pension, if I'm right I get a shot to run."

Biden officially entered the race months later and the voters barely noticed him. But at least one fellow Democrat thought he was the best Biden he could be.

Standing there interviewing him at the Galivants Ferry stump, I would have never guessed Joseph Robinette Biden, Junior would be the next vice president of the United States.

Red, White and Blue

The two Romney staffers went to look for an American flag. They wanted it behind the former Massachusetts governor—off his right shoulder, not his left. They also wanted to make sure we were using two portable lights and not just one. This interview wasn't in the television studio after all, but in a hotel ballroom, where lighting wasn't properly designed.

As one of few television political reporters in South Carolina, it was not unusual to get random calls from perspective candidates and their campaigns. With no incumbent president or vice president in the running, many politicians decided to start making the rounds early.

It was December 2006, a full year before the South Carolina primary. Mitt Romney had not officially announced his candidacy but it was clear he was in the race. The former governor was coming off years of positive publicity following his rescuing of the 2002 Winter Olympics in Salt Lake City and after one term as the moderate Republican governor of one of the bluest states in the country.

The precision for detail by the Romney staff at this early stage of the game was slightly upsetting for my photographer, Kevin Abadie, who was a bit of a perfectionist himself. We looked at each other as the Romney staff triumphantly brought in the flag and tested where it would be folded around the pole so it looked just so.

This would be the final presidential primary season without the influence of social media. There would be no Instagram or Twitter posts and no picture of Romney in front of the flag to promote on Facebook. That would all have to wait for the next campaign in 2012 where Romney and I would make a bit of news together from another interview.

But first things first.

I was anxious to sit down face-to-face with Romney and get a sense of his personality. This is true about every interview I conduct. How many Americans get that rare chance to look into the eyes of presidential candidates and watch their expression and reaction as they answer questions? Frankly, it's a responsibility I have always taken very seriously. National candidates can find local television interviews more relaxed, not carrying the weight of a showdown with someone like the late, great Tim Russert. Through the years, this has allowed me to get an up-close assessment of most of our top national politicians—call it my "electability meter."

Preparing questions for presidential candidates, for me, involves at least a few days of homework to establish what viewers would want to ask, what issues are timely and need to be asked, and some personal insight that may force the candidate to open up a bit—or at the very least—share something interesting outside the usual talking points.

And, yes, let me make it clear: I always determine my own list of questions. So many times I'm asked "did management make you ask that?" as if there is a hidden left-wing or right-wing conspiracy.

There isn't.

Romney strode into the room with a grin and strong handshake, looking every bit as if he had come from central casting. I had interviewed Howard Dean, John Kerry, and John Edwards during the last primary season in South Carolina, but Romney seemed like an entirely different type of politician.

A Republican from Massachusetts who had at first been soundly defeated by Senator Edward Kennedy—the liberal icon—only to come back and win a statewide race. He was a moderate who had disavowed the Reagan economic plan in the 1980s and had supported allowing gays in the boy scouts. Romney had also voted for former senator Paul Tsongas in the 1992 Democratic Presidential primary in Massachusetts. He especially hated Newt Gingrich's Contract with America, the crown jewel of the modern conservative playbook.

After his election as governor, Romney had worked with Kennedy and state Democratic lawmakers to create and implement a statewide healthcare program mandating everyone pay into the system—later called "Romneycare." A plan, incidentally, Senator Barack Obama ridiculed during a presidential debate I covered in Myrtle Beach prior to the 2008 South Carolina Democratic primary.

The irony, as it would turn out.

The "new" Romney had taken a sharp turn to the right. He was banking on conservatives giving him a second look. Gone were any negative statements about "Reaganomics" or talk about working with Democrats. Even his pro-choice position on abortion flipped to pro-life just in time for his White House run.

By every objective measure, Mitt Romney is one of the most fascinating political figures of our time.

As we took our seats, and as Kevin tested our lapel mics, I studied Romney for a moment, trying to picture one of the wealthiest men in the country—with an estimated net wealth of $500 million—trying to relate to what was a quickly deteriorating economy for the middle class.

During the last half of 2006, economic growth and job growth had both slowed as the housing bubble burst. The nation was running its largest deficit in history as the ongoing war in Iraq cost more than anyone in Washington had expected.

President George W. Bush's approval rating had shrunk to 35 percent and was still falling. GOP candidates across the country refused to be seen at campaign rallies with him. By Election Day, congressional Republicans were spanked so bad that Democrats recaptured both the House and the Senate.

Many top political strategists had become convinced that the only way Republicans could win the presidency for the third straight election—something accomplished only once in my lifetime—was to nominate the "anti-Bush"; someone with independence and national recognition for taking on the administration.

Gallup polling suggested that would be either Arizona senator John McCain—a maverick who had opposed Bush for the nomination in 2000—or former New York City mayor Rudy Giuliani, who had gained fame and respect during the aftermath of 9/11.

The same polling also showed Romney in the low single digits, almost completely off the voters' radar. With the three cameras now focused and rolling, I started our conversation there.

"Well, I think it's pretty natural that the frontrunners at the very beginning days of the race are people who have been known on the national stage," Romney told me. "The familiar names, McCain has been around a long time, Mayor Giuliani has been well known by the American people for a long time. Governors tend not to be well known outside their own states."

This was true enough. Bill Clinton came from nowhere to defeat George Bush in 1992 without ever having run a national campaign. The same with Jimmy Carter, who defeated President Gerald Ford in 1976. Ronald Reagan was a well-known actor prior to entering politics, so his name recognition was already high—although it took him three times at the presidency before he finally achieved it.

But Romney wasn't without some national recognition. In fact had he not stepped in, it is possible the 2002 Winter Olympics would have been a complete disaster.

In the late 1990s, a bribery scandal forced several Salt Lake City Olympic officials—and the mayor—to quit. Corporate donations—critical to a large event like the Olympics—were quickly drying up. With the clock ticking, Romney was asked to leave Boston and take the helm.

During the Opening Ceremonies of the 2002 Winter Olympics—with billions of people watching on television around the planet—Romney was introduced alongside President Bush and International Olympic Committee president Jacques Rogge.

It was just months after the horrific September 11, 2001 terrorist attack that left nearly 3,000 innocent people dead. An American flag that had flown over the fallen World Trade Center was carried into Rice-Eccles Stadium by eight Olympic athletes—and escorted by New York City firefighters.

With wind gusts blowing throughout the stadium, the Mormon Tabernacle Choir began to quietly sing the National Anthem.

"They did something people hadn't expected," Romney told me when asked about this moment. "They were singing an old 1930s version of our national anthem, where you repeat the last line one octave higher. As they repeated that line a gust of wind came into that flag. One of the flag bearers that was holding it, Derek Parra, said to me that for him it was as if the spirits of all those who had fought for American liberty had just blown into that flag."

The Winter Games proved to the world that America was back on its feet. The $1.3 billion dollar event made tens of millions in profit and it gave Romney some old-fashioned red, white, and blue credentials that he hoped would play well in future campaigns.

But it didn't solve the "elephant in the room" problem that was widely whispered as Romney set his eyes on a White House run.

America has never elected a Mormon president and many evangelical Christians in South Carolina were determined to keep it that way.

Influential South Carolina Republican and conservative leaders told me privately that Romney could expect fierce opposition from the religious right, especially in the voter-rich upstate—the key area for Republicans to carry to win the state.

The religion did not help in practical political terms either. It prohibits drinking alcohol—even iced tea for that matter—which meant there would be no smiling picture of Romney (as there had been for Reagan and about every other presidential candidate) in a bar holding up a beer to demonstrate they were the working man's candidate. And not only was he from that elusive 1 percent world but, unlike say the Kennedys or Bushes, he didn't have those cool drunken stories to tell which a majority of voters relate to.

The religion issue was certainly not new to a presidential candidate. Shortly before the 1960 election, Democratic nominee John F. Kennedy addressed Protestant leaders about being a Catholic. There were rumors he would get direct orders from the Pope.

"I am not the Catholic candidate for President. I am the Democratic Party's candidate for President who happens also to be a Catholic. I do not speak for my church on public matters and the Church does not speak for me," Kennedy said at the time.

And he offered this warning for the future: "For while this year it may be a Catholic against whom the finger of suspicion is pointed, in other years it has been, and may someday be again, a Jew or a Quaker or a Unitarian or a Baptist. Today I may be the victim, but tomorrow it may be you until the whole fabric of our harmonious society is ripped at a time of great national peril."

39

JFK won, but remains our only elected Catholic president to date.

With that in mind, I asked Romney if he was preparing to draft a similar speech.

"I know that the theology of my faith is different than the theology of other faiths, but this is the time to talk about political leadership. As one great evangelical leader said the other day, 'we're not looking for a pastor in chief.'"

I pressed Romney on whether he envisioned a JFK-type speech in the future.

"I get asked about my faith a great deal and I'm happy to respond to it anytime someone asks a question. Maybe there will be a speech that goes into it in some depth. What's encouraging to me is that evangelical Christian leaders and faithful members across the country are supporting my campaign."

Almost a year to the day after our interview, Romney delivered his "Faith in America" speech, which echoed Kennedy's words.

"Let me assure you that no authorities of my church, or of any other church for that matter, will ever exert influence on presidential decisions," said Romney.

Before the South Carolina primary, Bob Jones III, Chancellor of the evangelical Bob Jones University—who once called Mormonism and Catholicism "cults which call themselves Christian"—endorsed Romney.

"To have the support of Bob Jones III means a great deal to me, I appreciate it very, very much," Romney told me following the endorsement.

This, coupled with the support of conservative U.S. senator Jim DeMint, led Romney's campaign team to believe that the Mormon issue had been adequately addressed.

As we continued our first interview, I was surprised with just how little difference Romney was offering in contrast to Bush in both domestic and foreign affairs.

"I believe I would make America a more prosperous and more secure country for my kids and my grandkids," was the way he summed up his potential candidacy.

No criticism of the failing economy. No disagreement on the handling of Iraq. No strategy on how to be the "anti-Bush" Republican.

When the interview was over, Romney said "see you soon," and left the room. Kevin and I looked at each other and as if reading each other's minds, shook our heads.

Romney looked and acted the part of a presidential candidate. But there was little empathy on the economy, little emotion on the Olympics, and little thought to the war in Iraq.

It was a completely robotic interview.

As we drove back to the television station I said to Kevin that hopefully we would have the chance to sit down with Romney again. Maybe it was an off day? Or maybe he wasn't quite ready for a national campaign?

The following year, Romney's fortunes grew. In an October 2007 American Research Poll, he led in Iowa, New Hampshire, and South Carolina. If that held, he would unquestionably be the GOP nominee.

Shortly after the poll was released I received a phone call from the Romney camp. They asked if I wanted to do another profile interview during a day he was spending in Pawleys Island. This was the opportunity we had wanted.

The breakfast they were serving at Applewood House of Pancakes that sunny October morning looked delicious. But sadly, I decided a long time ago—along with most journalists—that free food is a no-no at political events. The chumminess of eating and drinking with candidates and their supporters is not acceptable in my mind. The bacon would have to wait.

Romney strode in for our interview with his shirt sleeves rolled up, this time seeming even more confident about his chances, with the polls showing him leading just about everywhere.

There was no American flag positioned behind him this time, although Kevin had managed to find a bouquet of fresh flowers that added some color behind his white shirt.

I started our talk by pointing out that Romney could be on the verge of the coveted trifecta—winning the first three presidential contests in Iowa, New Hampshire, and South Carolina.

"There has never been a Republican, other than a sitting president, who has won Iowa and New Hampshire," Romney said with an energetic tone.

"So if I can do well in both of those and can go on and do well in South Carolina, Michigan, and Nevada, that would give me a heck of a start."

I pushed Romney more on what would happen if he achieved the trifecta—personally believing that it would wrap up the nomination for him early.

"It would be unbelievable, fabulous. But that's something you only dream about."

While most polls showed him ahead, there were also some ominous signs that his opponents were effectively tagging him as the "flip-flop" candidate; a term no candidate wants and can rarely survive.

The most recent example was Senator John Kerry, the 2004 Democratic nominee for president. Kerry had voted against the Gulf War in 1991 after Iraq took aggressive military action against Kuwait. But then he supported going to war in Iraq in 2002, despite Iraq having nothing to do with 9/11. The two positions were at opposite ends on the issue of war.

Perhaps most famously in 2003—a year after he had supported going to war in Iraq—Kerry voted against funding troops in Iraq and Afghanistan. During the campaign, Kerry argued he had actually voted for the $87 billion before he voted against it.

It left Americans shaking their heads.

The Bush campaign exploited the flip-flopping in effective television ads. And President Kerry was not to be.

Four years later, Romney was watching his credibility slip as he struggled to answer questions about his changing position on abortion. He had been pro-choice running for the Senate and for governor, now he was pro-life running for president.

The record couldn't have been clearer.

In 1994 during a debate with Ted Kennedy, Romney said, "I believe that abortion should be safe and legal in this country."

Eight years later, during a debate for governor, Romney said, "I will preserve and protect a woman's right to choose and am devoted and dedicated to honoring my word in that regard."

But at some point between 2002 and 2008, Romney changed his position. By the time he entered the presidential race he said he was solidly pro-life and went so far as to support the reversal of Roe v. Wade.

I pressed Romney on how anybody could see that as anything but a flip-flop.

"What the people of Massachusetts have realized, and you can't see it here, is I was governor for four years," Romney explained. "When I became governor and the first piece of legislation that came to my desk would have ended human life in the case of an embryo, I could not sign it."

I pressed Romney again on how his actions as governor were not completely opposite from what he had promised during his campaign.

"Actually, what I did was honor the promise I made to the people of Massachusetts. I said I would not change the laws, I would keep the laws exactly as they were."

For the first and only time in my interviews with Romney, he became clearly irritated. I don't think my question about abortion was unexpected, but I think in his mind he was hearing the completely unsatisfactory answer he was giving to voters.

He had changed his position on the most thoroughly debated social issue of our time. He should have just admitted it and moved on.

I ended our interview with a question about Hillary Clinton. At the time she was way ahead of little-known Senator Barack Obama in the polls.

"I'm actually surprised to see I'm doing pretty well in the head-on-head polls with Hillary Clinton and the polls will jump all over, but I'm encouraged by that."

Who could have known then that it would be Barack Obama, not Clinton, that Romney would face four years later.

As we left Pawleys Island, Kevin and I agreed the interview was better than the first, but there was still a strange distance about Romney and it was hard to put a finger on it. He was personable and obviously very close to his family, but like Bob Dole and Michael Dukakis before him, that didn't translate to voters on television. My hunch was that if Romney didn't get the nomination this time I would probably never interview him again.

My hunch was wrong.

JUDGE ME ON MY RECORD

It was the Friday night following the September 11, 2001 terrorist attack on America. As I had all week, I was anchoring the 11 p.m. news live when we aired a three-minute story about families and individuals at Ground Zero passing out "Missing" flyers. They were still holding out hope their loved ones had magically survived in the fallen towers.

At one point, a young man started talking about his younger brother. Holding a flyer with his brother's picture on it, he talked about how they had shared a room growing up and he couldn't imagine life without him. Then he started sobbing.

At that second, for me, days of pent-up hidden emotion flooded my head. The horrible attack had left nearly 3,000 innocent people dead in a single morning. It had happened on our own shores, the scope of the destruction almost beyond comprehension. The tallest buildings in our nation's largest city brought down in two hours. The Pentagon in Washington, DC, the symbol of our military might, now had a huge smoldering hole in its side. A third plane, brought down by heroes on board, had been on its way to destroy either the U.S. Capitol or the White House.

How could this happen in America, the most powerful nation on Earth? The family members and loved ones and the entire country were still trying to make sense of it all.

As the story ended, the camera came back to me. For a split second I couldn't move. I looked down, trying to regain my composure, but a tear was already making its way down my cheek. Feeling suffocated was a new experience for me on live television, but that story—especially the young man looking for his brother—had been too much. Another second or two went by before I looked up and quietly said, "excuse me," and ignoring what was on the teleprompter, ad-libbed:

"Whatever you're doing right now please join us in remembering the thousands who died earlier this week and send a prayer to their families."

It was the single most difficult moment in my television career.

One year later, I traveled to New York City to report on the progress being made at Ground Zero. Life had gone on in America's largest city, but there were reminders everywhere of the scar the attack had left. I stood and looked at the giant hole in the ground, where the tallest buildings I had ever been in had collapsed, and felt ill. After five or ten minutes, I told my friend Peter Barden (a proud New Yorker who was acting as my cameraman) I'd had enough. Instead of focusing on the giant pit left behind from the fallen towers, my story instead focused on the buildings nearby that were still being repaired because of falling debris.

A fence around the property still had thousands of tribute items on it. The faces a reminder of the humanity lost in a single morning. Church groups regularly performed there, so I interviewed a few people about that.

New York City police and firefighters would stop and take pictures with the endless tourists. Who could ever forget the faces from photographs of those first responders who were running into the burning buildings as many tried to exit? Some of them spoke to me about their experiences—most had been on duty on 9/11.

There were the businesses near Ground Zero still struggling after reopening. I remember one Brooks Brothers clothing store in particular that I had shopped at when visiting Manhattan, and spending time at the World Trade Center, in 2000. Now in 2002 there were no customers. Tourists wanted to see Ground Zero but not shop for clothes.

There were some signs that New York City was recovering—it had to with millions of people living and working there. I reported on a parade honoring Polish Americans that happened on 5th Avenue. There was the Italian festival, which drew quite the crowd in Little Italy. And a street fair along Broadway from 47th to 57th Avenues was packed.

Still, conversation after conversation I had with New Yorkers revealed lingering disappointment, mixed with anger, that our government had yet to bring al-Qaeda leader Osama bin Laden to justice.

We now know, from the 9/11 Commission Report, thirty-six days before the terrorist attack, President George W. Bush received a Central Intelligence Agency briefing paper called **"Bin Laden Determined To Strike in U.S."** The brief warned of terrorism threats from bin Laden and his supporters:

"Al-Qaeda members—including some who are U.S. citizens—have resided in or traveled to the U.S. for years, and the group apparently maintains a support structure that could aid attacks."

The CIA memo pointed out bin Laden's history of aggression during the Clinton presidency including the bombing of U.S. embassies in Kenya and Tanzania, and the bombing of the USS Cole, which left seventeen American sailors dead. The brief also stated the CIA had not been able to corroborate the "sensational threat" that bin Laden planned to hijack a U.S. aircraft.

Thirty-six days later, a total of nineteen hijackers attacked America. Ten flew two commercial jets into the Twin Towers at the World Trade Center in Manhattan—both 110-story towers crumbled to the ground in less than two hours. One jet with five hijackers crashed and blew a huge hole into the Pentagon in Washington, DC—the symbol of America's military might. A third jet with four hijackers was set to target either the White House or U.S. Capitol but it was courageously brought down over rural Pennsylvania by the passengers on board.

Osama bin Laden, as he later publicly admitted, personally directed all nineteen hijackers.

In the end, 2,973 innocent people were killed in a single morning, making it the worst terrorist attack on American soil in history.

Despite the long-held view that bin Laden's hatred of America started during the Gulf War in 1991, in a speech in 2004, he said his plans for the attack started shortly after Israel invaded Lebanon in 1982 during the Reagan administration:

"As I looked at those demolished towers in Lebanon, it entered my mind that we should punish the oppressor in kind and that we should destroy towers in America in order that they taste some of what we tasted and so that they be deterred from killing our women and children... So with these images and their like as their background, the events of September 11th came as a reply to those great wrongs."

One thing is certain: bin Laden had left the American government plenty of clues through several administrations. Despite a Tomahawk cruise missile attack by Clinton on bin Laden's suspected training camps in Afghanistan in 1998, he had alluded capture or death until it was too late.

During a State of the Union address in the late 90's, I left the media center in the U.S. Capitol, walked up the stairs and then out the front doors on the west side. As I stood there on the balcony, on a chilly January night, looking out at the Washington Monument, I could hear the faint applause coming from inside the well of Congress as the President of the United States Bill Clinton delivered his speech. It was quite a moment for a political geek who loves presidential history. It saddens me to this day to think in the aftermath of 9/11, no one will ever have that much freedom to roam around our Capitol, and most of our public monuments and buildings, again.

In the days following the September 11th attack Bush said about bin Laden, "I want him, I want justice. And there's an old poster out West as I recall that said, 'Wanted: Dead or Alive.'"

Six years later, with wars in both Afghanistan and Iraq ongoing, the question on the minds of many voters was, "where is bin Laden?" The lack of an acceptable answer promised to be an issue in the upcoming 2008 campaign.

Immediately following the attack on 9/11, one of the first people Bush spoke with was New York governor George Pataki. A fellow Republican, Pataki had shocked the political world in 1994 when, seemingly out of nowhere, he defeated incumbent governor Mario Cuomo.

In mid-2007, Pataki was eyeing a potential presidential bid and that's what brought him to South Carolina. I interviewed him in a three-camera shoot outside on a beautiful day with the Atlantic Ocean as our backdrop.

"How quickly did you speak with the president that day?" I started.

"I called President Bush at that conference in Florida, and we spoke and I asked him to shut down the airspace over New York, and he said, 'we're already shutting down the airspace over America.'"

"How soon were you made aware that this wasn't an accident but a terrorist attack?" I followed up.

"I'll never forget that, Jim. I saw the plane had hit the first tower, and like everybody else, wasn't sure what was happening, and then when the second plane hit I knew immediately that we were under attack."

Pataki said he remembered how proud he was of the New Yorkers who remained in Manhattan to help.

"There was a line of people waiting out in the soot and the dust and the debris from the towers and they weren't waiting to get the bus or a subway uptown—they were waiting to give blood."

But the lingering question about bin Laden remained.

"As the governor of the state of New York what do you say to the families of all those victims, have they had justice yet?" I asked him.

"Jim, of course not. And I don't know that you can ever have justice for a horrible barbaric attack like that. Certainly we're going to have disappointments, like the fact we still have not gotten Osama bin Laden. Regardless of what it takes, the War on Terror is something we have to prevail in."

After trips to early primary states, Pataki decided not to jump in the presidential race (he would in 2016) but his political rival—and fellow Republican—Rudy Giuliani, did decide to run. The former New York City mayor is forever linked in many Americans' minds to that tragic day.

I was scheduled to interview Giuliani in early April 2007 on the field prior to the home opener of the Myrtle Beach Pelicans baseball game. Giuliani, a die-hard Yankees fan, was scheduled to throw out the first pitch. At the time, he was leading in the South Carolina polls and had an impressive campaign team which included state treasurer Thomas Ravenel. Locally, he was backed by Myrtle Beach Mayor John Rhodes.

Giuliani's campaign spokesman Elliott Bundy called me about an hour before the game to say they were running late. "How about interviewing him in the stands for an inning during the game?" Bundy asked. "We can do that," I quickly responded.

The interview turned into an extensive four-camera shoot—that's the most hardware I've ever seen for a political interview. A Giuliani staffer asked Mayor Rhodes to move as I took his seat in the stands. Kevin, leading our camera crew, told me later the mayor's expression was one of "really?" when he sat down at the end of the row.

As the inning started, I began my conversation with Giuliani about the importance of America's pastime in the aftermath of 9/11. Very few people can forget the sight of President Bush at Yankees Stadium in New York confidently walking out to the pitcher's mound to throw the first pitch before Game 3 of the World Series. He threw a strike over home plate, sending a signal that America was getting back on track.

After he left office Bush told *TIME*, "It was the most nervous I had ever been. It was the most nervous moment of my presidency."

"Baseball went a long way in helping America heal?" I asked the mayor.

"It sure did," Giuliani responded. "It did a lot for me. I mean, baseball games and my son's high school football games were the only things that got my mind off all the terrible things we were dealing with and the tremendous pressure of it. When I'd watch baseball it would remind me that life was going to go back to normal."

I pointed out that Giuliani and his rival for the nomination, John McCain, had actually sat together during the 2001 World Series, which the Arizona Diamondbacks went on to win in seven games against the Yankees.

Giuliani laughed and said, "We sure did! John continues to be a very good friend. We watched game six and game seven together. We had a bet on it and he won that bet."

Our conversation then turned serious. I told Giuliani that America got to know him on 9/11. In the middle of chaos and destruction, the mayor of the nation's largest city was seen on television walking the streets, his head and shoulders covered with ash. Fearless of the press, he answered reporters' questions with the little facts he had in an attempt to portray a sense of calm.

"Every day of my life I remember it, I remember parts of it every day of my life," Giuliani said.

"Sometimes it's the very sad parts, the very tragic parts. Sometimes it's the very brave and unbelievably wonderful things people did and tremendous spirit they had. So it's a mixture of very bad memories and very good memories. Seeing people twenty minutes before they died, seeing some of the horrible things that happened to people when things were falling off the building or people jumping off the building. I've learned I'm going to think of it every day of my life."

As for bringing bin Laden—the person who claimed responsibility for directing the attack that wreaked so much havoc on his city—to justice, Giuliani said:

"It's also something I think about every day. I think it's very, very important that in addition to everything else we're doing on the war on terror, that we catch him. We need to crush al Qaeda because they were the ones responsible for it, but it really is important we don't lose sight of the fact that we need to catch bin Laden and bring him to justice."

Despite leading in the South Carolina polls for a good part of 2007, there was the political reality that eventually conservatives would turn away from Giuliani due to his liberal positions on social issues.

He was pro-choice on abortion, which is almost a certain disqualifier for Republican activists. Add to that his support for domestic partnerships and sweeping gun control laws (meaning he was an enemy of the powerful NRA) and I questioned whether there was any conceivable way he could be the nominee: "Whatever, judge me on my record," he responded.

"Judge me on what I've accomplished in my public life. If you think that's adequate and I'll be a good president and I'll be able to lead the country the way I led New York City or the New York Attorney's Office or the other things I've done, fine. If you don't, well, that's what a democracy is all about. But I think it should be focused on public record. All of us that are running have very extensive public records. You can get a pretty good idea of what kind of presidents we're going to be by what we've done already."

There was also the fact Giuliani had been married three times and had gone through a very nasty and public divorce. That bitterness had led his son Andrew to announce he did not support his father's campaign.

So I asked him about what were expected to be very personal negative commercials and comments by his opponents in the months ahead.

"You know, part of being mayor of New York sort of gets you ready for that. It was going on every day. You had to deal with those things. You have to learn to say to yourself, everything about you is going to be brought up. Some fair, some unfair, but you stick to the issues. You stick to the things that are important."

In 2000, Giuliani had been widely expected to oppose First Lady Hillary Clinton for the open U.S. Senate seat in New York. But a diagnosis of prostate cancer created a health scare and forced him to drop out of that race. At this point in 2007, the polls suggested the two New Yorkers could finally face each other.

"She's tough, Hillary Clinton would be a very, very tough candidate," said Giuliani. "So would Barack Obama be a tough candidate. John Edwards would be a tough candidate. You don't get to pick and choose the Democratic opponent. I have enough to do to deal with the Republican primary."

As the inning ended, I asked Giuliani to sum up for me the rationale behind his candidacy.

"I have the ability to keep this country on offense against terrorism. I understand it in a way no one else does. I think these are things I've done already and these are things I can do for the country."

As we wrapped up the interview, we concentrated on baseball for a few moments. "This is a great game, it really is," he laughed. An inning later his entourage, including Ravenel, left the ballpark.

As we headed back to the station, Kevin and I agreed that Giuliani was a tough, experienced politician who was fearless of the press. At the time, he led in the polls in the state, and despite his views on social issues, we thought his leadership on 9/11 may be enough to overcome them for GOP primary voters.

His endorsement by Ravenel, a rising star in state politics, was also a critical component for his campaign. Ravenel was part of a well-known and respected Charleston political family (the landmark Cooper River Bridge is named after his father Arthur) with deep pockets and resources. I first met Ravenel in 2004 when he was seeking the GOP nomination for the U.S. Senate. I moderated a live debate between the six candidates and while Ravenel lost that primary to Jim DeMint, many across the state believed he would be back on the ballot soon.

Two years later, he won the GOP nomination for state treasurer and faced a Democratic incumbent who had been in office since 1966. When Grady Paterson, then eighty-two, refused to participate in our scheduled live television debate, my General Manager Billy Huggins gave the green light to broadcast it anyway. The "debate" featured me asking Ravenel questions for thirty minutes with an empty chair at the table "in case Patterson changed his mind," I told the audience. He didn't. After four decades of public service, Ravenel sent Patterson into retirement.

Six months into his new office—and two months after he attended the ballgame as Giuliani's state chairman—Ravenel was indicted on federal cocaine charges. He would quickly step down from the Giuliani campaign and later resign as state treasurer. It was the beginning of the end for Giuliani in South Carolina.

About two weeks after the indictment I interviewed Giuliani at a campaign stop in Myrtle Beach. "Sure, it came as a shock," Giuliani told me. "It's a terrible thing when something like that happens to someone. It's something he's going to have to answer for. But, you know, it's one of those things that is highly personal."

Ravenel was later found guilty and sentenced to ten months behind bars. Federal Judge Joseph Anderson Jr. said, "We have an awful lot of cocaine parties at the house of a state constitutional officer." Ravenel would resurface in 2013 in a reality television show on Bravo about young aristocrats and southern plantations.

A new American Research poll released shortly after Ravenel's indictment showed Giuliani slipping and McCain rising to the top of the Republican field. The momentum for "America's Mayor" stalled and it never reignited.

HIGHEST GLASS CEILING

Accepting the Republican nomination in 1996 Bob Dole proclaimed, "And with all due respect, I am here to tell you, it does not take a village to raise a child. It takes a family to raise a child!"

GOP delegates in the San Diego Convention Center stood and cheered as Dole took a direct swipe at First Lady Hillary Clinton. But I remember thinking at the time, "that is a softball that she could hit out of the park if she wants to next month."

Clinton had written *It Takes a Village* as her husband Bill prepared for his reelection campaign. In the book, which was on the *New York Times* bestseller list, she described a society where "children have caring and nurturing adults around them." Conservatives hated it. They claimed it was a book with a political agenda and no village was necessary if a child had a mom and dad.

Sure enough, at the Democratic National Convention a month later in Chicago, Hillary responded:

"For Bill and me there has been no experience more challenging, more rewarding and more humbling than raising our daughter. We have learned that to raise a happy, healthy and hopeful child it takes a family. It takes teachers. It takes clergy. It takes business people. It takes community leaders. It takes those who protect our health and safety. It takes all of us!"

The delegates stood and roared their approval. Then Clinton delivered the knock-out blow to Dole.

"Yes, it takes a village!"

The convention speech was a huge hit. One poll showed over 70 percent of women voters aged twenty-five to fifty loved it. And despite being viewed as "pushy" following her controversial effort for nationalized healthcare two years earlier, Clinton's approval rating had gone up from 38 to 53 percent according to Pew Research.

Despite Bill Clinton's low 37 percent approval rating in 1994, which coincided with the Democrats losing control of the House of Representatives to Republicans for the first time in forty years, the Clintons—backed by a stronger economy—easily defeated Dole and Independent candidate Ross Perot in 1996.

For fifteen years, no woman had dominated the political discussion more than Clinton. Eight years as first lady and then—think about this accomplishment for a moment—overwhelmingly elected and reelected a U.S. senator from New York.

In early 2007, the phone rang at my desk in the newsroom. It was a long time coming. After five intense months of badgering her press secretary Philippe Reines, I was finally going to get to interview Hillary Clinton as she made her first campaign trip to South Carolina as a candidate for president. Clinton was leading the primary race in every major poll.

The campaign said Kevin and I would be the only news crew allowed to interview her in Florence—one of just three stops she made that day.

As Clinton addressed a packed room at a barbeque lunch at Osborne's, we were led upstairs to prepare for the three-camera shoot. For lighting and background purposes, Kevin decided it was best if we stood for the interview instead of being seated. We also quietly discussed the secret service members who were watching our every move. I told Kevin he was putting on her mic.

With Clinton still speaking downstairs, I had a few moments to reflect on her often difficult and unpleasant political climb.

While her husband Bill left the presidency with a high approval rating, Americans still had endured nearly a year of impeachment proceedings after he lied under oath about having an affair with a young office intern; a lie that turned Hillary Clinton's world upside down.

Shortly before the New Hampshire primary in 1992—with Bill Clinton's campaign on life support after allegations of adultery—the Clintons had their first joint television interview on *60 Minutes*. It aired immediately following the Super Bowl and had a huge TV audience. Bill Clinton denied during that interview that he had ever had an extramarital affair with Gennifer Flowers (during a deposition six years later he would admit he did have an affair with her). As reporter Steve Kroft pushed for more details—and with a presidential campaign hanging in the balance—Hillary Clinton famously said:

"I'm not sitting here like some little woman standing by my man like Tammy Wynette."

The interview is credited for having helped steady the campaign. Bill Clinton placed second in New Hampshire but went on to win the nomination and the presidency.

Six years later, now as First Lady, Clinton found herself doing another television interview defending her husband who was now accused of lying about having "sexual relations with that woman"; White House intern Monica Lewinsky.

"I think the important thing now is to stand as firmly as I can and say that, you know, the President has denied these allegations on all counts, unequivocally, and we'll see how this plays out," she told NBC's Matt Lauer. "The great story here for anybody willing to find it and write about it and explain it is this vast right-wing conspiracy that has been conspiring against my husband since the day he announced for president."

Hillary Clinton was still playing offense for her husband, saying publicly she believed his denials and that their political enemies were responsible for making all of it up. But less than eight months later, Bill Clinton told the nation in a live televised address:

"Indeed, I did have a relationship with Ms. Lewinsky that was not appropriate. I misled people, including even my wife. I deeply regret that."

Bill Clinton was impeached by the House for lying under oath about Lewinsky but survived a trial in the Senate. With just over a year left in his presidency, Hillary Clinton—the scorned political wife—could have decided to hide or go away. Instead, she announced she was running for the U.S. Senate in New York—one of the top political jobs in the country.

And she won. Big.

By every objective measure, Hillary Clinton is one of the most fascinating political figures of our time.

When Clinton finished her speech in Florence she was brought upstairs, escorted by several secret service members and staff members. No other press, with the exception of a photographer, was allowed there.

I'll be the first to admit that I had a preconceived notion about Clinton.

After so many years in politics, and after putting up with her husband, I thought she would be, for lack of a better word, icy.

That preconceived notion was completely false.

As Kevin was putting the lapel mic on her, Clinton started discussing some of the artifacts in the room—various pots and fine china the owners had collected—which she said triggered memories of some of the trips she and daughter Chelsea had made overseas.

Here was Hillary Clinton talking to me like an old lost friend. I remember telling Kevin after the interview that if her campaign staff got her into enough living rooms in Iowa, New Hampshire, and South Carolina, she would erase whatever other preconceived notions others might have about her and be a cinch for the nomination.

We now know in her "inevitable nomination" frontrunner-driven campaign, that didn't happen. At least not enough.

Another word here about my preparation for an interview with a presidential candidate. Typically, you will have around ten to twelve minutes and—with the glaring exception of Barack Obama, which we'll get to later—I've always honored that time limit.

That means you have to ask a variety of questions quickly and depend on the candidate to give you precise soundbites in return.

I like to call it a form of "interview tennis." I lob a question at the candidate and they hit it back. Every now and then I'll attempt a backspin, never surprised when there is a volley in return. We continue until match point—or until a staff member says, "last question." With really prepared candidates—almost always at the national level—you can have a great game of "interview tennis" even when it sometimes covers uneasy ground.

And Hillary Clinton is among the best at it.

Our interview was just weeks after Clinton had raised eyebrows during a speech in Iowa where she had repeated a question from an audience member, "What in my background equips me to deal with evil and bad men?"

As Clinton said it, she smiled and paused for effect.

The crowd howled with laughter as reporters looked on in confusion.

Pundits went on television suggesting she was referring to her husband and the years of defending him only to learn he had lied about numerous affairs.

So I started our interview there, asking her what she would do with her husband, the former president, if she were elected.

As I asked this question, Clinton made her trademark laugh—a bit awkward, a bit intimidating—made so famous by Amy Poehler on *Saturday Night Live.*

"I think that the work that Bill has done in the last years with his foundation and outreach to other countries gives us a leg up in terms of rebuilding the alliances that we need in order to be successful in leading the world," she told me.

When I pressed her on what exactly that meant in context to what he would do if she were President, she smiled and continued without offering specifics.

"One of the things I admire about our presidential system is that presidents use former presidents. I will certainly call on the former presidents."

Thinking about it now, Hillary Clinton is in this weird position where she wants the job once held by her spouse. She gives no indication of what kind of working relationship they'll have if she wins, maybe because it is impossible for her to know herself.

While Clinton is painted as a liberal by Republicans, many are surprised to learn she actually started in politics in 1964 as a young Republican supporter of Barry Goldwater, often called the "father of modern conservatism."

"His emphasis on individual responsibility was exactly in line with the way I was raised," Clinton told me. "I supported him strongly in that election and I was a Goldwater girl."

Four years later, now a junior at Wellesley College, Clinton drove to New Hampshire on the weekends to volunteer for the anti-Vietnam war campaign of Eugene McCarthy. Her political views had shifted drastically.

At the time of this interview, Clinton led in every major poll and Obama was in third place trailing John Edwards. Many believed Clinton would win the trifecta—winning first in Iowa and New Hampshire, and then wrapping up the nomination fight in South Carolina.

Privately, however, the Clinton team were nervous about all the talk of inevitability and she worked to downplay expectations.

"I'm not going to make any predictions because we have a strong field of people competing here and elsewhere," she told me. "But I've been very heartened by my trip here today. I have a great personal fondness for South Carolina. I see it as an important state because of the issues it presents and I would hope to do very well here."

As she campaigned for the first time in South Carolina, Clinton's sights were more on Edwards than Obama. The former North Carolina senator was second in the polls and a native of the Palmetto State. After seeking the Democratic nomination four years earlier, Edwards had been tapped to be John Kerry's running mate. The ticket lost to Bush in a close contest determined by the electoral votes in Ohio.

Entering the 2008 campaign, Edwards had publicly apologized for his vote supporting the Iraq War, which had become increasingly unpopular. He was now calling on Clinton to do the same. "If she believes her vote was wrong then, yes, she should say so," Edwards told Tim Russert.

"Why shouldn't you apologize if you feel your vote helped get us in a war we shouldn't be fighting?" I asked her.

"Well, I've taken responsibility for my vote and I've called on the president and his team to take responsibility because clearly they went head-long into this war without adequate planning or even understanding about what they were getting our country into," Clinton told me in response.

While Clinton refused to mention Edwards by name, she had no trouble adjusting her sights on Bush, who had failed to capture Osama bin Laden.

"It bothers me greatly and for the life of me, I can't understand why bin Laden is basically at large," Clinton told me. "We have reports that he is still funding the training camps that are sending Taliban and al Qaeda fighters across the border to battle with our NATO forces. This is a very serious matter and I would have never diverted attention away from bin

Laden until we had gotten the job done and I'd like to see it done now."

Clinton would see it done eventually but in a role, at this point, she could have never imagined.

THEY DIDN'T TOUCH

We jumped in the news van in the morning wanting to make the two-and-a-half hour drive from Myrtle Beach to Orangeburg by noon. It was a very big political day; the first formal debate between the Democratic presidential candidates. MSNBC was set to broadcast it nationally, Brian Williams would moderate. Everyone was anxious to see how well Hillary Clinton would compete with "the boys."

Besides Clinton, Joe Biden, Chris Dodd, Dennis Kucinich, Bill Richardson, Barack Obama, Mike Gravel, and John Edwards would be on the stage. So many candidates, so little time.

And that presents a big problem for those of us in TV news. As the co-anchor of our 11 p.m. newscast, I would be live from Orangeburg to offer highlights and analysis of the debate—but only have three minutes total at the top of the show. Believe it or not, that is a huge chunk of time when you consider there are only about twenty-two minutes total during a thirty minute show—thanks to commercials. With eight candidates, plus the voices of experts like CNN's Candy Crowley whom we planned to interview following the debate, that doesn't leave much time at all.

So what do you do? Do all the candidates deserve equal time during three minutes of coverage? It's certainly easy to say yes (and everyone says yes when I ask the question to various groups). But now seriously ask yourself whether Mike Gravel is as truly competitive in the race for president as Hillary Clinton, or Barack Obama, or John Edwards, who were then each polling over 20 percent support in major polls?

And who is Mike Gravel?

One of the things I am most grateful for in my career is the trust my bosses—in all the TV markets I've worked—have given me to provide fair and objective coverage based on my many years of experience around politics. The only thing they have said to me is "be prepared to defend your decisions." And I have on occasion.

The fact is, not all candidates are created equal. True, some candidates who receive little coverage at the start of a campaign can climb and become part of the bigger narrative. But when you start out with little traction in polling, little fundraising ability, limited staffing and organization then, well, you are unlikely to be as successful getting out your vote. That all goes into determining how much airtime we give.

My first news director Bruce Kirk taught me an important lesson during my first year in the business. We were set to have a live televised debate between the candidates for mayor of Yuma, Arizona. Like most elections, there were the Republican and Democratic candidates, but this one also included an Independent who was a perennial city council candidate and political gadfly.

As the moderator, I made the case to Bruce before the debate that the Independent did not have the same right to equal airtime as the major party candidates. There was no way he could win based on any formula you could come up with and he would be taking time away from the "real" candidates who would be discussing the serious issues. Bruce listened patiently but didn't change his mind and the debate moved forward with all three candidates.

As Bruce predicted, the Independent gave us a priceless performance. Seated between the other two, dressed in a tuxedo and bow tie, he held up newspapers to make his points and challenged the others to be more honest. I told Bruce afterwards it certainly made for more entertaining TV, but I had not changed my mind about candidates meeting a minimum requirement for free airtime. (By the way, despite his debate appearance, the Independent candidate ended up with less than 1 percent of the vote.)

Still, there is part of me that remains sympathetic to the underdogs in campaigns, and because this was the first presidential debate featuring all the Democratic candidates, we managed to include a brief soundbite from all—including Gravel, a former senator from Alaska—who gave us: "I got to tell you, after standing up with them, some of these people frighten me! They frighten me!"

The charged-up atmosphere at South Carolina State blew me away. There were hundreds of supporters of various candidates chanting outside, there was the university band playing, MSNBC had their anchors outside analyzing the debate as if it were a preseason game (which, thinking it over, it was). Standing there taking it all in, I realized my job was the equivalent of having a front row seat at the circus.

This first debate spent a great deal of time on the war in Iraq and various disagreements emerged. Edwards pressed Clinton to apologize for her vote supporting military action, Clinton said Bush should be doing the apologizing, while Obama played up the fact he had opposed the war from the start. Iraq was on the voters' minds as approval on the Bush policy continued to slip and most of the Democratic candidates were scrambling to justify their initial support.

The debate provided some interesting moments. Clinton had to answer why a majority of voters had an unfavorable view of her. "I tried to achieve universal healthcare back in '93 and '94, and I still have the scars from that experience." Richardson had to defend being a Democrat with the support of the NRA. "I'm a westerner. The Second Amendment is precious in the West." Obama was asked his view on the confederate flag, which still had a prominent spot on the South Carolina statehouse grounds. "I think that the Confederate flag should be put in a museum. That's where it belongs."

The best moment of the evening was when Williams turned to Biden and quoted a sentence from a *Los Angeles Times* editorial calling him a "gaffe machine" and asked if he had the discipline to be on the world stage. Biden answered "yes" and said nothing more. The crowd laughed and the debate moved on.

Following the debate, Clinton, Obama, and Edwards took off without making an appearance in the spin room. These areas—where candidates meet the press for one-on-one interviews—are becoming less relevant with every election. The second-tier candidates were all there, each claiming they had clearly "won" the debate. And Elizabeth Edwards was around, spinning the good word for her husband.

The Edwards campaign had contacted me several weeks prior to the debate to see if I'd be interested in talking to their candidate and doing a profile piece in our newscast as we had for others. Edwards was a South Carolina native, he had won the primary four years earlier, and he was the former Democratic vice presidential nominee. Of course I said yes.

We had scheduled the interview for the day following the presidential debate, prior to the start of the state Democratic Party convention in Columbia. It took days for the Edwards camp to respond when I requested a joint interview with both the candidate and his wife. A month earlier they had held a joint press conference in North Carolina to announce that Elizabeth's cancer, which had previously been in remission, had returned.

The campaign informed me that a joint interview would not be possible—that wasn't overly surprising—but what was surprising was being told I could speak to them separately. Following the debate, I met up with Elizabeth Edwards and asked her first about her health.

"I'm feeling fine, but I do try to deflect the conversation from my individual circumstance to the circumstances of people who face exactly what I'm facing but without an incredibly supportive husband and without healthcare coverage. If I can do that I'll feel invigorated as opposed to tired because of this disease."

It was impossible not to ask her about "hairgate"—after an admission by her husband that he had paid over $500 for a recent haircut. This along with news that the Edwards were building a $5.3 million dollar 28,000-square-foot house on 102 acres near Chapel Hill were damaging his reputation as the working class candidate.

"I don't want to know what your haircuts cost," she answered with a smile and laugh. "I promise I won't ask you, Jim." It was actually quite a brilliant way to deflect the topic.

That night, Elizabeth Edwards was full of energy as she worked the crowd and the press. What we didn't know at the time is that she was fully aware her "incredibly supportive husband" was having an ongoing affair with a former campaign videographer that threatened to destroy his presidential ambitions.

There are some candidates you meet and immediately like. For me, that's how I would describe John Edwards when I interviewed him first in 2004. He was in a battle for the nomination that year with John Kerry and Howard Dean. Both of them had charisma issues and Edwards seemed like the future of the Democratic Party.

In fact, Edwards placed second behind Kerry in the Iowa Caucus that year, knocking frontrunner Dean to third place. I interviewed Dean days after his infamous "scream" speech in Iowa—"We're going to South Carolina and Oklahoma and Arizona and North Dakota and New Mexico, and we're going to California and Texas and New York. And we're going to South Dakota and Oregon and Washington and Michigan, and then we're going to Washington, D.C., to take back the White House! *Yeahh-hhhhhh!*"—and was not surprised he placed blame for his campaign mess on the media.

"It went sideways when *TIME* magazine and *Newsweek* and all those folks decided I was the frontrunner," he told me. "Usually voters like to decide who the frontrunner is, not the news media. Most people seem to know that my speech was the entertainment side of the media. They've played it 937 times over the week. But it was attempt to fire up the troops and we did. It wasn't very presidential."

But it sure was funny.

At the end of the interview, Dean told me on air he was cheering for the Patriots against the Panthers in the upcoming Super Bowl. Days later, he received 5 percent of the vote in the South Carolina primary. And that was that.

Kerry picked Edwards to be his running mate later that summer and the ticket came close to winning, with Ohio's electoral votes sinking their fate. The race was so close, most pundits agreed Edwards would be in a strong position to seek the nomination again.

Four years later, as Kevin and I set up the two cameras and lights for our street corner interview in Columbia, we assumed the friendly Edwards would be back.

You know what happens when you assume.

Edwards arrived being driven in a black presidential-looking SUV. As he exited the car, he grabbed his coat from the backseat and started shouting at his staff. This went on for minutes—he was clearly irritated at something. This demeanor was opposite from the guy I interviewed four years earlier.

On a side note, politicians who treat their staff poorly—especially publicly—are bush-league. Yes, we elect a candidate to make the final decisions on issues, but we also expect them to hire a qualified and experienced group of people who comprise a team. When the leader of that team has little respect for the individuals working for them, you can bet they think even less of the voters who put them there. End side note.

Edwards approached and we shook hands. I pointed out that my voice was nearly gone after having a severe allergy attack in Orangeburg the night before (my allergist the next day told me to avoid going to Orangeburg, which I have, and it's worked perfectly). I started questions on his push to get Clinton to apologize for her vote in support of war in Iraq.

"I thought my vote was wrong, it was important for me to accept responsibility. I think the next President of the United States needs to be honest with the American people. For Senator Clinton I think this is a question for her, and anyone who supported the war, it's a question of their own conscience and that's something she has to resolve for herself."

While Obama was still polling low in South Carolina at this point it was clear that the African American vote—which had helped Edwards easily win the primary in 2004—could overwhelmingly go his way. I asked if that made him nervous.

"I think growing up in the South and South Carolina when I was young, I understand the civil rights movement. I understand the history of race and segregation in South Carolina and because of that I feel a huge responsibility on issues of inequality and race. I talk like this so I think I have a natural connection here..." I interrupted and asked if his southern accent is what he meant—"you got it, it's still there."

So how is it, I asked, that someone so concerned about inequality and those less fortunate could so easily pay $500 for a haircut?

"Well that was just a mistake," he responded. "That should never have happened. The bill got sent to the wrong place and the campaign should have caught it and sent it to me. If they had sent it to me I could have seen how much it was, which I didn't know. So the whole thing was a series of stupid mistakes. But I'm responsible for it, I'm the candidate and I can't blame other people."

Edwards was also responsible for something far worse and he couldn't blame anybody but himself. On this he wouldn't fess up for a long time but it was explosive enough to end his political career. And we sensed it before it ever went public.

After returning to the television station, I took the tapes from Kevin and started looking at the video (b-roll as we call it in the industry) to see if there was anything I should write to and include in my profile. At one point I paused the tape and thought, *something is wrong with this picture.* Following our interview, Kevin had run with his camera in front of the Edwards as they walked with enthusiastic supporters down a street. But there was absolutely no touching. No holding hands, no hugging, not even many smiles.

"That's odd," I said to Kevin.

The visual reminded me of the Mondale/Ferraro campaign in 1984. Former vice president Walter Mondale had made a historic choice putting a woman—Congresswoman Geraldine Ferraro—on his ticket. But there was debate within his campaign on how touchy-feely the two should be in public. In the end, they decided to stand and walk arm-to-arm rather than hug or clasp hands for those victory poses.

And that's exactly what we were seeing the husband-wife team of John and Elizabeth Edwards do down the streets of Columbia.

Very odd, I thought.

What we didn't know then was what the tabloid *National Enquirer* (that's still a bit embarrassing for us political journalists) exposed several months later.

At the time of our interview, Edwards had been having a fourteen-month-long affair with campaign videographer Rielle Hunter. In an interview with *GQ* magazine Hunter said it started at the beginning of 2006, and Elizabeth learned about the affair in December of that year after finding a secret phone her husband and Hunter had been using.

By all accounts, Elizabeth was furious—what wife wouldn't be—but for whatever reason she wanted the presidential campaign to continue. That decision by the Edwards to stay in the race would later infuriate many supporters and former staff members who were embarrassed by his risky behavior.

Edwards and Hunter would conceive a daughter just weeks after our interview where he had lectured about the next president being "honest with the American people."

By every objective measure John Edwards was an epic fail.

Dumb As Hell

"Mr. Butterfield, are you aware of the installation of any listening devices in the Oval Office of the President?"

A simple question asked by the Minority Counsel to presidential deputy assistant Alexander Butterfield during the 1973 Watergate hearings.

"I was aware of listening devices, yes, sir" Butterfield replied.

That question and answer were the beginning of the end for President Richard Nixon. The tapes would provide so much damaging information that it would lead to the first—and to date, only—presidential resignation in our history.

Fred Thompson was the attorney who had asked that critical question. It was on my mind as we drove from Myrtle Beach to Columbia to interview the former senator and actor. He was making his first stop in South Carolina and—in a first—his campaign had called us and asked if we wanted to have an exclusive interview. Of course we did, and Kevin was especially excited because *The Hunt for Red October*, in which Thompson had appeared, was one of his favorite movies.

We arrived in Columbia where Thompson delivered a speech to a few hundred people, most of them supporters. Others just wanted to see the TV and movie star up close. At one point during the speech he hit on the topic of illegal immigration and singled out Cubans, saying:

"I don't imagine they're coming here to bring greetings from Castro. We're living in the era of the suitcase bomb!"

The statement, one of his first as a candidate, raised eyebrows. Hillary Clinton wasted no time responding, telling a group of Hispanic leaders, "Apparently he doesn't have a lot of experience in Florida or anywhere else, and doesn't know a lot of Cuban Americans."

Even the conservative National Review called the statement the "first unforced error" of Thompson's campaign. Writer Jim Geraghty wrote, "Aw, man. Of all the groups Fred Thompson could cite as a potential security threat, did he have to pick the Cubans? The one group of Hispanics that leans Republican?"

The immigration issue wasn't a new one during recent campaigns. Despite the fact President Ronald Reagan signed the last amnesty bill—"I believe in the idea of amnesty for those who have put down roots and lived here, even though some time back they may have entered illegally," Reagan said in 1984—many conservatives were now solidly committed to building a big fence on the border with Mexico and shipping back the estimated eleven million illegal residents in the country.

Perhaps the most sensible answer to this immigration question, in my view anyway, came during an interview with a national politician you'd probably least suspect.

In 2002, while doing a story on the growing number of deaths on the U.S./Mexico border by people attempting to enter the country illegally, I asked former vice president Dan Quayle about our border policy. He answered:

"One of the things I have urged throughout my life in politics and speaking on public policy issues is to concentrate on economic development south of the border. Because if you have good jobs, a better quality of life, there will be more of a tendency to stay in your neighborhood."

In other words, instead of taking years to build a great big wall that will never be high enough, and spend billions of tax dollars on increased border patrol that will never be enough, just help stabilize northern Mexico's economy. Quayle's theory is, people and families who can find jobs and a steady income will not feel the necessity to risk everything—including their lives—to come here illegally.

Imagine if we had spent the last fifteen years doing what Quayle proposed instead of all the endless bickering we've witnessed that still has us nowhere near solving the problem.

Back in Columbia, after Thompson's speech we jumped on board his luxury campaign bus. These were really becoming the "in thing" for presidential candidates. Fully decked out with TVs, leather chairs, plenty of room for family and even their favorite foods. John McCain had one. So did Mitt Romney. Now we were on the Thompson express, although it remained parked during our interview.

Thompson is probably best known by millions for his television character on *Law and Order* along with over a dozen movies. But his starring role in helping bring down the Nixon administration will probably be what historians find most fascinating about him.

As the cameras rolled, I asked Thompson to take us back to that time, the summer of 1973.

"Well, I was thirty years old, a young man in the center of the most important thing going on in our country at the time. I was sitting at the right hand of Statesman Howard Baker (just what did the President know and when did he first know it?), Sam Irvine was one seat over, and I got to watch American history be made."

But what about effectively asking the question that led to a fellow Republican resigning from the presidency?

"I had to do my duty," Thompson said. "I started as a loyal Republican and ended up a loyal Republican, but you have to call them as you see them, and we knew there was a taping system in the White House and it was our obligation to bring it out."

On one of Nixon's tapes, his aide H.R. Haldeman informed him that Thompson had been appointed as the minority counsel.

"Oh shit, that kid?" a dismayed Nixon responded.

On another tape from May 1973, Nixon would say about Thompson to his White House Chief of Staff Alexander Haig:

"Oh shit, he's dumb as hell."

Three months later, the thirty-year-old Thompson would ask the not-so-dumb question that led to Nixon's embarrassing departure.

To say Thompson waited too long to enter the busy 2008 GOP field is an understatement. He fiddled around for most of the spring and summer as conservatives tried to coax him into the race. The sixty-five-year-old actor first had to quit his TV show and leave Hollywood. He and his family also had to worry about his non-Hodgkin's lymphoma, which was now in remission.

Conservatives had spent months wishing for a savior who could deliver them from the current pack of McCain, Giuliani, and Romney, each of whom they viewed with suspicion. So in September, just months before the first votes were cast, Thompson went on *The Tonight Show with Jay*

Leno and declared, "I'm running for President of the United States."

The announcement brought a collective yawn and worse.

His Republican opponents, who at that exact same time were debating in New Hampshire, had a field day with the timing of his decision. "I was scheduled to be on Jay Leno tonight, but I gave up my slot for somebody else because I'd rather be in New Hampshire with these fine people," said Mike Huckabee to enthusiastic applause. Mitt Romney suggested Thompson wait until January to make his decision while John McCain quipped, "maybe we're up past his bed time."

I asked Thompson what was the final turning point in his decision to enter a competitive presidential race so late and what message he was sending to the other candidates.

"It had to do with what I perceive to be my relationship with the people," he told me. "I've been traveling around the past few months and I feel like there's something different and something special going on in the country. When I put my name in play, the response was just extremely more than I expected and I had to think seriously about this. So it's no aspersion on anyone else."

From his late entry into the race to the questions of the day; I started by asking whether he would defend the ongoing neo-conservative strategy in Iraq despite polls showing support for the war falling.

"I think sometimes there's only two bad choices. If we had not gone in there, Saddam Hussein would be down there well on his way, in my opinion, to nuclear weapons. He and his two crazy sons would still be in power, having defeated the United Nations and the United States with regard to the embargo attempts."

But what about the fact that we had failed, thus far, to capture the terrorist who was responsible for organizing the events of 9/11?

"Well, we gotta find and kill this guy," Thompson told me.

"I mean, he represents everything that's dangerous to this country. But we should not be fixated on one personality. There is gonna be somebody to replace him once we catch him and administer justice. They are a broad network around the world, certainly in the United States, trying to get their hands on Weapons of Mass Destruction. And of course we need to do anything possible to catch this guy because of what he's done to our people, but it's not going to be over once we do."

Thompson was widely known due to his appearances in movies and on television—especially as the District Attorney on *Law and Order*. My impression of his answers on the political questions I had asked were they were still a work in progress. He wasn't quite comfortable—or interested—in a lot of the details.

That is until I asked him what his favorite acting role had been. He smiled and his eyes lit up as he said, "My favorite movie? *The Hunt for Red October*." Kevin said "yes!" loud enough behind the camera to make Thompson smile even more.

He had the memorable scene in that film where he said, "This business will get out of control. It will get out of control and we'll be lucky to live through it!"

Thompson continued, "I got to go out on the USS Enterprise for a little while. It was a great story and I got to play a great character. I mean, I got to play a fellow, the kind of people I admire."

Fred Thompson told me he needed to win South Carolina to be the nominee. He would finish third, and as quickly as he had entered the race, he was gone.

FAITH AND LIBERTARIANISM

Fred Thompson entered the race late in 2007 with conservatives hoping he would be the "rallying" candidate that could prevent John McCain from winning the nomination.

But late in the year Thompson wasn't igniting much of anything. Nor was Mitt Romney, who was watching his lead in the first three critical states drop. So the focus shifted to the former governor of Arkansas, Mike Huckabee.

A likeable guy with an "aw-shucks" demeanor, Huckabee was an ordained Southern Baptist minister with very conservative social views. Even though he was receiving little national media attention, it was becoming clear to those of us in South Carolina that evangelicals, and home-school proponents, were beginning to pay close attention to his candidacy.

Huckabee organized those groups and shocked everyone by winning the Iowa Caucus. And this leads to yet another example where I feel a caucus fails the process. Had Iowa conducted a primary instead—where the turnout would have increased and the convoluted process been eliminated—Huckabee may not have been the winner.

The victory put him in the national spotlight, slowed down any momentum for Romney, pleased McCain, who was expecting a victory the following week in New Hampshire, and set up South Carolina as the GOP showdown between the establishment candidate and conservative alternative.

Huckabee had few campaign dollars, but was effectively pushing the buttons of the religious right. He said in South Carolina that opposing abortion was a "critical" reason why he was running for president. He also picked up the endorsement of former South Carolina governor David Beasley, a conservative who had warmly introduced George W. Bush at Bob Jones University eight years earlier.

The Romney campaign, stinging after the Iowa loss and sinking in polls from New Hampshire, accused Huckabee of wearing a "Christian leader" hat in states like South Carolina but dropping it in other states where social conservatism was less important.

I interviewed Huckabee before the primary and asked if his campaign, so deeply rooted in religion and the issues it raised, was polarizing for the Republican Party.

"A lot of people want to make it the issue," he told me. "I think it's only the issue where people want to actually know that you have convictions. That you have core principles that you stand by and that those core principals are consistent and authentic. If they are, then I'm not sure that it matters what faith you profess as much as it is that you have something that you truly believe in more than just getting elected."

Huckabee was out of the race by the first week of March. He decided not to seek the nomination again in 2012, but announced as a GOP candidate for 2016 in a very crowded field.

Another candidate I was covering believed Huckabee's only claim to fame in the nomination fight was his religion. In fact, when Huckabee released a Christmas time TV ad in South Carolina that featured a bookcase in the background that looked like a cross, congressman Ron Paul responded, "It reminds me of what Sinclair Lewis once said, 'when fascism comes to this country, it will be wrapped in the flag, carrying a cross.'"

Ron Paul stood out—I mean, really stood out. The one-time Libertarian nominee for president was widely dismissed by Republicans in 2008 mainly due to his anti-neo-con views on foreign policy. He had been the only GOP presidential candidate to oppose going to war in Iraq and he was jeered at a live presidential debate in Columbia:

"I think the party has lost its way because the conservative wing of the Republican Party always advocated a non-interventionist foreign policy... Republicans were elected to end the Korean War. Republicans were elected to end the Vietnam War. There's a strong tradition of being anti-war in the Republican Party."

Paul was then asked if those non-interventionist views still held in the aftermath of 9/11:

"Have you ever read the reasons they attacked us? They attack us because we've been over there; we've been bombing Iraq for ten years... We don't understand the irrationality of Middle Eastern politics... I'm suggesting that we listen to the people who attacked us and the reason they did it, and they are delighted that we're over there because Osama bin Laden has said, 'I am glad you're over on our sand because we can target you so much easier.' They have already now since that time killed 3,400 of our men, and I don't think it was necessary."

At this point in the debate Rudy Giuliani, who was making his leadership as mayor during 9/11 the narrative of his campaign, interrupted and chastised Paul's position:

"That's an extraordinary statement, as someone who lived through the attack of September 11th, that we invited the attack because we were attacking Iraq. I don't think I've heard that before, and I've heard some pretty absurd explanations for September 11th and I would ask the congressman to withdraw that comment and tell us that he didn't really mean that."

At that point, the Republican crowd erupted in large cheers for Giuliani, as Paul tried to have the last word:

"If we think that we can do what we want around the world and not incite hatred, then we have a problem!"

To say Ron Paul was not fully accepted by conservatives as a Republican presidential candidate in 2008 is an understatement. After being booed at this debate he was left out of many others. His point about considering the ramifications of our actions overseas was not selling in the GOP primary even as support for Bush and war in Iraq was quickly dropping in polls.

Paul's campaign crowds, however, steadily grew throughout 2007. This strange political coalition of college students, anti-war liberals, and anti-government libertarians had the potential of expanding the GOP brand, if—and this was doubtful—the neo-cons in the party could share space.

Paul made his first campaign visit to Myrtle Beach in November 2007. Many of the hundreds of cheering supporters were wearing "Ron Paul Revolution" tee shirts. He told reporter Mike Essian, "I never believed it was necessary to go to war, because I never believed it had anything to do with 9/11, or anything to do with Weapons of Mass Destruction, and it turned out to be so." That put him completely at odds with the Bush-Cheney foreign policy.

One night before the primary, I was anchoring live from the Myrtle Beach Convention Center, the sight of an upcoming presidential debate. With a few minutes to go before the 6 o'clock news, I looked over and saw Ron Paul walking alone on a sidewalk. I dropped my microphone and went over to thank him for allowing our station to use his campaign blimp that afternoon for some aerial shots. Paul looked up at the blimp—with RON PAUL REVOLUTION boldly printed in red, white, and blue—and back down at me and said, "I wish I knew who did that."

The blimp was not officially connected to Paul's campaign and had been shadowing him in New Hampshire and South Carolina for weeks. It was also a very effective gimmick because we in the local news business didn't have many other campaign blimp stories to tell and it generated a lot of free publicity.

What I appreciated most about Ron Paul is that he seemed as bewildered as the rest of us on why he was treated like a rock star by his incredibly enthusiastic supporters. He also seemed equally dumbfounded that a gigantic blimp was following him around the country.

After he placed fifth in both Iowa and New Hampshire, I interviewed him one night via satellite and asked whether he would eventually bolt the GOP and run an Independent or third party campaign:

"I have no plans and no intentions on doing that. I've done it before, and the system is so biased against third-party and Independent candidates, if you're not a billionaire it's difficult. So we lack in our defense of democracy here in this country. But as far as supporting other candidates, if they would come around to supporting these views I would certainly consider it."

Paul would seek the GOP nomination again in 2012, and there were a lot less boos over his foreign policy views during debates. In fact, by 2016, many of the leading Republican presidential candidates—including Bush's own brother Jeb—had started to mimic his position on Iraq.

Ron Paul's son, U.S. senator Rand Paul, also entered the race in 2016, sharing many of the same views as his dad.

Paul may have failed as a presidential candidate, but his revolution was only beginning.

Against The Odds

It was a full two years before the presidential primary when Senator John McCain's press secretary called and asked if we wanted to have the first television interview in South Carolina since he lost the GOP primary six years earlier.

"Of course!" I replied.

We then worked out details to have a wireless microphone on McCain (C-SPAN style) for his book signing stop and the two speeches he would be delivering in the upstate. I thought, "we can call it 'A Day with John McCain!' It could be a great two-part sweeps piece!" My news director liked the pitch.

As we discussed the upcoming two years of coverage, we agreed it would be best to have a designated photographer for all future campaign events. Thus, my partnership with Kevin Abadie—expert photographer and editor—was born. Our coverage in South Carolina would take us all over the state, to the lawn of the White House, and even an Emmy nomination.

But first thing first, "A Day with John McCain."

To say the return to South Carolina was painful for McCain is an understatement. Six years earlier, he had arrived in the Palmetto State after beating Texas governor George W. Bush by nineteen points in the New Hampshire primary. Bush's one-time fifty-point lead in South Carolina had evaporated, and a win by McCain would have likely propelled him into the Republican nomination and a general election win (the Democrats had held the White House for eight years and rarely does the same party win three presidential elections in a row).

With McCain's fortunes rising, a conservative and evangelical coalition devised a smear campaign against him that is still discussed by political strategists everywhere.

There were first rumors floated that McCain had fathered an illegitimate black child. Then, rumors he had slept with prostitutes and given his wife V.D. A third rumor suggested McCain was 'mentally unstable' after returning from Vietnam.

All of them patently untrue.

Christian-fundamentalist Bob Jones University in Greenville—with a controversial long-standing ban on interracial dating—played a huge role in turning out the evangelical vote. Texas governor George W. Bush accepted the university's invitation to address hundreds of voters before the primary telling the crowd, "it feels a lot warmer here in the state of South Carolina if you know what I mean." McCain was told to stay away and he replied angrily, "If I had been invited I would have told them to get out of the 16th century and into the 21st century. What you're doing is racist and cruel. Governor Bush went there and never said a word. I would never, ever do such a thing."

McCain must have hit a nerve because the university quietly ended the ban a few months later.

Rumors about McCain "siring children without marriage" were being spread by a bible professor at Bob Jones. Flyers were being distributed with a picture of a little black girl with the McCain family—leaving it to the imagination rather than the truth that she had been adopted after his wife Cindy met her during a relief mission in Bangladesh.

Most of the gossip, reporters learned later, was being provided to the evangelical right by Karl Rove, Bush's top strategist. While researching the ugliness of the primary fight, Dr. Eddie Dyer of Coastal Carolina University told me, "The allegations have never been proven so you can classify them as scurrilous, but that took McCain out of the race."

On primary day, Bush beat McCain by eleven points backed by a huge voter turnout in the conservative upstate. McCain, with clinched teeth in Charleston, told supporters, "I want the presidency in the best way, not the worst way. I won't take the low road to the highest office in the land."

Several months later, after he had dropped out of the race, a subdued McCain told supporters his biggest regret from his 2000 campaign was not publicly calling on South Carolina to remove the confederate flag from the statehouse grounds in Columbia. "I feared that if I answered honestly, I could not win the South Carolina primary. So I chose to compromise my principles. I broke my promise to always tell the truth."

(South Carolina would remove the controversial flag fifteen years later, after nine African Americans were murdered by a white man in a church in Charleston.)

So here we were six years later waiting to interview McCain in a state that had created such bitter memories, and just a stone's throw away from Bob Jones University.

As a disclaimer, I've known McCain since my teenage years growing up in Arizona. As a kid I circulated brochures in neighborhoods for his first congressional campaign and volunteered when he ran for the U.S. Senate. When I started my television career in Yuma, Arizona, McCain and I did a live weather segment together, which earned 3rd place "best TV live shot" from the Arizona Associated Press. At one point, McCain started talking about the dangers of "fluctuating barometers" and he encouraged more snowbirds to visit saying, "we take all plastic!"

We laughed so much, one viewer emailed the station asking why we had been drinking so early in the day. The craziness of doing weather on TV with John McCain still makes me smile when I think about it.

So McCain and I had history in and out of television, and it raises a legitimate question here of whether journalists and politicians can be friends. Of course the answer is yes, with a caveat that being friendly doesn't mean at the end of the day if a scandal hits, you won't cover it objectively. That's a journalist's job, and sadly it's happened during my career more than once.

I've always liked McCain on a personal level for two reasons. One, he sat in a tiny dirty cell in Vietnam for five years as a Prisoner of War defending our freedoms. A lot of politicians talk about service, but McCain, following the lead of his father and grandfather, has walked the walk. His time as a POW was spelled out in detail in his 1999 book *Faith of My Fathers*, which was also made into a movie in 2005. Second, he's fearless with the press. The better politicians I've covered have always been comfortable speaking their minds and McCain has never been so overly partisan that he won't occasionally tell his own party to stick it. After covering hundreds of cookie-cutter politicians through the years, when a maverick comes along it's interesting.

I had last interviewed McCain nearly three years earlier on the U.S./ Mexico border. McCain was kept under an umbrella on that sunny day until just seconds before my live shot because of concerns about his melanoma. In 2000, after dropping out of the presidential race, McCain had five hours of skin cancer surgery on the left side of his face, which left a permanent scar. He would stand out in the sun, with a cap and long sleeved shirt, for only a few minutes at a time and most of his future campaign events would be indoors.

Our interview in Greenville was inside a Barnes and Noble bookstore where several hundred people were waiting for McCain to autograph copies of his new book. Kevin, along with colleague Marshall Staton, set up three cameras and two lights, positioned in the middle of the store so that the books were faded in the background for dramatic effect. Some customers stopped dead in their tracks at the sight of John McCain sitting in the middle of the store. It had all the appearances of a network news shoot.

McCain sat down, and after we discussed the irony of crossing paths again in South Carolina, I began by asking about Bob Jones University and the wounds left over from the 2000 race.

"After we were defeated here I slept like a baby—sleep for two hours, wake up and cry—sleep for two hours, wake up and cry," he laughed.

McCain insisted that he held no lingering animosity with the evangelical activists and instead suggested that Rove was the main culprit.

"I was defeated here in 2000 not by religious conservatives, although that was certainly part of it, but I was defeated by the Republican establishment. Bush had the entire Republican establishment behind him and all the money that entails."

Since losing the 2000 nomination fight, McCain had broadened his maverick—conservatives called it moderate—reputation.

In Greenville that night, he made 600 Republicans—each who paid $50 and up for a ticket to hear him speak—wait an extra hour so he could attend a Martin Luther King Jr. ceremony across town. At that event, McCain choked up and wiped away a tear while reading King's letter from a Birmingham jail—"Daddy, why do white people treat colored people so mean?"—something I later included in our report. A few days later, McCain's speechwriter and close adviser Mark Salter called and said he liked the piece, except for the inclusion of the tears. No time to appear weak heading into another South Carolina battle.

With support for the war in Iraq dropping, I played for McCain a clip from a debate he had with his Democratic challenger Richard Kimball in 1986 where Kimball had suggested the possibility of ground troops in Nicaragua:

"I would not support and will not support sending U.S. troops to Nicaragua," said McCain at that time, "I don't think a majority of the American people would support such a thing, and Richard, I think you should rethink your position on a very dangerous and reckless policy of sending young men to fight and die in the jungles of Central America."

Twenty years later, with thousands of young people fighting and dying in Iraq, I asked whether McCain had radically changed his position on war.

"It's vastly different in that Nicaraguans never had any remote possibility of acquiring weapons of mass destruction."

Still, McCain was no fan of the Bush-Cheney-Rumsfeld strategy in Iraq.

Months later, we covered McCain as he campaigned in Florence, South Carolina. Once again we sat down with him for an interview and he unleashed on Secretary of Defense Donald Rumsfeld.

"Shortly after the initial invasion I gave speeches that we had the wrong strategy. The president has a right to choose his own team, but for years I said I had no confidence in Secretary Rumsfeld." I asked why Rumsfeld was the focus of blame when the buck generally stops with the Commander in Chief. "Of course Bush is responsible, and he has taken responsibility and he's said serious mistakes were made. The president has acknowledged that."

It was a strange full circle. In 2000 McCain ended his campaign with contempt for Bush but the former POW had once again forgiven and moved on.

At seventy-one, McCain was one of the oldest presidential candidates in recent memory. Besides his skin cancer, there were other questions about his health. While in Vietnam, McCain suffered from a broken leg and two broken arms. None of the injuries were treated properly at the time, and it's common knowledge among reporters that McCain cannot lift either of his arms high enough to comb his hair—usually a staff member is nearby to help him prior to interviews. So I asked him during this interview if he was prepared for another national campaign.

"I feel great. I hiked the Grand Canyon with my oldest son at the Naval Academy last August. I work seven days a week, twelve to sixteen hours a day. And I love being back in South Carolina, I really do."

As much as McCain loved being back, there were questions of whether his wife Cindy would ever return. After the campaign in 2000 where rumors questioned whether she was addicted to drugs (she had become dependent on prescription painkillers after back surgery in 1989, but had stopped taking them in 1992), and where her adopted daughter came from, many supporters believed she was justified in campaigning elsewhere.

Shortly before the primary I spoke with Cindy about returning to the state that had done so much to end her husband's presidential dreams eight years earlier.

"I resisted for a number of reasons—not just because of what happened in South Carolina—but our family has changed, our kids are at different ages now, and families go on. I really had to think about it," she told me.

Cindy McCain traveled the state in the weeks leading up to the vote. On board yet another bus trip, McCain smiled and said about his wife, "The only problem it poses for my campaign is that so many people say, why isn't she the candidate?"

During the multiple interviews with McCain that year, Kevin and I had witnessed his campaign go from frontrunner, to also-ran, to under the radar. After spending millions of dollars too soon, McCain cut back his operation and started concentrating on personally speaking at every veteran's hall in South Carolina. Each time we covered one of his rallies—sometimes with fifty people, other times two hundred—I would whisper to Kevin, "all of these people vote."

Shortly before Christmas, just weeks before the first vote of 2008 was cast, the McCain campaign released—in my view—one of the most memorable political ads of the year. It aired in both New Hampshire and South Carolina and in it McCain shared the story of how Christianity allowed him and a Vietnamese prison guard to form a special bond. While viewers watched a cross being made in the dirt, McCain said,

"One night, after being mistreated as a POW, a guard loosened the ropes binding me, easing my pain. On Christmas, that same guard approached me, and without saying a word, he drew a cross in the sand. We stood wordlessly looking at the cross, remembering the true light of Christmas. I will never forget that no matter where you are, no matter how difficult the circumstances, there will always be someone who will pick you up. May you and your family have a blessed Christmas and happy holidays."

The ad, so simple and heartfelt, helped propel McCain to a come-from-behind win in New Hampshire. Anyone who doubted whether voters would consider a former POW an "American hero" needed only to look at the results: McCain beat Romney, the neighbor from the state next door, 37 to 32 percent despite being outspent by a huge margin.

After winning the first-in-the-nation primary, as he had in 2000, McCain headed back to South Carolina. This time, however, unlike the disaster of eight years earlier, there was a sense the Palmetto State could deliver the knockout blow in his favor.

"Did you ever think after you lost South Carolina in 2000 you'd be so close to the nomination again?" I asked him on board his campaign bus. "Frankly, at the time I didn't contemplate that," McCain laughed.

I asked whether his 2000 campaign theme of being Luke Skywalker fighting the Bush empire had changed to him now supporting Bush and his policies.

"It's pretty much the same themes, but the world has changed since 9/11. We're now in a struggle against radical Islamic extremism that's going to be with us for a long time. We didn't have that in 2000."

As the bus continued its trip from Myrtle Beach to Charleston, I asked McCain if he would agree that South Carolina, once again, remained vital to his political future. "South Carolina remains a key and vital aspect of whoever wants to get the nomination."

Indeed it was. I'll write more about his South Carolina showing later in the book.

Four years later, I asked McCain in an interview to think back on when he knew he was going lose the general election in 2008 to Barack Obama. He pinpointed a single day:

"Jim, I could tell that we were in trouble," McCain answered. "We were up three points on September 15th, the stock market went down 700 points and at the end of that day we were six points down as white male educated voters watched their 401Ks disappear."

With an incumbent president of his own party at 25 percent approval and an economy that was failing, McCain says he knew through the fall that he wasn't going to win.

"I give Obama credit for running a great campaign and I will take any blame for losing that anybody wants to attribute to me."

McCain would win another term in the U.S. Senate in 2010 and five years later, as he neared eighty, announced he would seek reelection again in 2016.

A FOREIGN-SOUNDING NAME

For 210 years, voters in our nation elected white men to be President of the United States. Like clockwork every four years. Initially, voter eligibility was left up to states (another "states' rights" thing) and most of them only allowed white guys to do the voting. The Fifteenth Amendment was approved in 1870 allowing African-American men the right to vote. Women were not granted that privilege until the Nineteenth Amendment in 1920. But as of 2008, no African-American male or female of any color had been elected to the highest political office in the land.

Oh, sure, we had a few presidents that were "different" than the others along the way. Thomas Jefferson and Abraham Lincoln were not Christians, as an example. In fact, Jefferson took the New Testament, tore it apart, and kept only the sections he liked (known as the Jefferson Bible). Can you imagine any politician doing that today?

George Washington had only one natural tooth left by the time he was elected president and had dentures made out of hippopotamus ivory (not wood so stop saying that). James Buchanan was a bachelor. Ronald Reagan was divorced. Franklin D. Roosevelt used a wheelchair. Teddy Roosevelt is the reason we have teddy bears. William Howard Taft was so heavy he once got stuck in the White House bathtub.

But despite their various quirks and differences, they were all still white guys.

So in early 2007, when former first lady Hillary Clinton and a little-known U.S. Senator named Barack Obama were leading the pack of potential Democratic nominees, it was really a historic thing.

Obama had announced his candidacy in the exact place where Lincoln had started his political career in 1834:

"It was here, in Springfield, where North, South, East and West come together that I was reminded of the essential decency of the American people, where I came to believe that through this decency, we can build a more hopeful America. And that is why, in the shadow of the Old State Capitol, where Lincoln once called on a divided house to stand together, where common hopes and common dreams still live, I stand before you today to announce my candidacy for President of the United States."

For months following Obama's announcement, the focus of many pundits—and I have to admit I was guilty too—remained squarely on Clinton on the Democratic side. The wife of the former president, with a huge organization and seemingly all the campaign money, the feeling was she would have no problem defeating her opponents.

But by the time I sat down for an interview with Obama in August, there was a slight shift of opinion in the air. While Clinton still led among Democrats nationally—eighteen points in a CNN poll, twenty-three points in Gallup—there was nonetheless some murmuring that her campaign was not galvanizing activists, especially in South Carolina.

So for days I prepared my questions, tilted toward the historic side of Obama's candidacy. What, I wondered, if he won and for the first time America had a non-white guy as Commander in Chief? And what if South Carolina, home to Strom Thurmond and his segregationist presidential campaign sixty years earlier, propels Obama to the White House?

Sometimes when you are living during historic times you don't see it. But after 210 years of doing the same thing—think of how many generations that is—Americans were potentially on the verge of doing something epic. And I was going to ask about it.

Kevin and I arrived in Dillon, South Carolina, at J.V. Martin Middle School for the interview. The school, built over 110 years ago in 1896 and still in use, had been featured two years earlier in the documentary, "Corridor of Shame," about crumbling schools along I-95.

The school superintendent, Ray Rogers, had been in the district for two decades and described to reporters how rags were used to fill holes, and buckets (of which there were many around) captured rain during storms. During the winter, without central heating, the temperature in the gym would sometimes drop to eighteen degrees. On this mid-August day it was so hot inside that Obama, and every reporter, took off our suit coats and rolled up our sleeves as we fought off the sweat. It was truly deplorable that any American child was attempting to learn under these conditions.

As we toured the school, and entered the gym, Obama grabbed a basketball, bounced it a few times, set up and nailed a basket from beyond the three-point line! It was about the only thing to cheer about in that school.

For the interview, Kevin and I had to undergo more security checks than we ever had for any other candidate, including Clinton, who was the former first lady. Our equipment was taken to a separate room, scanned and checked, and dogs were then brought in to sniff it out. Secret Service, already protecting Obama even though we were months away from his Iowa Caucus win, then used a wand to individually scan us.

I whispered to Kevin, "This campaign thinks he's already president." In reality, I'm sure he was receiving above the ordinary amount of hate mail and death threats, which had spurred the early Secret Service protection.

We had set up three cameras in a cramped little room in a trailer used by school officials. The wood paneling—popular I'm guessing in the 1960s—was not an ideal backdrop, but continued the narrative of just how lost many of these southern rural schools had become.

Obama entered the room with his trademark smile and offered a strong handshake to the crew and me. He was young, energetic, and smooth. About the same age, (I'm slightly younger) I remembered thinking, *our generation is on deck.*

As Kevin situated our mics, Obama and I chitchatted about the water shortage out west. I told him having grown up in Arizona everyone was concerned about the growth in Nevada, which receives just a small allocation of water from the Colorado River.

"They're bringing it in from the rural areas up north," Obama told me, "so the rural folks up north, the ranchers and all these folks are complaining. There's a real intrastate conflict there between water resources."

At some point, in my view, the ongoing drought in the West—especially in places like Las Vegas which was built in a desert but uses more water per capita than anywhere else in America without the resources to supply it—is going to catch up with us and a future president will have a potentially catastrophic problem on their hands.

During our discussion about water Kevin told me he was ready and with the cameras rolling, our interview began.

"We are sitting in a school built in 1896, leading to the question of whether all American children are getting a quality education?" I started.

"Well, I don't think they are," answered Obama. "I think the superintendent, the principal, and the teachers here are doing a heroic job trying to keep it together. But they're not getting a lot of help."

I followed up, "Let me ask you the bigger question. A white child born today, a black child, red child, brown child, an American baby—do they all have an equal opportunity to achieve in America coming right out of the gate?"

"You know, my instinct is that race is still a factor, but the biggest factor is economics," he replied. "If they're born to middle class parents then they're probably going to get a pretty good education. If they're born to wealthy parents they're going to get a very good education. And if they're born to poor parents, or live in a poor district, then they're going to suffer. That doesn't mean that money solves all our problems. Parents have to parent. My own mother wasn't wealthy but she instilled a love of learning in me, even when I resisted sometimes, and I ended up getting an excellent education. But money does make a difference in terms of being able to hire quality teachers and retain those teachers. It makes a difference if children see that the school building is run down while a prison is new or the mall is new. That sends a signal to them about the value that society places on education."

Still, I questioned why many of the struggling school districts across the country were located in predominately minority areas.

"I think part of where race and class intersect is that the larger society sometimes feels that black or brown children can't learn, or we shouldn't expect them to learn, or it's not important if they're not doing well. But one of the things I try to emphasize is that the U.S. workforce is going to be about half-black and brown pretty quick. And we will rise and fall as an economy depending on how skilled our workforce is. So we all have an investment in every child."

Just days before the interview, Obama had made news by suggesting America should begin the process of normalizing relations with Cuba.

Many conservatives, and some Democrats, were outraged. But at least one Republican, Congressman Jeff Flake of Arizona, said he agreed with Obama.

"There's been criticism this week about your stand on Cuba," I asked. "Yet, there are some conservatives in Congress, like Jeff Flake, who have called for a complete lifting of the embargo so you do have some bipartisan support. Are you surprised how political the response was rather than a discussion of whether this is a good idea?"

"No, look, Cuba's been a hot button political issue for quite some time," Obama responded. "The fact is, what I called for was not an end to the embargo. It was relatively modest; it said, let's make sure family members can travel to Cuba. So let's lift the travel ban so that people can visit their mother or grandmother. And let's make sure that that we loosen up the remittance mechanism so that Cuban Americans here can send money to help their family members in Cuba. I think it is possible as Fidel Castro dies, that we then have an opportunity to start opening up a new dialog with Cuba. And I hope that over time, we can bring them back into the community of nations and that they will release political prisoners and we'll start seeing a normalization of relations. But that is probably a bit further down the road."

While doing research on Obama, in preparing for my questions, I have to be honest and admit I was less than impressed with his resume. As a candidate for the state senate in Illinois eight years earlier, he had managed to get all of his opponents kicked off the primary election ballot, but there's nothing wrong with playing hardball if your opponents can't get valid signatures on their petitions. There was also his losing bid for Congress but that wasn't earth-shattering either. The lack of substance after his legislative career started, however, didn't lead me to think of any questions.

Yes, he had given a speech opposing the war in Iraq at a time just about everybody else, except congressman Ron Paul and few others, were supporting it. And he had gained notoriety with a memorable keynote speech at the 2004 Democratic National Convention:

"There is not a liberal America and a conservative America — there is the United States of America. There is not a black America and a white America and Latino America and Asian America — there's the United States of America!"

In the fall, that speech helped propel him to a landslide victory for a U.S. Senate seat in Illinois. His African-American GOP challenger, Alan Keyes, claimed during a debate that Obama wasn't black enough because he had not descended from American slaves. Obama ended up with 70 percent of the vote.

"We'll be hearing a lot more from Barack Obama in the course of the next several years," Tom Brokaw said when declaring him the winner on election night.

Obama was sworn into the Senate in January 2005, and two years later, after a successful book tour, he was seeking the presidency. There was, objectively, not a lot of material to work with here.

Except that infamous elephant in the room. The "never been done before" political reality.

For Romney it had been his Mormon faith. For Obama it was his biracial heritage and whether America was ready—210 years into this grand experiment—for its first non-white president.

Obama was born in Honolulu, Hawaii in 1961 to a white mother from Kansas and a black father from Kenya. His mother and father divorced when he was only two and his mother remarried. His stepfather moved the family to Indonesia where he lived from the ages of six to ten. While there, he attended schools with a predominately Muslim student population. He then moved back to Hawaii to live with his grandparents and was enrolled in one of the best private schools—Punahou in Honolulu— in the country. There he was known as "Barry O'Bomber" for his skills on the basketball court, something we had witnessed in Dillon before our interview when he sunk that three-pointer.

After graduation from high school, he moved to Los Angeles and enrolled at Occidental College. It was while at "Oxy" that he admits being in the party scene—drinking, smoking marijuana, and doing cocaine.

"It was typical of a teenager who was confused about who he was and what his place in the world was, and thought that experimenting with drugs was a way to rebel," he told *60 Minutes.*

After attending Columbia University in New York, and later Harvard in Boston where he got his law degree, Obama moved to Chicago. It was there—despite his father and stepfather having been Muslim—where he would be baptized a Christian and become a member of Trinity United Church of Christ. That church became controversial during the campaign when a tape emerged showing Rev. Jeremiah Wright, a close friend of Obama's, saying from the pulpit, "America's chickens are coming home to roost," in response to the terrorist attacks on 9/11.

Two months later, Obama said he was outraged by his pastor's behavior and resigned from the church.

It is against this backdrop that I asked a series of questions to Obama about race. There was his middle name, Hussein, which he shared with the former Iraqi dictator whom the American military had removed from power. There was the lingering question—brought up by Democrats and Republicans alike in his past political campaigns—of whether he was truly "black enough." In fact, *TIME* magazine had posed that very question on its cover. And then there was the bottom line: Americans had never voted for anyone other than a white man for president.

So I started there. "In 2008, can Barack Hussein Obama be elected President of the United States?"

Obama smiled and said, "That's the question that we'll find out in coming months. So far, it's going pretty good. I don't get a sense that I'm getting a lot of resistance because of my race. Or the fact that my father was from Kenya and so I've got a foreign-sounding name."

A Clemson University poll that month had Hillary Clinton slightly ahead of Obama in the state. It reported: "Over half of the expected Democratic vote in 2008 will be in the African-American community. As expected, Barack Obama is drawing heavily from this group, over three-quarters of his supporters are African American."

That led to questions of whether Obama could attract enough white voters to win the state against a well-organized Clinton effort.

"You know, right now people have been inspired and are enthused about the campaign," Obama told me.

"I would say here in South Carolina we have by far the best grassroots organization I think people have seen in a very long time. We have volunteers coming out of the woodwork. Young people are getting involved. We've got just a terrific operation. But ultimately, people are going to make a judgement based on, 'is this a guy who can deliver on universal healthcare, is this a guy who can build schools in areas like this one, is this somebody who can get us out of Iraq, and stabilize the country and protect the country from terrorism?' And if people think I'm the best guy for the job, even if I was green, I think I'd end up getting the nomination."

I followed up with, "*TIME* magazine asked on a cover recently, 'Is Obama Black Enough?' Is that a relevant question in the campaign?"

"You know, I think that this is an issue that's been manufactured not just by the press but by political pundits," Obama answered.

"The fact of the matter is, when I go into a barber shop on the Southside of Chicago, nobody's asking whether I am sufficiently and authentically black. It speaks I think to some of the issues we still have as a culture in terms of race. And one of the things we're trying to do is—and when I say we, I say myself and my wife, whose grandparents came from Georgetown in South Carolina—one of the things we're trying to project is that there's no one way to be African American. And we're not going to play into stereotypes about how we should behave. We're Americans. We have full claim on this country. And we want our children to feel that regardless of their skin color, or their name, or their background, that they have an opportunity to be part of the American community."

It had been clear early on that Obama, and his wife Michelle, had been irritated by the attacks from the Clinton campaign. Days before this interview Michelle Obama had said, "One of the most important things that we need to know about the next President of the United States is, is he somebody that shares our values? Is he somebody that respects family? Is he a good and decent person? So our view was that, if you can't run your own house, you certainly can't run the White House."

Many pundits were quick to suggest she was speaking about the Clintons.

"Speaking of your wife, a little controversy this week," I asked Obama. "She mentioned 'family values' in a speech, and many pundits immediately suggested she was aiming at the Clintons. True?"

"You know, I found it fascinating that people would think she was talking about anything other than us. She didn't mention the Clintons in her comments. What she was talking about, which she has talked about for months, is that when we were making the decision on whether I would run for president, the first question we asked was how will our kids respond, and can we create a sense of normalcy for them. And her point was, and I think this is close to the exact quote, if we're not taking care of our own kids in our own house, then it's pretty hard for us to suggest that we can run the White House. Somehow people took that as a comment on the Clintons and, actually, one of the things I admire about Bill and Hillary Clinton is that they did a good job raising Chelsea, she seems to be a terrific young lady. So, again, this is part of the craziness of presidential campaigns."

But I noticed during Obama's answer a slight indifference in his face when he mentioned Bill Clinton. So I pushed further:

"If national Democratic Party leaders came to you tomorrow and said, 'the best thing we can do for the Party in 2008 is put Bill Clinton front and center on the campaign stump,' would you support that idea?"

Obama paused, looked down, and showed agitation.

"Well, I think Bill Clinton is extraordinarily talented. He was a successful president, by and large, on a lot of important issues. But I think that what will ultimately determine whether we win is how well we project into the future. You know, what we want to be able to say is, 'we can bring the country together' and what I believe is that I can unify this country, get out of the red-state-blue-state divide, get out of the racial divide. Let's solve our problems in a common sense kind of way; that's what I think America is hungry for."

In other words, the Clintons did not "project into the future," they divided the country with too much partisanship and Obama planned to stop and change it. The bickering, including over race, between Obama and the Clintons would get much worse in South Carolina before the

January primary.

At this point in the interview I felt nervous excitement behind me. I also noticed that Obama's facial expression had turned from conversational to confrontational. While Kevin typically gave me time cues during interviews, this time he was behind me. And then I instinctively realized I was over time.

"Let me ask you if you've kept your promise to your wife to quit smoking during this campaign?" I asked with a smile, hoping to squeeze in a few more quick topics.

"Yes."

The one-word answer was accompanied with a stern look, as if I had asked a question so beyond the realm of dignity he couldn't believe it.

But the question was coming about twelve minutes into an interview that was supposed to be only eight. So I stopped and thanked him for the conversation.

Obama shook my hand, smiled, and looked up at one of his campaign staffers and said, "He was pretty good. He fit in five questions after his last question."

I had waited eight months for the interview and told Obama that I was sorry, but I wanted to cover more ground. In truth, I only got in about five topics—way short of many of the other national politicians I've interviewed.

That was the Obama style. Sit down with reporters but only for a strict four to eight minutes. As a lawyer, he can filibuster about every answer, leaving a journalist time to ask only two or three questions. It was a trick he would perfect in the coming years.

As we drove back to the station, I asked Kevin why Obama had acted like we were holding him hostage after only ten minutes. "There was no way for you to know his staff was seemingly getting upset we were keeping him in there," Kevin replied. "You had no way to catch those time cues, but Obama saw everything and his face, when you see the tape, goes from very jovial to very upset by the time you asked the smoking question."

I was concerned about how we left the interview and told Kevin, "He isn't soundbite ready and that was part of the problem. He reminded me of interviewing a state lawmaker; way too wordy."

"Well I'd be looking out for your IRS statement if he wins," Kevin laughed. "And an Oval Office interview won't be happening."

After sitting down with Obama that day I felt clearly his time would come. Just not in 2008.

WE CAN NOW PROJECT

With all the presidential candidates crisscrossing the state, both of South Carolina's Republican senators endorsed a candidate before the January primary. Jim DeMint backed Mitt Romney while Lindsay Graham supported John McCain.

DeMint said of Romney at the time, "There's no one in the race like Mitt Romney who has proved in business, and his volunteer work, and as governor of Massachusetts that he can solve a problem, not by creating more government but by making freedom work for everyone."

DeMint also praised Romney's healthcare plan, known as Romneycare, which required all Massachusetts residents to have health insurance or face a financial penalty:

"Well that's something I think we should do for the whole country," DeMint told Fox News. "The governor just looked at the numbers like a good businessman and realized we could give people private insurance policies cheaper than we could provide free healthcare. We've got probably over twenty states now that have tried to copy what he did and that's a good sign that people think he's on the right track."

DeMint, and other Senate Republicans, would later strongly oppose the federal healthcare act, or Obamacare, which was based on the same principal. He would also refuse to endorse Romney prior to the South Carolina presidential primary four years later.

Graham, meanwhile, had been actively working on South Carolina conservatives for years to prevent the scathing treatment his close friend and colleague McCain had received in 2000. Two years before the primary, Graham told me at a GOP dinner in Greenville:

"South Carolina is the third primary in 2008, it's the first primary in the South; it will be a hugely important event. John has been well-received and for conservatives who believe in controlling spending, John McCain is your guy."

Graham, who rose to fame in the late 1990s by leading the congressional impeachment trial against President Bill Clinton, would be a close adviser and confidant to McCain throughout the campaign. (Graham threw his hat into the ring for the GOP presidential nomination in 2016 with foreign policy views very similar to McCain's).

But the most prominent Republican politician in the state was not getting involved. While as a congressman eight years earlier, Mark Sanford had endorsed McCain in the brutal primary with Bush. This time around as governor he refused to do so.

Sanford was a fascinating politician. Part conservative, part libertarian, part maverick.

I first met him in 2003 while working on a three-part special series with producer Scott Trabandt examining the highways and roads leading into Myrtle Beach, one of the top tourist destination spots on the East Coast. Those roads were becoming increasingly clogged with bumper-to-bumper traffic and with hurricane worries each summer, local officials were becoming increasingly nervous. (In fact, during Hurricane Charley in 2004, we announced during our coverage Sanford had ordered state troopers to direct traffic inland from Myrtle Beach and all lanes on Highway 501, one of the busiest stretches of road in the state, reversed to allow for evacuations.)

We wanted Sanford's input for the roads story and his staff helped arrange for photographer Nate Zinnel and me to ride along and interview him on Highway 501. As Nate positioned himself in the front passenger seat recording Sanford and I, who were seated in the middle row of his SUV, we made a critical error in deciding not to wear our seat belts because they interfered with the lapel mics. After the story aired, several angry viewers called in to express their outrage with our lack of safety and the message it sent.

It was duly noted and I've never made the mistake of interviewing someone in a vehicle without wearing a seat belt again.

What I found interesting during our conversation is that Sanford didn't blink an eye blaming state lawmakers, a majority of them fellow Republicans, for playing politics with road money. "If you look at the way locals here anted up for the infrastructure improvements on the Grand Strand, it's frankly at odds with what happened with the Cooper River bridge (a

$6 million bridge built in Charleston). I mean there's a real disconnect there, and it's based solely on politics."

The public loved Sanford and the way he needled other politicians. Those politicians, however, didn't care for it much and never forgot.

Once, at a fundraiser for the Long Bay Symphony at Brookgreen Gardens in Murrells Inlet, I observed Sanford work the crowd. Or I should say not work the crowd. He stood next to a wall and let people come up to him. He didn't circle around every table reaching for hands and patting people on the back like most politicians. Sanford struck me as a number cruncher at heart, although he did have one thing going for him that many other politicians didn't. He looked great on television.

Sanford provided one of my favorite career live television debate moments. As he sought reelection in 2006, I moderated the final gubernatorial debate between the governor and his Democratic challenger Tommy Moore. A few prominent elected conservatives in South Carolina had expressed their dissatisfaction with him—payback for that maverick style—and they had endorsed Moore, much to Sanford's obvious annoyance.

At the start of the debate, as voters across the state and the nation on C-SPAN, looked on, I left my position behind a lectern and approached Sanford with this question:

"Governor, we've seen these 4 x 8 signs all over the state that say 'Republicans for Tommy Moore.' There are some Republicans here tonight, some of Horry County's most popular officials, who support the Democratic nominee. When you look back, what is it with Mark Sanford and your administration and your governing that has angered so many in your own party?"

"Who would they be?" Sanford shot back challenging the question.

"With legislators, state senator Jake Knotts; we can start there," I responded without hesitation. "We can run through other lawmakers—Horry County Auditor Lois Eargle is in the audience tonight—she's supporting Tommy Moore." At this point I started to back up toward my lectern to grab a sheet that had another dozen names on it. Sanford raised an eyebrow.

"I can continue on," I said, "but you would agree there are some?"

"Absolutely, absolutely," Sanford quietly said and then continued his answer.

The exchange provided an important lesson for journalists. A live debate or interview with politicians is like entering a courtroom. Never flippantly throw out a question without understanding the background, and be prepared to offer more details. Had I been unprepared in this situation, Sanford would have made me look ridiculous in the first minute of a live debate. Instead, I called his bluff and it firmly established who was piloting the debate.

It would have never occurred to me that night that Sanford, after his huge reelection and popularity with voters, would go on several years later to embarrass his family, himself, and all of South Carolina. For six days in 2009 Sanford went missing, his spokesman claiming he was out hiking the Appalachian Trail. In fact, he was in Buenos Aires, Argentina, with a mistress he had started a relationship with a year earlier while on an "economic development" trip. With whispers growing about his hiking story, in a bizarre circus-like press conference, Sanford acknowledged the affair, calling his mistress his "soulmate." That prompted his wife, the First Lady of South Carolina Jenny Sanford, to leave him and file for divorce. Lawmakers in both parties, never enamored with Sanford, started impeachment proceedings against him. He survived the remaining year of his term as a wounded incumbent—becoming the butt of many national jokes—and all talk of a future presidential bid ended. Remarkably, voters in Charleston returned Sanford to Congress in 2013. (Incidentally, Sanford and his "soulmate" went their separate ways. I'm not sure if he ever actually hiked the Appalachian Trail.)

After a year of following the presidential candidates around South Carolina, in late August 2007, Kevin and I found ourselves in Washington, D.C. working with the ABC News crew on the lawn of the White House. We were there to record a special one-hour program profiling the upcoming primary called *South Carolina: On The Road To The White House.*

ABC News provided their crew, which was helpful on a day it reached 95 degrees in Washington with 100 percent humidity. As I fought the sweat standing outside in a dark suit, the ABC team offered plenty of water and towels. We used their photographers for the main shooting and Kevin worked on b-roll and side shots we later used as cutaways.

"We are surrounded by the ABC News crew treating us like we're network," Kevin whispered to me at one point. "I know, just don't forget we're not," I responded.

At one point, with the ABC guys as our guide, we checked out the old swimming pool between the White House and the West Wing, now located under the floor of the press briefing room. It had been designed as a therapy pool for FDR and the four following presidents used it. But the press has its needs, and during the Nixon presidency the pool was covered and now eighteen miles of cable are housed there. First Lady Hillary Clinton in the 1990s had talked about building a new area for the media and restoring the pool, which is still intact, but for now it just remains a buried historic artifact.

With the White House as a backdrop I started the show: "For the first time in South Carolina's history, the nominees of both the Republican and Democratic parties could be determined by voters in our state. South Carolina is going to be a very important state on the primary calendar in 2008, and perhaps no city will be more important than Myrtle Beach, with the eyes of the world on two presidential debates."

That's right. Two presidential primary debates were headed to Myrtle Beach.

The Debates

Earlier that summer I got a phone call from Brad Dean, CEO and President of the Myrtle Beach Area Convention and Visitors Bureau, who wanted to know if Kevin and I could edit together highlights of the political interviews, debates, and profiles we had produced that year so that he could use it to help land one, perhaps two, presidential primary debates.

"That would be incredible for Myrtle Beach!" I replied, excited but a little skeptical. I wasn't sure Myrtle Beach would be taken seriously enough to land a rare presidential primary debate, let alone two of them.

But we made a four-minute documentary that showed off our station's political coverage and the Grand Strand's growing importance in the presidential primary process.

With the backing of influential South Carolina congressman Jim Clyburn and the Congressional Black Caucus Institute, Brad convinced CNN that the Grand Strand could support the logistics for a Democratic primary debate shortly before the primary on January 26th.

"We have chosen to hold the debate in Myrtle Beach," Clyburn confirmed to me in an exclusive interview that broke the news to South Carolina. "Myrtle Beach is just a natural. The difficult part was convincing other members of that; many had never heard of the Grand Strand, but it went well."

At the same time, working with state GOP Chairman Katon Dawson, Brad put together a package that convinced Fox News they should broadcast live a Republican candidate's debate in Myrtle Beach before their primary on January 19th.

"We cannot overstate how important this debate is going to be for the Republican Party," I told viewers while breaking the news during one of our newscasts. "It will follow the Iowa Caucus and New Hampshire primary, and be just nine days before South Carolina votes."

Dawson said during an interview the debate, "May provide an opportunity for the candidates to throw a Hail Mary" after results from both Iowa and New Hampshire.

The Grand Strand had never before hosted such high profile political events with such a huge international audience. But Myrtle Beach was quickly shedding its image as the "Redneck Riviera." Gone were the cheap motels on Ocean Boulevard replaced by new high-end hotels on a sixty-mile stretch of some of the nicest white sandy beaches in America.

It had seemed almost impossible for Brad to convince Republicans and Fox News not to head to the conservative upstate and Greenville, or Democrats and CNN to the capitol city of Columbia. But with the strong backing and support from Mayor John Rhodes and the city council, they got it done. Between the two debates, there would be over 1,300 credentialed members of the media from all over the world.

Brad arranged for giant sand sculptures of the heads of all the presidential candidates be made outside both debate venues. The international press corps ate it up. ABC News especially loved it, White House correspondent Jake Tapper telling me the uniqueness of it was the only reason producers let him come to Myrtle Beach (after covering so many prior primary debates).

The night of the Myrtle Beach Republican debate on January 10th, a new Rasmussen poll showed McCain taking the lead with 27 percent support. Huckabee was second with 24 percent. Romney was third with 16 percent followed by Thompson with 12 percent. Giuliani was down to 6 percent, with Paul at 3.

Prior to both of the debates, I produced and anchored a live thirty-minute debate preview show featuring clips of my interviews with each candidate and analysis with Dr. Eddie Dyer of Coastal Carolina University. On a mild January evening, standing in front of the Myrtle Beach Convention Center, I started our GOP debate coverage by pointing to the poll and how far Romney and Giuliani had slipped. About McCain and Huckabee I said, "These two candidates were at the bottom of this poll a month ago, it demonstrates how quickly things can change in a presidential race."

Inside, the clash between the six candidates started early, with Romney accusing McCain of being too pessimistic about the economy. "I know that there are some people who think, as Senator McCain did, some jobs have left Michigan that are never coming back. I disagree," Romney said.

McCain looked at Romney during his response and told the crowd it was time for some "straight talk" and said, "There are some jobs that aren't coming back to Michigan. There are some jobs that won't come back here to South Carolina."

Thompson, who had fallen back in the polls, launched a stinging attack on Mike Huckabee:

"He would be a Christian leader, but he would also bring about liberal economic policies, liberal foreign policies. He believes we have an arrogant foreign policy and the tradition of, blame America first. He believes in taxpayer-funded programs for illegals. He has the endorsement of the

National Education Association, and the NEA said it was because of his opposition to vouchers. He said he would sign a bill that would ban smoking nationwide. So much for states' rights. So much for individual rights," as the crowd applauded.

For his part, Huckabee dismissed Thompson and struck a more populist tone, "We need to make sure that we communicate that our party is just as interested in helping the people who are single moms, who are working two jobs, and still just barely paying the rent, as we are the people at the top of the economy."

He also received the loudest round of applause of the night when he defended the Southern Baptist Convention's declaration: "A wife is to submit herself graciously to the servant leadership of her husband." Huckabee responded, "I'm not the least bit ashamed of my faith or the doctrines of it."

Giuliani, who was watching his presidential dreams slip away, pointed his attack at McCain, "John gets great credit for supporting the surge in Iraq. But, John, there were other people on this stage that also supported the surge. The night of the president's speech, I was on television. I supported the surge, I've supported it throughout."

McCain calmly responded, "I condemned the Rumsfeld strategy and called for the change in strategy. That's the difference."

The Fox News format allowed—perhaps encouraged—audience participation, which was criticized afterwards for more resembling the *Maury Povich* show than a presidential debate. There were wild moments of applause, blended with plenty of boos, especially aimed at Ron Paul during a discussion of foreign policy.

He was first asked if he would condemn the rhetoric of some of his supporters who were 9/11 "Truthers" (those who believe the U.S. government and/or corporations had something to do with the attack) and Paul responded, "I don't endorse what they say and I don't believe that."

Then he was criticized by several of his opponents for arguing the U.S. should not have invaded Iraq. All five of his GOP challengers strongly backed the Bush policy. Paul responded,

"We used to support Saddam Hussein and we used to be allied with

Osama Bin Laden, and what I want to do is stop that. Who are our friends one day turn out to be our enemies. Right now, we finally got rid of Saddam Hussein. And what are we doing now? We're re-arming the Sunnis, the old henchmen of Saddam Hussein. And what are they going to do with it? There's all those weapons we're giving the Sunnis in Baghdad. So look out, believe me, that war is not over and right now they're demanding more troops in Afghanistan and some people, like the Senator, he thinks we should be there for 100 years if necessary. How can he commit the young people of this world, five more generations, to be in Iraq if it's necessary? I say it's time to come home!"

Paul's message, met with boos in 2008, would be greeted by Republicans with more enthusiasm four years later.

After the debate, during our 11 p.m. news, I offered this assessment: "It's still unclear who will win in South Carolina, although the headline of the hour belongs to Fred Thompson for his feisty exchange with Mike Huckabee who he views as his number one enemy in this race for the nomination." Dyer agreed, "I thought Fred Thompson came out swinging. So did Mitt Romney. Both of them up until tonight had appeared wooden to me."

I then pointed out that Thompson and Romney were "on the ropes" after terrible showings in both Iowa and New Hampshire. "They had to change their tone tonight because what they've been doing hasn't been working," Dyer added.

Katon Dawson, the chairman of the South Carolina GOP, told me after the debate that he couldn't have been more pleased with the "can-do" attitude of Myrtle Beach in hosting the debate, despite some flak he took for not choosing Greenville.

Nine days later, on the anchor desk in Myrtle Beach, I broke into ABC prime time programming with this:

"Good evening—we break into the movie to bring you a major story in the race for the White House tonight. In a stunning reversal from his loss in South Carolina just eight years ago, Arizona senator John McCain is now our projected winner in the South Carolina primary. Again, he lost here in 2000 and it knocked him out of the presidential race then, but now we can call it—John McCain has won the primary. Mike Huckabee comes in second. We'll have more coming up at 11."

In the end, McCain, with the strong support of veterans across the state, won the primary with 33 percent. Huckabee, almost out of nowhere as the new conservative alternative to McCain, placed second with 30 percent. Fred Thompson placed third with 16 percent, Mitt Romney forth with 15 percent, Ron Paul with 4 percent and way back, Rudy Giuliani with only 2 percent of the vote.

What was clear is that had conservatives united behind a single candidate, let's call him Huckabee-Thompson-Romney, they would have beat McCain easily with around 60 percent of the vote. No matter how he did it, McCain left the Palmetto State with a sizable bounce that would help propel him to the GOP nomination.

The night of the Democratic debate on January 21st, it was clear the stakes couldn't be higher. Obama had won in Iowa, Clinton in New Hampshire and Nevada. The 'first-in-the-south' primary would tell the world who was really leading in the battle for the nomination.

The most coveted endorsement for Democrats in South Carolina remained Clyburn. I pressed him the night of the debate on whether he would get involved. "People are torn," Clyburn told me. "I made a commitment to stay out of it, and I'm not going break faith with any of them."

Local political activists were pleased about all the attention, with a dozen TV live trucks parked outside the Palace Theater. "For Grand Strand residents to see the Democratic candidates up close is just wonderful," former Horry County Democratic Party chairwoman Sally Howard told me.

My television station, as it had prior to the Republican debate, aired a live preview show the night of the Democratic debate. I started the program by saying, "Good Evening. Thirty minutes from now, perhaps the most important event for the Democratic candidates running for President of the United States in 2008. They find themselves here in Myrtle Beach, in the Palace Theater behind me, in a showdown that ultimately could determine whether it's Barack Obama or Hillary Clinton as the nominee for the Democratic Party."

John Edwards was also in the debate. He had won the South Carolina primary in 2004, but polls at this point had him behind running a distant third. Once, during the ninety-minute slug-fest, Edwards was forced to say, "There are three people in this debate, not two!"

It was a much colder January evening as we reported live from outside—at one point I couldn't feel my lips move—and the security much tighter. Reporter Mike Essian pointed out both Clinton and Obama already received Secret Service protection (at this point none of the Republican candidates qualified) and over forty members of Congress were in attendance. In addition, "Security had to cut anywhere from 200 to 300 seats in the audience just to make things safe," Mike said, which made scoring an invite to the debate the equivalent of finding a Willie Wonka golden ticket.

With five days to go until the primary, the eyes of politicos, and the world, were on the debate, which everyone knew would be one of the last of the primary season. The debate made international headlines with Clinton and Obama attacking each other's integrity, both of them unleashing the most intense and personal exchange of the campaign.

It started early on, after Obama was asked by CNN's Suzanne Malveaux if Clinton was right that he couldn't account for $50 billion worth of new programs he had proposed:

"What she said wasn't true. We account for every single dollar that we propose. Now this, I think, is one of the things that's happened during the course of this campaign, that there's a set of assertions made by Senator Clinton, as well as her husband, that are not factually accurate."

With the crowd applauding, Obama kept going, steering away from his spending plan and onto the topic of the war in Iraq:

"When Senator Clinton says—or President Clinton says—that I wasn't opposed to the war from the start, or says it's a fairytale that I opposed the war, that is simply not true. When Senator Clinton or President Clinton asserts that I said that the Republicans had had better economic policies since 1980, that is not the case."

This was the first of many salvos Obama aimed at Bill Clinton by who he believed was distorting his views. As it had been clear in my interview,

Obama was anxious to move beyond the Clinton era.

Hillary Clinton responded with her own put-down of the junior senator from Illinois:

"I do think that your record and what you say does matter. And when it comes to..." (the audience burst out in applause) ... a lot of the issues that are important in this race, it is sometimes difficult to understand what Senator Obama has said, because as soon as he is confronted on it, he says that's not what he meant."

The two then spent a few minutes debating what Obama had said about Ronald Reagan, which was a bit surreal in a Democratic debate.

"You talked about admiring Ronald Reagan and you talked about the ideas," Hillary said.

"Hillary, I'm sorry. You just..." Obama interrupted.

"I didn't talk about Reagan," Clinton said.

Obama, more heated and angry than at any moment in his political career, replied, "What I said was that Ronald Reagan was a transformative political figure because he was able to get Democrats to vote against their economic interests to form a majority to push through their agenda, an agenda that I objected to because while I was working on those streets watching those folks see their jobs shift overseas, you were a corporate lawyer sitting on the board at Wal-Mart!"

The crowd erupted into applause, some booed, with the Democrats now providing their own version of the Maury Povich show.

"I just want to be clear about this," Clinton followed up. "In an editorial board with the Reno newspaper, you said two different things, because I have read the transcript. You talked about Ronald Reagan being a transformative political leader. I did not mention his name."

"Your husband did," Obama, on the verge of losing his temper, interrupted.

"Well, I'm here. He's not!" Clinton responded to a cheering audience.

"Okay. Well, I can't tell who I'm running against sometimes," Obama snapped.

And then Clinton went where she had never gone before.

"I was fighting against those ideas when you were practicing law and representing your contributor, Rezko, in his slum landlord business in inner-city Chicago!"

It was the first time during the campaign Clinton had tied Obama to Tony Rezko, a longtime Chicago fund raiser, who had been indicted on federal charges of business fraud and influence peddling. Obama had done legal work for Rezko and later returned more than $40,000 in campaign contributions linked to him.

The crowd booed, applauded, and groaned. Obama looked down and said, "no, no, no" as if he had suffered a body blow. Clearly this give-and-take showed the importance of the South Carolina primary, and sent a message to Democrats nationally that this fight was far from over.

That night, at the start of the 11 p.m. news I said,

"You get the sense we're right on the edge of history. You have the first woman who could potentially become the president and the first African American who could do the same thing, and South Carolina is going to be critical in helping them become the nominee. The Obama campaign told me tonight an expected win here on Saturday will propel his momentum into Super Tuesday where he could finish up this fight. The Clinton team says a win here after her victory in New Hampshire would make her the inevitable nominee."

Our analyst Eddie Dyer said the fireworks didn't help the Democratic Party, "For those two to go at each other like they did tonight really doesn't do either campaign that much good. I think if I had to call it, Obama probably did himself a favor tonight; he came off a little more statesman-like than Hillary Clinton. If those two keep going at each other like that, the big winner will be John McCain."

Eddie and I then got into the biggest surprise of the campaign thus far, Bill Clinton's decision to become the "axe man" for Hillary's campaign. Just days before the debate, Clinton claimed Obama had put out a "hit job" on him for the accusation he had brought race into the campaign. He also blamed the media for buying into that narrative. Those comments led our newscasts and received statewide attention.

Half of South Carolina's Democratic primary voters were expected to be African American, and Clinton was using that fact to acknowledge his wife had fallen behind in polls. "They are getting votes, to be sure, because of their race or gender, and that's why people tell me that Hillary doesn't have a chance to win here," Clinton said while in Charleston.

Former South Carolina Democratic chairman Dick Harpootlian openly complained Clinton's campaign resembled the race tactics used by Lee Atwater, who we discussed earlier in this book.

"To see the former president Bill Clinton begin to do some of this dirty work for his wife, some suggest it's a little unbecoming of a former president," I said on air. Eddie agreed and added, "It's a very odd strategy to have Bill Clinton out in front for her and I just don't understand. There are a lot of people you could put out front but he seems to be willing to do that."

I asked Clinton strategist Mark Penn following the debate whether the former president was now an axe man for his wife's campaign.

"He's no axe man," Penn told me, trying to spin optimism for a campaign that had watched its huge South Carolina lead slip away. "Senator Clinton is running her campaign talking about the issues—the war, our energy future, and how we do something about the economy. And I think President Clinton has been a tremendous asset throughout this campaign. He raised the issue of Senator Obama's votes on the war and his actual record on the war. And as Senator Obama has said himself, records are fair game in a campaign."

Former state superintendent of education Inez Tenenbaum, who lost the 2006 Senate election to Jim DeMint, was an early backer of Obama. After the debate, she was quick to link the Clintons together. "Well I believe the candidates need to pull their own weight," Tenenbaum told me. "The candidates need to be the ones who have interchanges with each other, not the candidates' spouses, and that does concern me a great deal. So every candidate has to stand on his or her own two feet, that's the only fair way to do it."

Edwards' advisor Joe Trippi perhaps gave me the best soundbite of the night: "They were fighting over which one was a slum lord and which one was a Wal-Mart board member!"

As to those wondering about the impact for a community hosting two presidential debates, Brad Dean later told me when added up, the economic benefit from the two debates was $10.3 million. In addition, the publicity value from the print and broadcast coverage totaled just over $12 million.

A week later, I was back interrupting network prime time programming again, although much earlier this time. It was clear from all the polling we had that Barack Obama was going to defeat both Hillary Clinton and John Edwards by a comfortable margin. In the end he received 55 percent of the vote to Clinton's 27 percent and Edward's 18 percent. That 40 percent lead of Clinton's when I interviewed her a year earlier had evaporated. Obama's ability to get out the African-American vote, and excite younger voters, was key to his overwhelming victory.

After Obama won the primary by a huge margin, Bill Clinton compared the win to that of a prior black candidate: "Jesse Jackson won South Carolina in '84 and '88. Jackson ran a good campaign. And Obama ran a good campaign here." The comment further inflamed the tensions between the Obamas and Clintons, and worried national Democrats began to wonder if the wounds were becoming too deep.

During a later interview, Jackson told me he was not offended by Bill Clinton's comparison, but pointed out his presidential campaigns had led to rule changes that cost Hillary Clinton the nomination.

"We changed the rules to proportionality, as opposed to winner-take-all which is a way of suppressing votes," said Jackson. "By '88 I had as many delegates as I had popular votes. When Barack ran in 2008, Hillary Clinton won, at the end, California, Ohio, Pennsylvania, and Texas barely. She would have been the winner except we had democratized democracy and opened the process up."

And Jackson said his campaigns made it possible for both Obama and Clinton to be so close to making history.

"The most significant thing is we answered the question of whether a black man or a woman could be accepted and the answer now is yes," Jackson told me. "I tried to advance the cause of inclusion for all Americans. I remain concerned, passionately, about Appalachia. I think in some sense it's a measuring stick of our character. If you ignore Appalachia, we can ignore anyone at our peril."

With wounds from the 2008 primary fight still fresh, Democrats at least had one bit of good news. They could leave South Carolina and not look back. It was as good as lost in the general election.

Come November, as expected for all the reasons we discussed earlier, Obama lost South Carolina to McCain in the general election 54 to 45 percent, while winning the presidency by a comfortable margin.

At the end of all our coverage in 2008, Kevin and I were nominated for a news Emmy award for our work. "You stayed on these people phone call after phone call, the truth is you got these interviews by pestering these people but it worked," Kevin told me later. The fact is the candidates, and voters, needed us to cover the campaign and we had done our best.

Days following the Inauguration of Barack Obama in January 2009, my time in South Carolina came to an end. As evidenced by the events in this book, it had been a fantastic six years.

At a farewell party after my final newscast in Myrtle Beach, co-hosted by the local Democrats and Republicans, Myrtle Beach mayor John Rhodes, who I had so unceremoniously bumped from his seat at the baseball game with Rudy Giuliani, presented me with a plaque that read:

PROCLAMATION HONORING JIM HEATH FOR HIS SERVICE TO MYRTLE BEACH TELEVISION MARKET

WHEREAS, *for six years, Jim Heath was the well-known face and voice of WPDE-TV serving as the station's co-anchor and lead political reporter; and* WHEREAS, *in this capacity, Heath was nominated for an EMMY for his political reporting and was selected "anchorman of the year" four times by readers of the Myrtle Beach Herald; and* WHEREAS, *Jim Heath's strength in political reporting is indicated by the many candidate debates he moderated and the background specials he produced; and* WHEREAS, *The Myrtle Beach area will greatly miss Jim Heath's knowledge of the local, state and national political scene and its players, as well as his detailed and personable on-air presentation;*

NOW, THEREFORE, BE IT RESOLVED *that the City of Myrtle Beach thanks Jim Heath for his six years of service to the community as co-anchor and lead political reporter at WPDE-TV and extends best wishes for the future; as he embarks on a new position at WBNS-TV and the Ohio News Network in Columbus, Ohio.*
Signed John Rhodes, Mayor of Myrtle Beach.

GOD BLESS OUR TROOPS

"Is your job ever fun?"

From time to time people will actually ask me that question.

Being in broadcast news is what I've always wanted to do in life, so until that question is asked, I never think about some people actually disliking the news or thinking my job is actually boring.

Boring? Are you kidding?!

Here are two examples of my favorite moments as a reporter, and what makes it a great career.

SANTA IS FOGGED OUT

"Are we sure we can make it out?"

It was a simple question I overheard several U.S. Marines discussing at the Grand Canyon airport.

My photographer and I had flown with several U.S. Marines from Marine Corps Air Station Yuma to the Grand Canyon that morning as part of the Toys for Tots program. Our goal—called "Operation Havasupai"—with U.S. Marines from Marine Medium Helicopter Squadron-764 was to make a quick twenty-minute flight from the rim of the Grand Canyon to the bottom in order for Santa to deliver toys to the Supai children. It was 10 a.m., and the goal was to be back in the air no later than noon.

Sometimes simple plans go haywire.

When we arrived at the Grand Canyon airport, there were several inches of fresh new snow on the runway. Plows were working to clear the snow as a Marine crew was busy scraping the twin blades of the gigantic Marine CH-46E helicopters.

A small group of Marines were huddled with Hal Jensen, a retired Marine from Flagstaff who had started the Toys for Tots effort in 1995. Jensen—known affectionately around Northern Arizona as "Head Elf"—had meticulously laid out the agenda for the day. He appeared to be busy inventing a backup plan—much like a coach with an unexpected opponent—on the spot.

The opponent this day was Mother Nature. It wasn't snowing hard—as it had overnight—but it was only twelve degrees with dark skies and the possibility of a high layer of clouds in the canyon.

Clouds in the canyon? I thought out loud. *These are great combat helicopters but can they fly themselves in between the walls of the freakin' Grand Canyon?*

The mission could not be easily scrapped. Besides Santa and all those toys, the four helicopters would be carrying more than 16,000 pounds of food and other supplies.

The Havasupai Indian Reservation is one of the most isolated places on the Earth, sitting 2,000 feet below the rim of the Grand Canyon. Perhaps known best for the stunning Havasu Falls waterfall, the Supai village is accessible only by helicopter, mule, horse, or by an eight-mile hiking trail. So making a quick run to Home Depot for building supplies or Subway for a quick bite to eat is out of the question for the 450 residents.

It was important to get down there.

"The weather could be better, but we can safely fly and land," Major Marcus Malais, aviation safety officer at HMM-764, and our pilot, told us. "At no time will there be risk to man or machine."

So we loaded up and entered the freezing cargo bay. The plan was for the first two helicopters to leave approximately twenty minutes ahead of the third and fourth. That final helicopter would have Santa and Mrs. Claus on board. We needed the extra time to set up the toys, and our cameras, before the "big moment" for the kids.

As we strapped in our seats—just a long bench really—Yuma County Supervisor Bob McLendon and I noticed the rear loading ramp of the CH-46 had been left open for the flight. Any thought of warming up was quickly gone. We lifted off from Grand Canyon airport and soon Malais was flying us through one of the seven natural wonders of the world. He gently, like a boat on the sea, rolled us slightly left to right, giving us a great view.

About five minutes into our descent, however, the winds picked up blowing fresh snow off the canyon walls. Our visibility quickly became limited; in fact I could see the second helicopter following us but nothing behind them.

"Santa is going to have quite a ride," I said to Bob, who nodded in agreement.

Soon our helicopter landed and we were greeted by over one hundred happy and cheering Supai children. This was the seventh time the Marines had made the Toys for Tots run, but it still had to be exciting for the kids to see those giant mechanical birds fly in from the sky.

"One little girl came up to me yelling, 'Santa is here! Santa is here!'" Malais told me after landing. "I asked her, 'how do you know Santa is here?' And she said, while giving me a big hug, 'because the Marines are here!' How awesome is that?" he said.

The kids had made a big banner, which was hung in the recreation center: "Welcome Toys 4 Tots!"

"The children are so excited they can hardly stand it," Velma Eisenberger, principal at Havasupai Elementary School told reporters.

Here at the bottom of earth's most famous canyon, I noticed several satellite dishes on the top of homes. In the technological age, the Havasupai were not as disconnected from the world as you might have thought. But school board President Roland Manakaja estimated nearly 60 percent of the tribe was unemployed and the supplies from the Toys for Tots run made a big difference.

As we moved into the recreation center, I noticed some excitement from a group of Marines. I wandered over and one whispered to me, "Too much fog, Santa and Mrs. Claus are stuck above and can't make it."

"Santa is stuck because of bad weather?" I shook my head in disbelief.

The man set to play Santa was really good too—I had met him at the airport and noted he had a real beard. The good news was the toys were here. The bad news is there was no jolly old elf to hand them out.

But never doubt the magic of the U.S. Marines.

Thirty minutes later a very tall and slender Santa, complete with red suit and bushy white beard, appeared to the delight of the children. As luck would have it, one of the volunteers had been told earlier in the week that the original Santa may not be able to make it and he had packed his suit in a duffle bag just in case.

"Incredibly, the guy with the suit just happened to overhear our conversation and jumped in to save the day," Malais told me. "No one, including me, had any idea that Santa #2 would be walking out that day. I was as surprised and bemused as anybody; it truly was Miracle on 34th Street!"

As Santa handed out the presents, I noticed a bit of apprehension on the faces of the pilots. I followed them outside to see what the worry was all about. As I looked up, any hint of the sun had been replaced with a dark wall of clouds and fog that was quickly descending into the canyon.

"If we can't fly out, our only option is to hike out," one Marine told me.

At that moment we were literally stuck at the bottom of the Grand Canyon!

The clock continued to tick for about two hours until Malais determined the fog did not pose a safety risk.

"Normally, we never fly without a weather briefing and a detailed analysis of the conditions, but that analysis wasn't available here," Malais told me. So the seasoned pilot made the decision to lift out of the Grand Canyon from a self-described trick he had learned from the Supai themselves.

"In years past, I had chatted with the elders many times and the topic of weather came up often," Malais told me later.

"I was taught that when the birds and animals become silent or disappear, the tribes people prepare for rough weather, but as soon as the birds return and begin to sing, the tribespeople return to normal activity. Well, that's exactly what I did. I listened and watched carefully for the animals and spoke with the elders. Once nature started to come alive and the elders gave me the nod, I stated to my crew that the birds are singing so let's 'man up' and get out of here. Yes, they thought I was bat crazy!"

Crazy? We were taking off from the bottom of the Grand Canyon in thick fog because the birds were singing. That's not crazy at all.

With the Supai children—many now on their new bikes thanks to the Toys for Tots effort—waving goodbye we took off and soon were in an ocean of clouds. We were flying in the Grand Canyon and there was zero visibility.

"This was challenging no doubt, and the unknown still lay atop the canyon," Malais told me. "We use GPS to create a couple of waypoints for guidance, and a GPS point for the Grand Canyon airport. I briefed my other aircrew to stay close and emphasized to all the aircrew that we must maintain visual contact with each other at all times."

We could have been 300 feet from the canyon wall or an inch and not known. The strong winds were blowing snow all around us creating a white glow. Even the Marines on board, the best fighting soldiers on earth, seemed apprehensive.

"Grab a strap and hold tight, this will get bumpy!" shouted one Marine who had positioned himself at the open door in front of the cargo bay. McLendon looked over at me as if we might be sharing the last few seconds on Earth together. A longtime high school basketball coach, he had been in some tough games before, but I made a mental note that this one could come down to a lucky three-pointer.

After a slow, cold, and frightening half-hour we lifted out of the Grand Canyon. Despite it being below freezing, I made a mental note that there was sweat on my back.

"My Dashed 2 (the second helicopter) did a beautiful job staying tight, and Mother Nature was gracious enough to continually open a window of opportunity for us to get home safely," Malais told me. Truth be told, he was a bit relieved to be back on the ground too.

Flying back to Yuma I said to Bob, "What a great event for those kids, and what a great job by the Marines to get us there." He nodded and said, "Yes, true, but still we probably don't want to ever repeat that trip."

True enough. I made a decision when we landed at MCAS Yuma; from now on I was leaving military hardware to the military.

That is until months later when I arrived in South Carolina.

NO CODE 11

"Jim, do you like roller coasters?" Major Randy Redell asked me through the microphone on his headset as we sat on board the F-16 fighter jet now on the runway about to take off.

"Love them," I replied.

"Great, after what's about to happen in the next thirty seconds, no ride will ever compare," Redell chuckled.

I had only moved to South Carolina from Arizona a few months earlier and now I was strapped inside an F-16 roaring down the runway like a bullet. I nervously laughed to myself, wondering if this is what it was going to be like living in the South. In a few seconds we were off the ground heading straight up like a rocket. Within thirty seconds, we had reached 15,000 feet and pulled 4-Gs in the climb. I mentally applauded my decision to forgo breakfast that morning.

As we leveled off, Redell rolled the jet 45 degrees, stopped and repeated the fast movements several more times. Then we did some Cuban-8s and other loops and rolls which showed off the maneuverability of these $25 million fighting machines. It was like being in a live-action video game, only real.

I was seated behind Redell, both of us wearing oxygen masks and helmets that had microphones and earpieces. The inside of the aircraft was being recorded for all posterity (and the local news viewer that night at 6 o'clock) to enjoy.

When I had arrived at Shaw Air Force Base early that morning, I had to pass a physical and have my blood pressure and ears checked out by a flight surgeon. Being told I was in excellent health had already made the day well worth it.

Then came the task of putting on the gear associated with flying modern day fighters, which was no easy undertaking. The flight suit was heavy and fire-resistant. Additionally, I was issued steel-toed boots and a helmet equipped with an oxygen mask. A picture later confirmed that I looked less like Tom Cruise in *Top Gun*, and more like a news anchor way out of his league.

On the outside of the flight suit, I wore what looked to be ski pants with inflatable bladders over the stomach and each leg. For an hour we sat and practiced tightening the stomach and leg muscles along with inhaling and exhaling in sharp breaths—techniques I was assured would assist me in staying conscious during the upcoming sortie.

"Will this all be necessary?" I asked.

"You'll see," was the response from the flight surgeon.

As we arrived at the airfield, the USAF Thunderbird crew were busy preparing the aircraft, which, as I climbed up the ladder, proudly displayed my name on the side. *How incredible is that?* I thought, with the nerves slowly beginning to creep in.

I had actually looked into joining the Air Force when I was in high school, during the height of the Reagan 'proud to be an American' days. But recruiters said my poor eyesight would keep me out of the cockpit and down on the ground. My interest level quickly waned.

Before climbing into his seat in front of me, Redell pointed out there was a handle between my legs that I could pull to eject.

"Eject?! Let's not lead the newscast tonight!" I responded laughing— but serious.

In the pre-flight training, I was taught how to disconnect the parachute harness in an emergency. Sitting there, I realized this whole experience was like being strapped to a bullet, with only the pilot to guide it.

Redell was a stud; there is no other way to say it. A former college football quarterback, graduate of the U.S. Air Force Academy, and now the Operations Officer for the USAF Thunderbirds in their 50th year. He was also thirty-five with a wife and young family along with those Hollywood good looks. There was never any hesitation about putting my life in his hands.

Except at this moment.

After enduring the punishment of 6, 7, and 8-Gs, he warned we were about to do a maximum 9-G left turn.

"Breathe at my pace," Redell told me through the headset as the flight suit clenched me like a fist. We rolled left in what I can only describe as a crushing feeling—9-Gs is equivalent to nine times your body weight pushing down on you.

This extra force pulled blood from my brain. Which is not good. So those ski-type pants went into action. To describe the flight suit as it's inflating during all this, imagine having a blood pressure cuff on your stomach and legs squeezing as tightly as humanly possible in an effort to force blood back up to your brain. And then imagine it squeezing even more. Yup, that's 9-Gs.

We held it for eight seconds. I didn't pass out. But my body ached, and my lap felt like a huge rock was sitting on it. Sweat accumulated on my forehead and other places we won't mention. There is sadly no roller coaster in the world that can prepare you for what this feels like.

"Congratulations," Redell said to me. "You just pulled 9-Gs and lived to tell about it!"

We then did a supersonic run, breaking the sound barrier, Mach 1, scorching along at 750 miles per hour. *Can you imagine this baby in combat?* I thought to myself. Redell then leveled us off and we flew in and above the clouds. We were upside-down at one point, which was probably the most uncomfortable maneuver for me because the harness wasn't quite holding me tightly in the seat. But I didn't dare say anything because part of me believed what I had been warned on the ground— these pilots were looking for ways to make journalists vomit during the flight. And I was determined not to be one of them.

The South Carolina scenery below was fantastic with its green forests, sandy white beaches, and that endless blue Atlantic Ocean. For over forty minutes we floated around these big puffy clouds, waiting for openings where Redell would fly us through and gun us straight down toward the ground as fast as possible. With land approaching quickly—like you see in cartoons—I smiled and thought of my dad who would have absolutely loved being up here. He was the first call I made when we were back on ground.

"You shouldn't have been nervous, if you would have crashed, you would have done so in an F-16 with an American hero and that's a good way to go," pop said to me. A true father's perspective.

As we started our landing, I heard the ground crew ask Redell if he had encountered a Code 11. "Negative," he responded. I later learned that was the code for a journalist vomiting all over the insides of an F-16. Not me, not on this day.

The jet landed softer than any commercial airliner I've ever been in.

On the ground I told Redell that the only thing I didn't love was being upside down. He laughed and said that was actually his favorite attitude position. He also thanked me for enjoying the maximum amount of time he could be in the air.

"We train in these jets, and the only time we can let loose a little bit is with the media," Redell told me. "Most of the time your colleagues start to feel sick and we have to land, but you didn't and that made for a great day."

Redell pinned a 9-G pin onto my suit and the crew presented with me a plaque welcoming me into the 9-G club. Three hours later I was on the air—instead of flying around in it—sharing my experience with viewers, in the back of my mind slightly disappointed that this was a once-in-a-lifetime experience.

To all the men and women who have served in our Armed Forces to protect our freedoms, especially the freedom of speaking our minds and debating all these issues, thank you.

God bless America.

PART TWO:
BUCKEYE STATE

THE HEART OF AMERICA

O-H!

If you're a Buckeye or know anything about Ohio, you just mentally responded I-O!

You just can't help it.

Any successful national politician knows it too. Like President Obama, who started his speeches with the O-H chant at campaign rallies in 2008 and 2012 (it's also how he welcomed the 2015 National Championship football team to the White House).

Let's try it again. O-H!

This lingo is well known to me because I was born in Ohio. As were my brothers and sister. As were my parents and their parents, and their brothers and sisters, my cousins, my aunts and uncles. The truth is, my family has deep Buckeye blood.

There is a city, in fact, in central Ohio called Heath. It's about two-and-a-half hours from my hometown of Van Wert, where my grandparents lived literally right across the street from each other. That really made life easy as a kid, if you got tired of one set of grandparents you just ran across Washington Street to the other.

My grandfather, Rolden L. Heath, Sr. was elected to the Van Wert City Council for a dozen years without ever having put up any campaign signs. Those were the good old days when reputation and word of mouth was all a good candidate needed.

Van Wert is also home to Balyeat's Coffee Shop, which has the best homemade chicken and noodles over mashed potatoes you will find in the entire country! The restaurant has become a bit famous, having been around for generations. My parents, in fact, met there on dates as teenagers.

For the record, Fletcher Heath, for whom the city Heath is named, was a respected businessman originally from Indiana and we have found no direct family link. Still it's always fun to say, "let's head to Heath!"

Geographically, Van Wert is located in the northwest part of the state, near the Indiana border and about thirty miles from Wapakoneta.

"Wapa-a-whata?" I hear you asking.

Wapakoneta. It has the distinction of being the birthplace of Neil Armstrong, the first human being to ever take a step on the moon.

"That's one small step for man. One giant leap for mankind."

Since the early 1970s, Wapakoneta has been home to the Armstrong Air and Space Museum, which became a mandatory summer visit when visiting my grandparents. The entrance to the museum itself hasn't changed through the years and is like walking into an alien planet. As a kid it was so cool to see the moon rocks and the Gemini 8 in which Armstrong flew. Come to think of it, it's still cool to see them.

Armstrong was an American hero in every sense of the word. And he was a Buckeye.

For you non-Ohioans what does it mean, exactly, to be a Buckeye?

I feel compelled to answer this question, first because politicos and journalists from across the country who are not a Buckeye invariably ask me this every four years. And before that question can be answered, it's important for you to have an understanding of what makes Ohio voters tick.

First, the term "Buckeye" comes from a smooth chestnut-brown nut that falls from a distinctive tree that Ohio's first citizens, Native Americans, believed looked very similar to the eye of a buck.

Indeed it does. Thus the name Buckeye.

Back in the day, Native Americans would smash up the nuts and use them in meals. Today, if you ask for a Buckeye to eat, you'll probably get a peanut butter and chocolate candy that is just delicious! Seriously, order some Buckeyes today if you haven't had them. (You can substitute a Reese's peanut butter cup, which is sort of the same thing but not as good.)

The next thing you need to know is how Ohio became known as the "Buckeye State."

For the answer to that, like many things in life, we must turn to politics for the answer.

Specifically, the 1840 presidential campaign of war hero, general, and senator from Ohio, William Henry Harrison.

Incidentally, Ohio is the "Mother of Presidents", despite what Virginia claims.

Sorry to get sidetracked here, but it's important to establish Ohio's argument while discussing William Henry Harrison.

Let's compare the Ohio and Virginia lists of presidents:

OHIO: William Henry Harrison, Ulysses S. Grant, Rutherford B. Hayes, James Garfield, Benjamin Harrison, William McKinley, William Howard Taft, and Warren G. Harding.

VIRGINA: George Washington, Thomas Jefferson, James Madison, James Monroe, John Tyler, Zachary Taylor, and Woodrow Wilson.

That's eight Ohio presidents to Virginia's seven.

The controversy over which state has produced the most presidents always revolves around William Henry Harrison. Yes, he may have been born in Virginia, but he spent nearly his entire life in Ohio and was elected to both the House and Senate, which then propelled him to the presidency. Without Ohio you don't have a president William Henry Harrison. And that would be a shame.

So take him off your list Virginia!

As for further evidence, the symbol of Harrison's 1840 presidential campaign was not the Flowering Dogwood of Virginia. No, in fact it was a log cabin decorated with raccoon skins and a string of Buckeyes!

And the name "Buckeye State" (answering the previous question before I became distracted) comes directly from a Harrison campaign song:

Oh where, tell me where, was your buckeye cabin made? 'Twas built among the merry boys who wield the plough and spade, where the log cabins stand, in the bonnie buckeye shade.

Oh what, tell me what, is to be your cabin's fate? We'll wheel it to the capital and place it there elate, for a token and a sign of the bonnie buckeye state!

So there it is. Harrison's campaign song—widely popular and sung all across the country—was the creation of the term Buckeye State.

With the famous slogan "Tippecanoe & Tyler Too!" the proud Ohioan overwhelmingly won that election. But unfortunately, he gave such a long inaugural address in the cold and wind he caught pneumonia and died thirty days later. An extremely incompetent Virginian took his place.

Of course, it's impossible to say "Buckeyes" without thinking about The (do not forget THE) Ohio State University and its national championship-caliber football team, season after season. And unlike many of its SEC counterparts, OSU is more likely than not to have a basketball team playing in March Madness too. The Buckeyes are not a one-season-only sports school.

My Uncle Dillon and Aunt Bev, and my Uncle Gene and Aunt Sue are all OSU graduates. My brother Mick attended there too. My dad graduated from Ohio Northern (go Polar Bears!), but he took us to plenty of Buckeye football games in Columbus each fall.

The first sports event I ever attended in life was a Buckeyes football game when I was five. The blurry images in my mind are of Woody Hayes pacing the sidelines, snow falling, skin-piercing cold, and a thermos of hot chocolate my dad brought in with us. He and my mom always had a different thermos, and they confirmed to my sister and I years later theirs was full of coffee and bourbon—to take the edge off the freezing temperatures.

True, with all of its positive attributes, it's hard to think of Ohio without associating it with really brutal winters. It's the reason why my parents packed us up and moved out west to Arizona. In their mid-thirties, my mom and dad said they had shoveled enough snow in their lifetimes and that was that.

With my deep Buckeye blood I couldn't wait to get back, and discover for myself, why Ohio is so pivotal in presidential elections every four years.

Indeed, each election night, presidential candidates keep their eyes on just a handful of states. Most politicos right now could accurately predict which way forty states and their electoral votes will go in 2016. It's sad there aren't more competitive states, but it's true.

States like California, New York, Illinois, Hawaii, and Vermont are solidly blue. States like Texas, Tennessee, Alaska, Utah, and South Carolina are solidly red. In the small toss-up "purple" group, besides Ohio, obviously, Florida is a huge prize (but take it off the battleground map if a presidential nominee is from there). The other competitive purple states—Virginia, Nevada, and Colorado—are not as big as Ohio.

So what the heck is it about this Midwestern state that makes it THE battleground state election after election?

The simple answer is: **Ohio is the heart of America.**

It's really that simple.

But I suspect you need more explanation.

In every way, Ohio has a nearly perfect brew of people—business, labor, rural, big city, young, old, middle class, rich, poor—that can determine the pulse of the nation and determine who will be leading it.

Need suburban soccer moms for your election demographic? Ohio has plenty of them. How about evangelicals, farmers, small business owners, or government employees? No problem, you can count on Ohio. Need a mix of progressives, conservatives, and centrists with a batch of libertarians, greens, and tea partiers included? Don't worry, Ohio has all of those too.

That's my general answer, and it's supported with the evidence of the election results every four years, and I'll give you a specific example in a moment. But let's dig a little deeper into the statistics, because knowing about Ohio is really that important to understanding who leads America.

Ohio is still a big state, stretching from Appalachia to the upper Midwest, with over eleven-and-a-half million people. To judge the economic barometer and how it relates nationally, it has a nearly perfect blend of manufacturing, agricultural interests, large corporations, and smaller businesses. Spending a half-day driving across Ohio, you can feel all at once Northeastern, Midwestern, and Southern all within the same border.

Politically, the Buckeye State has a nearly even divide between registered Democrats, Republicans, and Independents. That means the millions and millions spent in the state during the presidential election are really aimed at just a handful of voters who remain truly undecided until they head to the polls.

It's an expensive state for candidates to advertise on television and radio. You have the Democratic northeastern stronghold of Cleveland (television market 19). The center of the state's seesaw (the swingiest part of the swing state is how I like to call it) in Columbus (market 1). The Republican southeastern stronghold of Cincinnati (market 36). You can also add Dayton (market 63), Toledo (market 76), and Youngstown (market 113) to the mix. Most of these television stations will sell out their available ad space in October, weeks before the presidential election.

Ohio is too big for a lot of that hand-shaking campaigning we see earlier in the year in Iowa, New Hampshire, and South Carolina. But Ohioans still expect dozens of campaign stops by the candidates from Labor Day to Election Day, along with more phone calls, more political mailings, and more commercials.

If you're running for president and come to the Buckeye State (which you will, a lot), for heaven's sake make sure you know how to spell out O-H-I-O with your arms before you get to a campaign rally!

O-H!

GOD SPEED

It is difficult for me to write about just one person that I could offer to you as the embodiment of Ohio. There are the many U.S. presidents, of course, and astronauts like Neil Armstrong and Judy Resnik, inventors like Thomas Edison and the Wright Brothers, singers like Dean Martin, Nancy Wilson, and John Legend, actors like Paul Newman and Clark Gable, directors like Steven Spielberg, activists like Gloria Steinem, college football coaches like Woody Hayes and Urban Meyer, and athletes like Cy Young, Jack Nicklaus, Pete Rose, Stephen Curry, and LeBron James (Curry and King James were born at the same hospital in Akron) and the list goes on.

Incidentally, when it comes to professional sports teams, Ohio has seven of them—representing football, basketball, baseball, hockey, and soccer. That's in addition to the National Championship Buckeyes and the Best Damn Band in the Land! And what about Lebron and Urban?! Both are worth mentioning again. One of the greatest NBA players ever, one of the greatest college football coaches ever, and both left the bright lights of Florida to come home—to Ohio.

When it comes to journalists, what about the late Erma Bombeck, with her quick wit and popular newspaper column? Or Sander Vanocur, one of our best television news White House correspondents? Or one of my favorites, Hugh Downs, the legendary broadcaster who juggled hosting the classic game show *Concentration* while also anchoring the *TODAY* show?

"How did you get away with being an entertainer and news guy at the same time?" I once asked Hugh during an interview in Phoenix. "The audience tended to stick with me and support me," he replied. "They were different departments, and I wore different hats, and the audience had no trouble sorting that out."

But despite all these great personalities, if it were up to me to choose the one person who is the embodiment of an Ohioan, it is (drum roll please):

John Glenn.

A son of Cambridge, Ohio, Glenn always had an eye on the sky and seemed destined to have the right stuff. When the Japanese bombed Pearl Harbor and the nation entered World War II, Glenn enlisted. He flew a total of 149 missions during both World War II and later on in the Korean War. Among his many awards, he received the Distinguished Flying Cross on six different occasions.

All of this made Glenn an American hero. But then NASA came knocking.

"God Speed John Glenn."

The Ohioan was picked as one of the seven original Mercury astronauts. With President Kennedy's dream of placing an American on the surface of the moon by the end of the 1960s you cannot understate what a very big deal this was for the country.

On February 20, 1962, Glenn became the first American to orbit the Earth. He circled the planet three times aboard Friendship 7 traveling at 17,500 miles per hour during a flight lasting nearly five hours.

He was strapped into a seat in a bulky pressurized space suit crammed into a tiny capsule. At one point he had to manually pilot the craft when the autopilot failed. When you watch the footage from inside Friendship 7, you can see the look of concern on Glenn's face as he watched huge chunks of the life-saving heat shield come apart and fly past his window as he reentered the atmosphere.

Glenn landed safely and instantly became a national hero.

"There are milestones in human progress that mark recorded history. From my judgment, this nation's orbital pioneering in space is of such historic stature, representing as it does, a vast advancement that will profoundly influence the progress of all mankind. It signals also a call for alertness to our national opportunities and responsibilities. It requires physical and moral stamina to equal the stresses of these times and a willingness to meet the dangers and the challenges of the future. John Glenn throughout his life has eloquently portrayed these great qualities and is an inspiration to all Americans." -President John F. Kennedy

Two weeks after his historic Mercury flight, the largest ticker-tape parade in New York City's history was held. Tens of thousands of cheering Americans waved as an estimated 3,474 tons of confetti and ticker-tape fell along the parade route.

Glenn was rightfully treated as a hero, especially in the Buckeye State where he was born. But heroism doesn't mean you have everything handed to you, and you won't suffer from setbacks, as Glenn taught us when he stepped into the political arena.

In 1964, inspired by the Kennedys, he planned to run for the U.S. Senate but was forced to withdraw after he fell while shaving in the bath, injuring his ear. Six years later, he again offered himself as a candidate but was denied. He lost the Democratic nomination to liberal millionaire businessman Howard Metzenbaum (who lost in November to the Republican Robert Taft, Jr.) After a decade of political disappointment, Glenn finally won a Senate seat in 1974 after yet another brutal primary fight with Metzenbaum who made the unfortunate error during the campaign of asking Glenn if he had ever had a job.

"You stand in Arlington National Cemetery where I have more friends than I like to remember," Glenn responded, "and you watch those waving flags and you stand there and you think about this nation, and you tell me that those people didn't have jobs."

Game, set, match.

With the help of popular former first lady Jackie Kennedy who recorded a TV ad for Glenn—" I have never done anything political for anyone before, but I feel that both I and the country have an obligation to John Glenn"—he won that November and was reelected three more times (the only Ohioan to ever be elected to a fourth term in the Senate) until his retirement in 1998.

Like the Democrats who privately would say during the Eisenhower years that they wished he had been in their party, Ohio Republicans would say similar things about Glenn.

Despite being an American hero, Glenn had to work to earn his spot in the political world. And even after establishing himself as a winner in Ohio, he would learn that meant very little to the nation.

As I wrote about earlier in the book, Glenn, along with a bunch of others including Fritz Hollings, sought the Democratic nomination for president in 1984. I remember as a young high school kid thinking—at least on paper—this guy had everything Americans looked for in a leader. He was a war hero, astronaut, admired senator to pit against Ronald Reagan (who in 1982 was so unpopular, his wife Nancy considered telling him not to seek reelection). In fact, with the economy still in a recession, Republicans in the '82 midterm election were trounced in House, Senate, and governor races all across the country.

Glenn was also from Ohio. The mother of presidents. The state that always backs winners. This looked, at least on that piece of paper, like a slam-dunk.

So how in the world did former liberal vice president Walter Mondale beat Glenn and end up with the nomination that year?

The answer to that question is the very reason why I believe Glenn is the embodiment of Ohio:

Glenn is a centrist at heart. A moderate. Someone who was middle-left in his partisan politics, but desired to work with all points of view, especially on foreign policy.

Like many Ohioans, he was from modest beginnings, had served his country with distinction, became a hero, but never expected anything to be handed to him. He battled extreme views in his own party while working with members in the other. He was much more interested in getting things done than shouting at each other.

Glenn is the embodiment of Ohio because like the state in presidential elections, nothing can ever be taken for granted. Victories have to be earned. If you're out of step or too extreme in a race for Commander in Chief, Ohio voters, much like a political barometer, will go the other way.

Some say it's easiest to be in the political center. But that's not true. It's the most difficult place you can stand. It drives party activists crazy. It drives conservatives crazy. It drives liberals crazy. It drives those of us in the media crazy. It's very difficult to rouse up a crowd—or have a horse race story to tell on air—when a politician is arguing compromise, working together, and diplomacy.

Partisans at a precinct meeting or a campaign rally want some "red meat" from their leaders. They want to hear why the other side is responsible for every single thing that has ever gone wrong in America. And if you take away that anger from them, don't expect much campaign cash. Nothing is better for fundraising than negative and fear-filled rhetoric.

Let me add another personal observation here. As a political reporter and interviewer, I have always appreciated moderates. I find them interesting because they are rare, having managed to find a way to navigate through partisan primaries and survive. But I am under no illusion how boring they can seem to my colleagues or to voters. It says something about our system that it usually takes a candidate on the far right or far left to get attention in a primary. Then come fall, the people who weren't paying attention earlier complain about how few candidates there are in the middle who actually want to work with everyone to get things done.

But that's where Glenn was politically. His record in 1984 was much more conservative than Mondale's, or Gary Hart's, or George McGovern's, or Jesse Jackson's. And his proposals were to the left of Reagan and the Republicans.

Add all of this up, and Glenn was a centrist in a presidential primary race that doomed him from the start.

Glenn's kickoff announcement in April, 1983 had gone terrifically. He announced for president in front of a couple thousand people in his hometown of New Concord, Ohio. With American flags all along the side of the road, he traveled down John Glenn Highway to John Glenn High School for his speech and then it was off to the John Glenn Gym at his Alma Mater, Muskingum College. There he proclaimed, "I say it's time America was on the march!"

As the primary campaign unfolded, Glenn, who hated campaign rallies and asking for money, watched the AFL-CIO and other labor organizations endorse Mondale. He was furious at what he viewed as the former vice president's pandering to labor interests and promising everything they wanted and not answering how he was going to pay for it. The anger built until Glenn could remain silent no longer.

In mid-January, 1984, Dartmouth College hosted a three-hour debate between the eight Democratic candidates for president. It was the first-ever talk-show style debate moderated for the first ninety minutes by ABC's Ted Koppel, and the second half by talk-show host Phil Donahue. It was aired live on PBS with an estimated audience of nine million viewers.

It would become one of my favorite political debates of all time.

At one point, a Dartmouth student in the audience stood and asked Mondale how he was going to pay for all the new programs he had proposed while still balancing the federal budget. Mondale answered:

"I would make cuts, but I would add something in terms of education and science in terms of promoting a competitive force structure and also in terms of restoring some fairness in American life. I've worked this out very carefully and I have pledged and can achieve it to reduce the Reagan deficits by more than half."

Glenn, who had been shaking his head in disagreement during Mondale's answer, responded, "Let me point out that's the same vague gobble-dygook of nothing we've been hearing all through this campaign! Let's just get with it! Let me say something here..."

As the crowd roared approval, Glenn continued,

"there wasn't a single figure attached to that except we're going to reduce it by half. I've put out a very specific program, other people here have too. This gentleman who just made that statement here—and I like Fritz, he's a good man—but when you go before labor and you promise you're going to match foreign governments subsidy for subsidy, dollar for dollar, and the cheapest estimate we can get on that is $50 billion, Reuben Askew who was the special trade representative estimates it's $130 billion. And then you go before other people and promise them everything else. Is this going to be a Democratic Party that promises everything to everybody and runs up $170 billion a year...?"

At this point a clearly irritated Mondale started to interrupt, but Glenn continued:

"Let me finish. That's $170 billion a year that will only help put more people out of jobs. That's ridiculous! I'm disgusted and tired of all the vague promises. I wish that the former vice president would in fact get some figures down so they can be compared to what the rest of us are proposing."

At this point, an angry Mondale looked over at Glenn and responded:

"The first point, Mr. Glenn, is that the reason we have $200 billion dollar deficits is that you and some others voted for Reaganomics..."

Glenn responded, "no, no, no...!" as Mondale raised his voice back, "hold it, hold it, hold it...!"

Glenn kept going, "No, it's because your administration gave us 21 percent interest rates, 17 percent inflation rates, and that's why we lost the White House and why we lost the Senate!"

At this point, Mondale jumped out of his chair, with the other seven candidates and the audience watching in amazement, pointed his finger at Glenn and said:

"Mr. Donahue! There has just been about a six minute speech, all of it bologna! And I need six minutes to respond!"

Glenn leaped out of his chair at this point and pointed back at Mondale. The debate continued—former Florida governor Reuben Askew went next and said Mondale and Glenn "were right about each other" as the audience laughed—but the wounds were real. Glenn would come in third in the New Hampshire primary, behind Mondale and Gary Hart, and dropped out shortly after also doing poorly on Super Tuesday.

Despite losing out for the presidency, in 1998, at age seventy-seven, he returned to space aboard the shuttle Discovery, the oldest person to ever do so. And a new generation learned about his remarkable achievements.

Standing by his side throughout this remarkable career was his wife Annie. John and Annie were childhood playmates growing up in New Concord, and they were high school sweethearts. Married in 1943, they recently celebrated their 73rd wedding anniversary!

How's that as an example of the All-American couple?

In John Glenn, America sees a politician who won and lost. But always a hero. The perfect embodiment of the nation—and Ohio.

OHIO, OHIO, OHIO

"Ohio, Ohio, Ohio," said the late Tim Russert to Tom Brokaw during NBC's 2004 election night coverage. "Whoever wins Ohio is the next president."

It was all down to the Buckeye State. Would George W. Bush be reelected or would Senator John Kerry do the almost impossible and defeat a war-time president?

"Ohio is effectively two states, North and South," Brokaw explained to viewers. "Cuyahoga County, which is Cleveland and the greater metropolitan areas, and then down south there's a whole cultural differentiation that is much more like Indiana and Kentucky and West Virginia, although Ohio is unique always."

Many believe the high drama of this election came down to the *Columbus Dispatch* endorsement in the closing hours of the presidential campaign. Bush and Kerry were dead even in the polls, and neither campaign could pull ahead in the Buckeye State.

In late October 2004, editor Ben Marrison said while the *Dispatch* had not endorsed a Democrat since Woodrow Wilson, John Kerry was being seriously considered. "Our endorsement is up for grabs; it has become a jump-ball," Marrison said at the time.

Knowing there was no strategy to 270 electoral votes without Ohio, the Bushes deployed former president George H. W. Bush to Columbus in late summer to meet privately with *Dispatch* publisher John F. Wolfe. The Wolfes had contributed tens of thousands of dollars to Republican candidates through the years, but John F. was no big fan of George W. Bush and *Dispatch* editorials often reflected that fact.

During lunch at the Hyatt on Capitol Square, Bush "41" (as Bush "43" called him) heard an earful from Wolfe about the ongoing war in Iraq, Federal Government spending, and the ballooning national debt. The elder Bush left without any promises of an endorsement from Wolfe.

In early September, the day before delivering his acceptance speech at the Republican National Convention in New York City, George W.

Bush invited Wolfe, associate publisher Mike Curtain, and chief political reporter Joe Hallett to fly on board Air Force One from Washington, D.C. to Columbus, where he was attending a rally at Nationwide Arena.

It is yet another example of how important Ohio—specifically central Ohio—is in national elections. Here was the President, the night before his acceptance speech, stumping in Columbus with First Lady Laura Bush, who had also left the convention in New York to fly there to be by his side.

Bush was introduced at the rally by golf legend Jack Nicklaus, a Columbus native. "Jack said he is from Columbus—so am I," Bush told a roaring crowd. "My grandfather was raised right here in Columbus, Ohio! So I'm here to ask that you send a home boy back to Washington, D.C."

It's true; Prescott Bush, later a U.S. Senator from Connecticut, father of President George H. W. Bush, and grandfather to President George W. Bush and presidential candidate Jeb Bush, was born in Columbus in 1895.

Hallett, who had to fly from New York to Washington where he had been covering the GOP convention, told me Bush wasted no more than fifteen minutes in the air before summoning the group to his office in front of Air Force One. After some chit-chat, Bush looked at Wolfe and said, "Want me to tell you what I'm going to say tomorrow?" The trip provided Hallett and the *Dispatch* a national exclusive for the morning paper.

But still no endorsement.

Kerry pushed back, not repeating the mistake Al Gore made in 2000 by refusing to meet with the *Dispatch* editorial board, and traveled to Columbus to do just that in late September. In addition, his running mate John Edwards had an open line of communication with editorial writers.

With the eyes of politicos across the nation on one newspaper, *TIME* magazine called the pending *Dispatch* endorsement, "the most coveted in the U.S."

The Bush team was growing increasingly nervous. In just over a year and a half, Gallup had tracked Bush's approval rating fall from a high of 71 percent in April, 2003, to 47 percent in early October, 2004. The growing unpopularity of the war in Iraq had a lot to do with it. No paper was more critical editorially of the invasion than the *Dispatch*—opposed from the beginning, one of the few newspapers in the country—despite its Republican leanings.

In a September 11th editorial—three years after the terrorist attack and less than two months before the election—the *Dispatch* ripped into the Bush administration for the failure to bring Osama bin Laden to justice:

"How did the destruction of bin Laden slip so far down the nation's to-do list? Why are the bulk of the U.S. military and intelligence assets tied up in Iraq, which posed only a hypothetical threat, while the pursuit of the man who slaughtered thousands of Americans on their own soil is on the back burner?"

The Kerry campaign and Democrats knew of the value of being the first Democrat in ninety-eight years to get the *Dispatch* stamp of approval. The endorsement could be used for momentum to tip central Ohio into their column and with it, the presidency.

At the editorial board meeting on September 24th, led by Wolfe, Kerry came across as "friendly, well-prepared, confident, and tough on Bush, playing the deficit card he knew would appeal to the publisher," Hallett told me.

In late October, with the newspaper endorsement in the most critical state needed to help make him president almost in hand, some inside the *Dispatch* believe Kerry made a tactical mistake.

A couple days before a campaign event in Pennsylvania, Kerry personally phoned Wolfe to tell him he would be making a "major policy speech about federal spending." Without giving specific details, Kerry told Wolfe the address would be sure to "please" him. Hallett was sent to Wilkes-Barre to cover it.

But the speech turned out to be nearly identical to one Kerry had given in Columbus two days earlier. At both, he accused Bush of having plans to privatize Social Security—the "January Surprise," as the speech became known. "I will never cut the benefits, and I won't raise the retirement age," Kerry had promised about 1,500 African-American parishioners at

Mt. Olivet Baptist Church in Columbus on Sunday. It was nearly the identical message Hallett heard in Wilkes-Barre on Tuesday.

The issue of Social Security privatization was not high on Wolfe's list—certainly nowhere near federal deficits and spending—and he felt duped by Kerry. In the end, Wolfe and the Dispatch stuck with Bush, although offering a less than glowing endorsement. Still, it may have slowed any Kerry momentum in a state that would determine the outcome.

At 3 a.m. on election night, forty-nine of fifty states had been called, and Bush was stuck at 266 electoral votes—four short of the 270 needed—while Kerry had 252. The twenty electoral votes in the hard-fought state of Ohio would be the difference. If Bush won Ohio, he would end with 286 electoral votes. If Kerry won, he'd have 272. With 99 percent of the precincts reporting statewide, with a difference of 118,000 votes out of over five-and-a-half million cast, Kerry refused to concede defeat until there was a thorough review of the Ohio votes.

"I don't see any basis right now for that at all," Ohio's GOP chairman Bob Bennett told reporters at 4:30 a.m. "I think the margin of victory is certainly beyond any margin of error in Ohio."

The networks decided not to call a winner (still reeling from the botched calls of Florida four years earlier) so the nation went to bed without knowing who had won the presidency.

"Karl Rove and company believes that cultural issues will help them in the Southeast and in the Southwest in Ohio," Brokaw had told viewers. "They think they lost votes in 2000 because in the closing days of the campaign, it was disclosed that George W. Bush had a drunk driving arrest and that kept some cultural conservatives at home, according to Mr. Rove and his operatives. They think they'll get them back this time and that will make the difference."

Indeed it was.

A proposed constitutional amendment to ban same-sex marriage—Issue 1—on the statewide ballot is what Bush's campaign manager Ken Mehlman credited later for the margin of victory. The Bush team had worked closely with Ohio Republicans earlier in 2004 to make sure the gay marriage ban was before the voters.

My first campaign event as a teenager. Behind me, Senator Barry Goldwater of Arizona. The finest public servant I've met.

Celebrating my high school graduation with a trip to Capitol Hill with my mom and dad. Congressman Bob Stump (center) welcomed us.

The most recognized place in Ohio—the 'Shoe at The Ohio State University in Columbus. Go Buckeyes!

It was all smiles with Barack Obama as my interview in Dillon, South Carolina started.

But after running over my allotted time, he was ready to leave.

This Capital University interview with Mitt Romney would make national news.

Our reunion several months later was friendly. We spoke again on board his campaign bus in Newark, Ohio.

Asking Hillary Clinton about what she planned to do with Bill if she won the presidency brought a smile to her face.

An interview at the ballpark with former New York City mayor Rudy Giuliani. Baseball helped America get back on its feet after 9/11.

We pushed our way through the crowd to get an interview with Joe Biden at the Galivants Ferry Stump.

There was a noticeable personality change in John Edwards between my first interview with him in 2004 and his 2008 campaign.

Marco Rubio told me the US Senate can "walk and chew gum" at the same time.

Photojournalist Kevin Abadie picked the Atlantic Ocean as our backdrop for this interview with former New York Governor George Pataki.

Talking with Senator Sherrod Brown at an Obama rally at Ohio State (left). Walking the streets of Charlotte with former Governor Ted Strickland hours before his primetime speech (center). In Washington, DC interviewing Senator Rob Portman who was on Mitt Romney's short list for Vice President (right).

Ohio delegates had great seats at both national party conventions. Republicans (on left) and Democrats (on right).

Watching actor Clint Eastwood speak to an empty chair at the Republican National Convention in Tampa.

A selfie with will.i.am from the Black Eyed Peas at the Democratic National Convention in Charlotte.

A behind-the-scenes look at our work station covering the conventions, a tangled mess of wires. We get everything ready here before you see us on TV.

What you see on television from our live convention coverage (left) and what we see when we're standing there (right).

Two TV news legends. Former NBC News anchor Tom Brokaw (left) and up in the CBS News booth talking with Bob Schieffer (right).

A conversation with John Kasich, who was a fascinating politician to cover on a daily basis.

I covered dozens of presidential campaign events in Ohio. This one for Romney in West Chester the Friday before election day.

A number of my press credentials collected during the fall of 2012 covering the presidential campaign in Ohio.

It was a career highlight—pulling 9Gs with the US Thunderbirds over the Atlantic Ocean (and no "Code 11").

Reporting from the ABC News location on the lawn of the White House.

Paul Ryan, the 2012 GOP Vice Presidential nominee, became a familiar face in Ohio during the final weeks of the campaign.

"Of course I did" was the answer John McCain gave me when I asked if he knew he had lost the presidency when Ohio went for Barack Obama in '08.

Interviewing famed historian Doris Kearns Goodwin at the Ohio statehouse where Abraham Lincoln learned the electors had officially made him president. Photographer Andy Wallace and producer Jeremy Naylor help prepare the interview.

The same-sex marriage ban passed in Ohio with 62 percent of the vote and carried Bush along with it. He beat Kerry 51 to 49 percent and Ohio not only went with the winner, but actually determined it.

The next morning in Boston, at around 11 a.m., with running mate John Edwards by his side, Kerry conceded to his supporters the vote margin in Ohio was too great and wished Bush well for the coming four years. In the end, if Kerry had won around 60,000 more raw votes in Ohio, he would have been President of the United States.

Those are the things that can keep politicians awake at night.

Now, fast-forward the clock four years to 2008.

The day after Barack Obama accepted the Democratic Party nomination, Senator John McCain, the GOP nominee, picked Dayton, Ohio to announce his selection of Alaska Governor Sarah Palin to be his running mate.

"I'm very happy, very happy today to spend my birthday with you and to make an historic announcement in Dayton, a city built on hard, honest work of good people. Like the entire industrial Midwest, Dayton has contributed much to the prosperity and progress of America."

Why did McCain choose to make this announcement, being watched with fascination all over the world, in Dayton, Ohio?

Simple. No Republican presidential candidate in American history has ever reached 270 electoral votes and the White House without winning Ohio.

Think about that for a second. That's an amazing record dating back to 1856. Let me repeat it: <u>No Republican has ever been elected president without winning Ohio.</u>

In fact, no Democrat has won the White House without Ohio since John F. Kennedy in 1960. And Ohio now has the longest streak of voting for the winning presidential candidate of any state in the country.

Over the last four presidential elections combined, just 144,818 votes separate Republicans from Democrats out of about twenty-two million votes cast. That's a difference of less than 1 percent.

That's why come fall in the race for the White House, the news usually centers around, as Tim Russert said, "Ohio, Ohio, Ohio."

In the fall of 2008, while campaigning in the Toledo suburb of Holland, Obama encountered Joe Wurzelbacher, who worked in the plumbing business, but was not a licensed plumber. During a five-minute conversation, Wurzelbacher asked several questions about Obama's tax plan. As he discussed the concept of a "flat tax", Obama said, "If you've got a plumbing business, you're gonna be better off if you've got a whole bunch of customers who can afford to hire you. And right now, everybody's so pinched that business is bad for everybody. And I think when you spread the wealth around, it's good for everybody."

Republicans took that last sentence and had a field day, believing it was the "smoking gun" proving Obama was just a socialist who wanted to "spread wealth around." Three days later, during the third and final presidential debate, McCain mentioned Wurzelbacher, or "Joe the plumber" more than a dozen times in the first ten minutes.

"I would like to mention that a couple days ago Senator Obama was out in Ohio and he had an encounter with a guy who's a plumber," McCain said. "Joe, I want to tell you, I'll not only help you buy that business that you worked your whole life for, I'll keep your taxes low and I'll provide available and affordable healthcare for you and your employees."

Obama didn't waste a chance to bring his conversation with Joe into the debate.

"The conversation I had with Joe the plumber, what I essentially said to him was, 'Five years ago, when you weren't in a position to buy your business, you needed a tax cut then.' And what I want to do is to make sure that the plumber, the nurse, the firefighter, the teacher, the young entrepreneur who doesn't yet have money, I want to give them a tax break now."

Thrust into the national political spotlight, Ohio's "Joe the plumber" took his fifteen minutes of fame and became an outspoken conservative critic of both Obama and McCain. He attempted a run for the House in 2012, but his congressional dreams went down the drain along with 23 percent of the vote.

Throughout all of October and into November, the Obama campaign pounded away at McCain in Ohio, linking him with President George

W. Bush, who was at a 25 percent approval rating after the economy came close to a complete financial meltdown. Wall Street titan Lehman Brothers had declared bankruptcy in September, setting in motion the worst economic crisis since the Great Depression. In response, Bush had signed a $700 billion bailout plan, using taxpayer money, to help keep the banking industry afloat. He also signed a $17.4 billion bailout for the auto industry. Conservatives in Ohio and elsewhere were livid, and many stayed home on election day. Meanwhile, Democrats increased their ground game in Republican-rich Hamilton County. Obama would be the first Democrat since Lyndon Johnson to carry it.

Palin, with no national political experience, added her own circus-like atmosphere to the campaign. While appearing first as a fresh face, the American people soon concluded she was in way over her head. When asked whether being a two-year governor of Alaska gave her foreign policy experience, Palin responded, "Well, it certainly does because our—our next-door neighbors are foreign countries, there in the state that I am the executive of. We have trade missions back and forth. We—we do—it's very important when you consider even national security issues with Russia. As Putin rears his head and comes into the air space of the United States of America, where—where do they go? It's Alaska. It's just right over the border. It is—from Alaska that we send those out to make sure that an eye is being kept on this very powerful nation, Russia, because they are right there. They are right next to—to our state." This rambling answer became immortalized by Tina Fey on Saturday Night Live when, as Palin, she quipped, "I can see Russia from my house!" In her only debate with Joe Biden, Palin asked if she could call him by his first name "Joe," because she couldn't stop calling him Senator "O'Biden" during debate prep. You just can't make any of this up. Palin, who was wildly unprepared for a national campaign, but became beloved by the far right, would return to Alaska and resign as governor halfway through her first and only term.

On election night, just minutes after the television networks called Ohio for Obama, McCain took to the stage before his supporters in Phoenix to concede defeat. There was absolutely no strategy for his campaign to reach 270 electoral votes without the Buckeye State.

Four years later in Columbus, shortly before the 2012 election, I asked McCain whether he knew instantly his campaign was over when Ohio went blue:

"Of course I knew it was over," McCain told me.

"Will Mitt Romney know it's over if he loses Ohio on election night this year?" I followed up.

"There's a way I can draw you on the electoral college map how Republicans can win without Ohio, but I'll tell you it is a tough, tough road."

"It's never happened before," I interrupted.

McCain agreed and said, "I mean, it's not an accident that the eyes of the world are on Ohio on election night. I promise you that."

All of this means for future presidential candidates, plan on camping out in Ohio. If voters don't see you, you'll lose. And make sure your spouse, your kids, your running mate, your best friends from college, your dog and every surrogate you have camps out there too. And please, if you don't think you can win in Ohio, don't bother to run.

TEA PARTY, GUNS & GAY MARRIAGE

After leaving South Carolina, I arrived back in the state of my birth to cover the Ohio statehouse and moderate a political show called *Capitol Square* for the Ohio News Network and then WBNS 10TV (the long-time powerhouse CBS affiliate).

10TV and the *Columbus Dispatch* newspaper were both part of the Wolfe family empire. The Wolfes owned the *Dispatch* for over 110 years before selling it in 2015 to New Media Investment Group. They have owned WBNS (Wolfe Banks, Newspapers and Shoes) television and radio since 1949. Members of the Wolfe family have been well-known community leaders in central Ohio for decades.

While the editorial page of the *Dispatch* during the Wolfe years always leaned right—and this goes to the issue of media bias, which I'll get to later—the working statehouse reporters did not. In fact, when I think of the *Dispatch* political reporters I worked with week after week, and had on my show each Sunday, I couldn't even begin to guess where they are at ideologically. They are just great journalists.

And if you're wondering if I ever received direction from management on what—or what not—to cover, the answer is no. Not once.

Capitol Square was a thirty-minute program that I inherited from a long line of previous hosts. One of the first changes we made was to make it relevant to that week's top political stories. I wanted Ohio politicians to think it was a "must appear" show if they wanted to communicate with the viewers (and voters) most interested in what they were doing.

Ohio's congressional delegation regularly appeared—Senators Sherrod Brown and Rob Portman, and Representatives Steve Stivers, Pat Tiberi, and Joyce Beatty. Speaker John Boehner, who represents Cincinnati, rarely speaks to the media (if it's not national press) and he was impossible to book. That was really his loss, a little more exposure back home wouldn't have hurt. Governor Ted Strickland was a regular guest, as would be Governor John Kasich (at least until he entered reelection mode in 2014).

This weekly show provided an insight into Ohio politics from Ohio's top statehouse reporters and analysts. In fact, that was the biggest challenge for me when I arrived in Ohio. I was surrounded by *Columbus Dispatch* political reporters like Joe Hallett, Daryl Rowland, Alan Johnson, Jim Siegel, Randy Ludlow, and Joe Vardon. Then there were the reporters who rotated on the show each week like Bill Hershey and Laura Bischoff from the *Dayton Daily News*, Bill Cohen, Karen Kasler, and Jo Ingles from *Ohio Public Radio*, Reggie Fields from the *Cleveland Plain Dealer*, and Mark Niquette from *Bloomberg News*. Add to this longtime Ohio political operatives like Bob Clegg, Dale Butland, Terry Casey, Sandy Theis, and Sam Gresham, and you had many, many years of Ohio political experience.

At times this new front row seat at the Ohio political circus could be a bit overwhelming!

There were a handful of elected officials who were absolutely fearless of the press and easily earned my respect. State Representative, and former Ohio Democratic Party chairman David Leland, along with Republican State Representative Jay Hottinger, were two of our go-to guests when something controversial was happening and no one else had the courage to appear. In fact, we started calling Hottinger our Ohio version of "John McCain" for his willingness to appear often on Sunday morning political shows.

Other regular guests included Secretary of State Jon Husted, who faced regular criticism for his role in enforcing Republican efforts to condense early voting opportunities in Ohio. Despite the heat, Husted—a likely frontrunner for governor in 2018—was always calm and prepared.

There is no question Republican lawmakers in Ohio and other states have looked at where the Democratic early votes are coming from—like the Sunday before the election "Souls to the Polls" effort where predominately African American parishioners go from church to the polling place—and attempted to eliminate or restrict them. Billionaire liberal philanthropist George Soros has bankrolled lawsuits against states like Ohio that have started rolling back early voting opportunities. Republicans claim they're doing it to prevent voter fraud, but Husted admits that is not an issue in Ohio. In fact, voter fraud in Ohio amounted to 0.002397 percent (135 "possible" cases out of 5.63 million votes cast) in 2012.

Hillary Clinton proposed in 2015 that every state have twenty days of early voting, but Ohio already has twenty-eight. Clinton's state of New York, with a Democratic governor and legislature, currently has zero. This points to a certain hypocrisy by Democrats, where early voting days in swing states can be litigated but, if you're a voter in a blue state—like New York, Michigan, Pennsylvania, Massachusetts, Rhode Island—no need for you to have any early voting days because the electoral votes are already in the bag.

Common sense tells us early voting should be available and uniform across the country. Polls should be open the weekend before the Tuesday election for the same reason a business stays open late on days before a holiday. Voters are the most informed and ready to cast a ballot the final week before an election, and that's when the voting booth should be most accessible.

While a state lawmaker, Husted also advocated for redistricting reform, but was unsuccessful in negotiating a bipartisan solution. After the census is taken every ten years, redistricting and reapportionment takes place to draw the boundaries of new congressional and state legislative districts. The process remains flawed in many states, including Ohio, because it puts the power to draw those lines in the hands of incumbents and the majority party. It's the explanation on how states like Ohio, the ulti-mate "purple" battleground state in presidential elections, is so "red"— like really, really red—in the state legislature. Non-Ohioans are usually shocked when they hear about the lack of political competition in the Buckeye State and will ask me, "How does the state that voted for Obama twice have so many Republicans running it?"

"It's amazing, even though we're a 50-50 state, there are almost no indi-vidual state legislative or congressional districts that are truly competi-tive," election law expert Daniel Tokaji from The Ohio State University said as we appeared on C-SPAN together shortly before the 2012 election.

"Around three-quarters of the congressional districts are drawn to favor the party currently in power, and almost two-thirds of the state legislative districts. For practical purposes here in Ohio, even though presidential elections are very competitive, legislative elections are not."

When the lines are drawn so lopsided politically, it means competition and any meaningful general election debate is eliminated, which in turn eliminates voter interest. Most of the time the competition in these stacked districts is in a primary election, where the most ideologically extreme candidates can win. In football terms it pushes the game away from midfield down toward the twenty, fifteen, and ten yard lines.

In an interview with ABC's David Brinkley just a month before leaving office, President Ronald Reagan was asked what one thing he didn't accomplish during his presidency that he regretted most. He answered: "Some people are going to erupt when I say it, but I think maybe our Founding Fathers made something of a mistake in the method of reapportionment. Every 10 years, when the census is taken, there are changes in the population. Growth here and loss of population elsewhere. Legislators lay out the new district lines. I think this is a great conflict of interest."

Reagan suggested the creation of a bipartisan commission, appointed every ten years, to redraw the districts. In 2015 the Supreme Court ruled that idea was constitutional, and six states—Alaska, Arizona, California, Hawaii, Idaho, Montana and Washington—now have an independent redistricting commission. Members of these commissions are not in elected office, and they are banned from running in the districts they draw. A bipartisan commission, to draw both state and congressional lines, is just common sense. A system that screws one team for a decade, while protecting the other just because they hit the "right" election cycle, is not a shining achievement for democracy.

"When you have safe seats, when incumbents just know they're going to get reelected, they don't have to listen to voters," Catherine Turcer of Ohio Common Cause told me. "They can listen to their buddies. They can listen to their parties. They don't have to pay attention to people in their districts." Voters should be skeptical of any plans to "change" the redistricting process that includes politicians who have a stake in the final maps. It's a conflict of interest pure and simple, and as Reagan said, the founders on this one simply got it wrong.

Another familiar name to those outside Ohio may be Attorney General Mike DeWine, a former U.S. Senator, who really never lets anything faze him. When DeWine suffered a serious bout of Vertigo before the 2014 election, I called and asked if he'd come on the show to talk about it. He did, without the slightest hesitation, and I think it helped quickly answer public concerns about his health. DeWine took a huge beating in his reelection campaign for the U.S. Senate in 2006, but he got right back up again four years later. He, too, is eyeing a campaign for governor in 2018.

DeWine's opponent for reelection in 2014 was David Pepper, who I had also covered when he ran for state auditor four years earlier. The son of former Procter & Gamble CEO John Pepper, David is young and ambitious with a law degree from Yale. Also fearless with the press, Pepper now leads the Ohio Democratic Party, and he's likely to have a very long political career ahead.

Other politicians in Ohio, and elsewhere, are not as transparent. On a personal note, I don't care if you are to the left or right ideologically, but if you are an elected official, be prepared to answer questions when they are raised. Too many officials in this social media age hunker down and hope the news will blow over. That's a bad strategy. What could be a one-day story often turns into something much longer when an official hides away and refuses to answer questions.

That is really the best advice I could give press secretaries and their bosses: Be upfront. Get in front of any controversy, even if it has some short-term pain. You are (or asking to be) on the taxpayer dime. The alternative is to hope questions stop being asked. And from experience that never, ever happens.

Along the same line, avoid the Friday news dump. That's so old school. Everyone in our newsroom knew that if a political press release hit late on a Friday afternoon in an attempt to avoid media scrutiny, I would personally stay as long as it took to make it a top story. The television show *The West Wing* devoted an entire episode on the technique called, "Take out the trash day." We're on to you, so just stop.

Capitol Square, which we taped in "real time" on Friday for air Sunday morning, usually ran smoothly. But on one show, just two minutes from the end of a particularly heated segment, one of my favorite political strategists looked at their counterpart and said, "that's fucking unbelievable!" For five seconds everything in the studio stopped. The strategist, realizing what had just happened said, "wait, can that be edited out?" Then in my IFB I heard producer Jeff Pullin scream, "OH MY GOD" as the floor crew pulled back the cameras.

If that had been live we would soon be off the air forever, I thought. Thankfully we weren't, and after a ten-minute delay we were back up and running.

That wasn't the only odd moment of my career. Once, while interviewing actor and comedian Paul Rodriguez, I asked a series of questions about his father who had immigrated his family to the United States from Mexico. The topic hit a nerve and the funnyman started to sob uncontrollably. "What are you doing to me, Heath?" he asked as the tears dripped down his cheeks.

Well, that was unexpected, I thought. Every now and then television tosses out a crazy pitch.

Once I recorded a commercial with Alex Trebek, the host of the game show *Jeopardy!*, in Los Angeles. He started the promo, "The answer, Jim, is: This is the name of the number one newscast in the American desert Southwest?" I answered, "Alex, I believe the answer is *Nightside!*" A stunned Trebek paused and responded, "You didn't phrase that in the form of a question. Get him out of here, can we get someone else?!" While we had a good laugh, he still refused to do a second take, insisting anything else would look too staged.

In Myrtle Beach, I anchored four live newscasts every weeknight for six years. That totals up to thousands of shows. On many summer nights (here's a visual for you) I would be wearing shorts and flip flops under the desk while sporting a suit and tie on air. Hey, it was a beach community after all! Some of my newscasts weren't perfect. Like the night—on a dare by a couple of station engineers—I used the word "voluptuous" to describe the very nice weather we were having. Or when I accidentally called a convicted murdered "Lemonade" instead of "Lemond" during a story—the crew pointed out the mistake during a commercial break and warned me to keep my windows locked in case he ever escaped.

The first station I worked at was an NBC affiliate. One night I made fun of Jay Leno during our late evening newscast. My general manager Paul Heebink had written a memo instructing the "front four" to mention *The Tonight Show* a minimum of four times during our late newscast. It was during a sweeps period and we were attempting to wrap our arms tightly around NBC programming. In a moment of rebellion one night I called out the memo live on air, and it resulted in what can only be described as a trip to the principal's office the following day. Paul equated what I did to "stealing my car and driving it into a ditch," and he sent me home to think about it.

I never made fun of Jay Leno (on air) again.

Another favorite moment occurred one night when we aired a health story about cataract surgery. Our very capable young reporter had unfortunately—and we never did figure out why—ended her report by showing a close-up of a butterfly with the worst eight seconds of soap opera-sounding music ever. It was just awful. Coming out of the story my incredibly fantastic co-anchor Heather Moore, in a tight camera close-up, lost it. "That music" is all she could say, laughing so hard she was in tears. Then she tossed it over to me. I tried to look and sound serious but it didn't work, I too had tears in my eyes. Angry viewers immediately called in to ask why Jim and Heather were so insensitive to people dealing with cataracts.

The second after we said "good night" on air our boss, Bruce Kirk, threw open his office door, which connected to the studio, and yelled "get in here!" As Heather and I sat and listened to his lecture about our responsibilities as "newsroom leaders," Bruce took one of his many Emmy awards off a shelf and slammed it on his desk. The little gold globe that is at the top of the statue broke and came flying off and ricocheted around his office. It was all Heather and I could do to not laugh out loud and get ourselves into even bigger trouble. But we apologized and committed to him it would never happen again. The word got out and the incident became infamous around the newsroom. Months later when Bruce, who also anchored the 6 p.m. newscast, signed off the air for the final time he apologized to "Jim and Heather for the Emmy incident" which made us all laugh. (Bruce was able to fix that Emmy by the way.)

Back in Columbus, my co-moderator on *Capitol Square,* Tracy Townsend, and I just clicked when we met. Together we were representative of the diversity of Ohio and a perfect team to ask the politicians what was going on. Sometimes in preparing questions each week, Tracy could tell when I was apprehensive about a topic and say, "you want me to take that one?" And she would. When one of us would get a negative viewer email, the other would volunteer to answer it. Winning an Emmy award with Tracy, and our *Capitol Square* team, including producer Jeremy Naylor, for a show we did from the lawn of the White House was a career highlight.

Covering politicians at every level of government has kept me close to the issues of the day. The challenge for me during any given daily newscast was finding ways to simplify those issues so that everyone could understand and find them as interesting as we politicos did.

My boss Elbert Tucker knew I loved baseball and would say to me endless times, "keep the ERA (earned run average) talk for your show, but just describe the most interesting part of the game in the nightly newscast." A lesson I thought about daily.

After spending most of the fall of 2009 covering the casino debate in Ohio (voters would approve four casinos in Cleveland, Columbus, Cincinnati, and Toledo) by early 2010, it became clear that the anger at President Obama over the new federal healthcare law was likely to result in huge Republican gains at the ballot box that November.

The first signal came from the very blue state of Massachusetts when a little-known state GOP senator, Scott Brown, won the U.S. Senate seat held previously for decades by Edward Kennedy. Brown's win, in the state where the Boston Tea Party ignited the American Revolution, was hailed by supporters as the modern tea party's first victory.

This new tea party movement had started shortly after Barack Obama took office. Supporters said they were concerned about excessive government spending, higher taxes, and a growing government debt. The movement's rallying cry was protecting the Constitution.

Several months after Brown's win I attended a tea party rally at the Ohio statehouse attended by a few thousand people. It was down from a rally a year earlier that attracted roughly 7,000, and missing were John Kasich and his running mate Mary Taylor, who had addressed the crowd the year before. There was a sense among Republican politicians that a huge anti-Obama wave was coming in November, so why risk being viewed as "too extreme" when the base was already sure to show up.

A Gallup survey showed that a majority of tea party activists were white (86 percent), Republican (80 percent), and male (59 percent). And while only eighteen percent of Americans said they belonged to the tea party, they were a huge political force in 2010 because the anger, pessimism, and negativity about Obama would almost assuredly mean they would vote come fall.

The most recognized face of the movement was the 2008 Republican vice presidential nominee Sarah Palin. Two days before the Ohio rally, Palin headlined a similar tea party event in Boston. There she told the crowd, "Is this what their change is all about? I want to tell 'em, Nah, we'll keep clinging to our Constitution and our guns and religion and you can keep the change!"

At the Ohio rally, one tea party leader told me, "Sarah Palin taps into what a lot of people are thinking. She's got some rhetoric, of course she does, that's what makes her popular, but she resonates with the folks."

While speakers at the Ohio tea party rally highlighted low taxes, gun rights, and less government, the activists clearly had Barack Obama on their minds. Conservatives were furious over the passage of the federal healthcare law—known as Obamacare—which sailed through both chambers of Congress without one Republican vote.

Some at the rally were holding signs accusing Obama of being a socialist. In fact, some tea party activists were wearing a shirt with Obama's face digitally manipulated to look like the Joker—the super-villain played by actor Heath Ledger in the movie *The Dark Knight*—and the word "socialist" underneath.

"When you do your policies that go against the American taxpayer, you're a socialist," one activist who was wearing the shirt told me. "The reason why it's the Joker on my shirt, if you've seen the movie, what did the guy want? He just wanted to watch the world burn."

And he, along with many others that day, honestly believed Obama intended to watch the world burn.

"When a movement is founded on this idea of independence, liberty, leave me alone big government, you are going to pull in the most absolute fringe individuals along with regular people," Jason Rink, author of *Ron Paul: Father of the Tea Party* explained to me.

The extreme images of Obama at the rallies had not gone unnoticed by Ohio's Democrat leaders. David Leland, the former state chairman, said Obama, the nation's first African- American president, created fear in some people.

"There is a segment in the tea party movement that is racially oriented," Leland told me. "They have a President of the United States who looks different than all the other presidents they've seen on their dollar bills. Things are different."

Even Boehner, the Republican leader in the House, admitted some tea party comments at rallies were "reprehensible and should not have happened."

"When John Boehner says the things that they do is over the edge, I think we have substantial evidence to support the contention that there are racist elements within the tea party," Sam Gresham of Ohio Common Cause told me during an appearance on *Capitol Square*.

But Alicia Healy had a different view. A young African-American woman who had become a leader in the Ohio tea party movement told me, "We don't agree with many of the things that people are saying that are racist statements against another group of people. We want all groups of people to be part of the tea party movement."

And many were. On Election Day, Republicans swept every statewide executive office in Ohio. They kept the state Senate and took back the House while increasing their numbers in the Congressional delegation.

Boehner became Speaker-Elect of the House of Representatives.

After the commanding victories, a state tea party activist and well-known libertarian, Chris Littleton, came on my show two years later to proclaim the tea party dead: "The tea party died because those of us at the protests refocused our energy, we've gotten far more precise and a whole lot better at getting something done."

The truth is, however, the tea party energy is still determining how far to the right many Republicans run in legislative districts across the country.

Another group with enormous political power in the state is the Buckeyes Firearms Association. Ohio's version of the NRA, they are a visible presence at the statehouse working with lawmakers on both sides of the aisle.

One afternoon, I headed to the Short North area of Columbus to cover an anti-gun rally backed by Michael Bloomberg's group Mayors Against Illegal Guns.

There I found supporter Blanche Luczyk who told me, "As a gun owner, I'm a responsible person, and I think it's responsible to ask to have all gun owners have a background check. It's just common sense. Any responsible person who is willing to take the ownership of a gun should be willing to have that background check."

Under the current federal law, licensed gun dealers are already required to do background checks. Felons, illegal immigrants, habitual drug abusers, and the severely mentally ill are banned from buying or owning guns. A proposed bill to expand background checks in late 2012 after the shooting massacre in Newtown, Connecticut failed to pass in Congress.

A non-partisan Quinnipiac University poll in mid-2014 found 92 percent of voters, including 92 percent of gun owners and 86 percent of Republicans, support background checks prior to all gun sales. The same poll, however, showed nearly half of Americans oppose stricter gun control, which they believed Bloomberg's group promoted.

Luczyk was one of a half-dozen members of the group who showed up for the rally. But soon, buses arrived full of pro-gun supporters, many carrying the American Flag, carrying Second Amendment signs and wearing rifles over their shoulders and handguns in hip holsters.

When Luczyk started her speech by telling the crowd that former president Ronald Reagan supported background checks, she was drowned out by shouts of "Germany, 1933" and "Hitler!"

I whispered to my photographer Dan Konik, "This woman has been consumed by the opposition, I've never seen anything quite like it." I started my live report that night, "This event certainly answered the question, what happens when you throw a political rally and no one shows up except your opposition?"

The counter-rally was another demonstration of the organizational power of the Buckeye Firearms Association and the NRA, which quickly took control of the rally and the message.

"There's no reason for Mayors Against Illegal Guns to be in Ohio," Linda Walker of the Buckeye Firearms Association, and an NRA board member, told me. "Ohioans stand up for our constitutional rights and that's the way it's going to be."

After Luczyk addressed the crowd for a few minutes to some jeers and boos, Walker, with a cheering crowd of dozens on her side, stepped up to the mic and replaced her as the speaker.

"People are fired up, people are concerned," said Walker. "It's overwhelming this many people show up on a Friday afternoon because our constitutional rights are that important."

All told, I did dozens of gun-related stories while in Ohio. The fight over legalizing concealed weapons in bars and restaurants (it passed). The debate, right after the Newtown school tragedy, to allow people to bring guns into the parking garages under the statehouse (passed). There was the bill to allow Ohioans to use silencers while hunting (passed) and reduce required training time for a concealed-carry license (passed). Another bill would allow concealed handguns to be taken into churches, day-care centers, airplanes, state buildings, airports outside security checkpoints, and publicly accessible areas of police stations (still being debated).

In fact, there were so many proposed gun laws—most rolling back regulations—that Ken Hanson, the legal chairman of the Buckeye Firearms Foundation, matter-of-factly told me, "Sometimes at the statehouse it's an embarrassment of riches."

My gun coverage in Ohio led to winning my first news Emmy award. From experience, you just can't do enough Second Amendment stories in this era we're in. The only political issue more popular on our website was marijuana—medical or otherwise. "Guns are a close second place, but nothing beats pot on social media," web manager Don Taylor often told me. In July 2014 I broke a story that a major marijuana referendum, backed by wealthy supporters, would attempt to make the Ohio ballot the following year. Indeed, the news was widely circulated on the web.

As much as pro-gun advocates are on a roll across the country, supporters of same-sex marriage are too. In fact, I can't think of an issue during my career where I've seen the public change its mind as quickly as approving gay marriage. By early 2015, major polls found support for same-sex marriage among all Americans above sixty percent, and support from those under thirty near eighty percent. Compare that to similar polls a decade earlier when opponents outnumbered supporters by a two-to-one margin.

As mentioned earlier, in 2004 Ohio voters overwhelmingly approved a constitutional ban on gay marriage. It was a primary reason why George W. Bush carried the state and won reelection that year. But just a decade later an Ohio court case, watched all over the world, would bring down that ban in Ohio and all across the United States.

In 2013, after a twenty year relationship, Cincinnati residents Jim Obergefell and John Arthur flew to Maryland to be legally married. Arthur was in the final stages of amyotrophic lateral sclerosis, or Lou Gehrig's disease. When he died several weeks later, the state of Ohio refused to recognize Obergefell on his death certificate. He sued, and when federal judge Timothy Black sided with him and ordered Ohio to recognize the marriage, Attorney General Mike DeWine dug in and prepared to take the case all the way to the Supreme Court.

On July 24, 2013 I led the 6 o'clock news with anchor Kristyn Hartman asking me, "Could this case be the game changer in Ohio, Jim?" I responded, "Kristyn, I think so. On both the legal and political front. If Ohio loses it will unravel the state's constitutional amendment." In fact, the case would lead to the historic June 2015 Supreme Court decision that made marriage equality the law of the land.

Appearing on *Capitol Square* after the Supreme Court announced they would hear his case, Obergefell, who never desired to be the focus of so much media attention, told me, "I want what any other couple in the state would receive and that's recognition." While the nature of his case had the potential to be historic, Obergefell insisted that for him it was a simple question of fairness. "When your spouse passes away, do you want your marriage recognized? Or when you pass away, do you want your spouse to have your marriage recognized? That's why it's important to me."

For his part, DeWine told me, "The case in Cincinnati is a real tragedy, but Ohio voters made it very, very clear what they wanted to do in regard to same-sex marriage. My job as attorney general is to support the law and defend the law if it's attacked in court." Pointing to a ten- year-old vote, and not the fairness of law, was an interesting fallback for the state's highest attorney. "Civil Rights shouldn't be adjudicated by popular votes, it's a matter for the courts," longtime Columbus residents Rick Neal and his husband Tom Grote, who had married in Massachusetts and had two adopted children, told me in response. As I left his office after the interview, I told DeWine's press secretary Eve Mueller that while I respected her boss, I really felt this case would put him, and Governor John Kasich, on the wrong side of history.

The Supreme Court decision was close: 5 to 4, with Justice Anthony Kennedy the deciding vote. Like the ruling on interracial marriage announced by the court in 1967, most younger Americans, more socially liberal than their parents and grandparents, were pleased and anxious to move on. "We started this fight for each other, and I've completed it for him and for our marriage," Obergefell said following the ruling. When history looks back and examines marriage equality in America, Obergefell and the state of Ohio will be key players.

This issue had another particularly stunning political moment in Ohio. On a Friday evening in March 2013, I was the lead story on the six o'clock news and started my report: "This news is sending shock-waves through Washington as Ohio Senator Rob Portman becomes the first sitting Republican U.S. Senator to endorse gay marriage."

It was a stunning reversal on a major social issue for Portman, who had adamantly opposed gay rights throughout his public career. In the House, he had supported a constitutional amendment to ban gay marriage. He also voted for the Defense of Marriage Act and supported a bill prohibiting gay couples in Washington, D.C. from adopting. His record had led 100 University of Michigan law school graduates to walk out of his commencement address two years earlier.

"If you know Senator Portman, he is extremely cautious," Jack Torry with the *Columbus Dispatch* told me that day. "I think he wrestled with this issue privately and finally concluded that he couldn't hold the position he had held on same-sex marriage after what his son had told him."

What his twenty-one-year-old son Will, a freshman at Yale, told him two years earlier was that he was gay.

"My son came to my wife and me, told us that he was gay, and that it was not a choice," Portman told me in an interview.

"This is one of those issues I think a lot of us maybe don't focus on until a friend or a family member or someone else talks to us about it. That certainly had a big impact on me. From the perspective of a father, it became an issue I looked at differently. I just believe in my heart it's the right thing to do. We shouldn't discriminate against people."

Immediately, opponents of gay marriage in Ohio made it clear Portman would be a target in his reelection bid in 2016. "The truth of the position is still that marriage should be between one man and one woman, and that doesn't have anything to do with whether you love your child or not," said Dr. Kent Spann of Citizens for Community Values.

When I heard the news I immediately thought back to 2012, and Mitt Romney's choice for running mate. Portman, who had endorsed Romney early in the primary process and was one of his most visible supporters, had been on the top of his list for vice president for weeks, if not years. In fact, on election night 2010, I said to 10TV anchor Jerry Revish, "Tonight, let me start the big rumor that Rob Portman will be on the very short list for vice president for Republicans in 2012. Republicans need Ohio in presidential elections. Portman has now been vetted and he's won an easy big race for the United States Senate. You might want to keep your eye on him, he may be the biggest winner of all tonight."

A senator from must-win Ohio, the popular Portman—who won his statewide race in 2010 by a 57 to 39 percent margin—had experience both in Congress and in the executive branch as George W. Bush's budget director. Yet, surprising many, including me, Romney went with little-known Congressman Paul Ryan of Wisconsin.

"Republican activists and strategists in Ohio are a bit disappointed, there is surprise here," I said on air early one Saturday morning after news leaked out about Romney's pick. "I think Portman and Ohio Republicans believed Portman would have helped carry Hamilton County, which President Obama won four years ago. I think the net impact of Paul Ryan in Ohio will be very little."

Seven months later I asked Portman, "Did you disclose to the campaign during the vetting process your son was gay?"

"Of course, they knew everything" he told me.

"Is that why you weren't chosen?" I asked.

"They told me no," he answered.

I remain skeptical. Romney's campaign, knowing Portman could be asked about same-sex marriage during the fall, and not knowing when he was going to publicly change his position, could not risk angering evangelical conservatives and give them a reason to stay home. In a close race, I'm guessing, they concluded it was too risky to put him on the ticket.

Portman, who is likable and on the "top tier" of politicians I've interviewed, will go down in history as the first sitting Republican U.S. senator who led to change his party's views on gay rights.

"I think here in Ohio and around the country, opinions are changing," Portman told me. "I don't think we should be telling people because they're gay they can't have a job. I don't think we should be telling people because they are gay they can't have the joy and stability I've had in my marriage and I wish for others." On the day the Supreme Court legalized same-sex marriage, Portman said, "As a father, I welcome today's decision."

After being seriously considered as a vice presidential pick in 2008 and 2012, many believed Portman was likely the next Ohioan to next seek the presidency.

It turned out someone else from Ohio would run instead.

A LIFE IN POLITICS

"Jim, put the microphone down and come over here!"

That's what gubernatorial candidate John Kasich said to me as my photographer Micah Riffle kept rolling.

Kasich had just voted early at the elections office in Delaware County prior to the 2010 election. We had covered the photo-op but Kasich took no questions, quickly left the building, and got into his SUV waiting outside. No sooner had Micah and I exited the building mumbling to each other that there wasn't much video to work with, than the passenger-side door of the black SUV flew open and Kasich jumped out.

"Put down the mic and that camera—I need to tell you something," Kasich repeated. I nodded to Micah that it was okay but it was completely unorthodox. Clearly this was something personal the former congressman wanted to share.

After putting the mic down I walked with Kasich about ten feet when he stopped, turned, and said, "Jim, I'm going to win this election and then some big things are going to happen."

My first thought was that maybe he had polling information or something specific about the election he was trying to share. Then it dawned on me maybe he just wanted a reporter to agree with him he was going to win after a long, expensive, and brutal campaign in the nation's seventh largest state.

"Congressman, when you say 'big things' what does that mean exactly?" I asked.

"Changes are coming in how we operate, but we can save the state," he told me. "You'll be amazed, these are cool things. Buckle in, Jim, because there are amazing things coming for Ohio!"

And with that brief pronouncement, Kasich turned and got back in his SUV and drove away.

"What was that all about?" Micah asked as we headed back to the station. "An insight into the thinking of John Kasich," is all I could reply.

Kasich is one of the most interesting politicians I've covered. On some days his eyes are bright, his speeches full of energy, and there are glimpses of the idealism of Ronald Reagan. On other days, perhaps a majority of them, his eyes are grey, his mood crotchety, and there are reminders of the gloominess of Richard Nixon.

Not that Kasich finds the comparison to Nixon necessarily bad. In 1970, just an eighteen-year-old college freshman at The Ohio State University, Kasich penned a glowing three-page fan letter to Nixon, begging to be invited to the White House. "I am a great admirer of yours," Kasich wrote, "I think you, as far as I can judge, are not only a great president but an even greater person." Kasich then offered the ultimate sacrifice a Buckeye student can give, "I would immediately pass up a Rose Bowl trip to see you."

Nixon received the fan mail and responded by extending an invitation to Kasich to visit him in the White House three weeks later. An excited college student then called home to tell his parents:

"I called my mother and said, 'I'm going to need an airline ticket,'" Kasich recalled to me during an interview on board his campaign bus in 2010. "You know, the mailman's wife, and I'm telling her I need an airline ticket to go down and see the president. I can still hear her yelling into the phone, 'honey, pick up the phone—something's wrong with Johnny!'"

Twenty days later, Kasich was standing in the Oval Office where he met with Nixon for twenty minutes. Kasich, already elected to the Ohio State student government, had made up his mind to spend a life in government.

At twenty-six, he became the youngest person elected to the state senate in Ohio. In 1982, in an overwhelmingly Democratic election year, Kasich won his first congressional bid, the only Republican in the country to defeat a Democratic incumbent that year. He would hold the seat for nearly two decades.

When Kasich was thirty-five, a young member of Congress, his personal life changed forever. He received a phone call late one night in Washington informing him that his parents had been in an automobile accident, hit by a drunk driver. His father had died, and his mother was going to die soon. Kasich reached the Pennsylvania hospital hours later, before she did.

"My whole world went black," Kasich said and he began a personal quest to figure out whether God existed. Kasich had been raised Catholic, but had drifted away from his faith.

"My mother and father died in 1987, and they didn't die in vain," Kasich told me. "I became a better man in a lot of different ways. I found a pearl in the middle of a rocky field. A terrible situation, but it was not all lost."

"Do you think about them and do you think they know about your career?" I asked.

"Jim, the way I think about it is they either know, or it's not important that they know, and I'm cool with all of that. My parents never met my wife, they never met my kids, but they either know or don't know. What do I suspect? I think they know. I'm very much at peace with that."

Kasich married Mary Lee Griffith in 1975, but the marriage ended in divorce five years later. In 1997, while a member of Congress, he remarried. He and wife Karen have twin daughters, Emma and Reese, now teenagers watching their dad in the national political spotlight.

Kasich became a born-again Christian following the tragic deaths of his parents. He is frank, though, in saying his faith remains a "constant effort" and he still has doubts and struggles. Kasich mentions his faith in more public appearances and speeches than any other politician I've covered.

During his nine terms in the House, Kasich had been a top lieutenant for Speaker Newt Gingrich, and was chairman of the Budget Committee. Part of his job was helping craft the GOP message following their takeover of the House in 1995.

During one meeting, Kasich and Republican Conference Chairman John Boehner bickered about whether the use of technical budget terms was clouding the GOP's message.

"John, John, John," Boehner said holding up his hand, "this is where, grammatically, we get into trouble. You're getting way down in the details..."

"...I know, but this is blatantly inaccurate," Kasich said, cutting off his

Ohio colleague.

His brash style landed him on Bob Dole's short list for vice president in 1996. Addressing delegates in San Diego, reading from a teleprompter, he mentioned his favorite topic, the budget:

"You may think that budgets are about green eye shades and numbers, but it's far more important than that. You see, budgets are about ideas. Budgets are about values. And most important, they are about people."

Kasich authored a bipartisan balanced budget deal in 1997 which also contained the first major tax cuts in sixteen years. The bill was signed in the Rose Garden by President Bill Clinton, with Kasich at his side. Former speaker Newt Gingrich told me in an interview Kasich was "a great chairman of the budget committee," and "we would not have had balanced budgets without his leadership."

In 1998, the year after the deal was signed, the country ran a budget surplus. It continued through both fiscal years 1999 and 2000. Both parties took credit, but there is no question Kasich was the architect of the deal.

In 1999, Kasich briefly ran for the GOP nomination for president. He had difficulty raising money and after five months dropped out of the race, endorsing Texas governor George W. Bush.

Kasich retired from Congress in 2001 and headed to Wall Street, where he worked at Lehman Brothers. There in his office at 3 World Financial Center, he worked on investment-banking deals. He was asked by a reporter in New York in 2001 about another potential presidential bid. "If I can fix my fund-raising problems, I will run again," he said.

First, he set his eyes on returning to Ohio and running for governor, where someone else already had the job and had every intention of keeping it.

Governor Ted Strickland invited me to visit his office about two weeks after I was back in Ohio. He was very gracious with his time, giving me some background on how difficult it was to manage such a big diverse state. He explained there were few things that could unite the interests of Toledo and Athens, or Cleveland with Cincinnati. Although, he pointed out, the Ohio State Buckeyes came close.

Strickland had a Reagan-like warmth that made it impossible not to enjoy speaking with him. He grew up as the second-youngest of nine children in rural Ohio, the son of a steelworker father and homemaker mother. Strickland was quick to tell audiences his family once lived in a chicken shack after a fire destroyed their home.

With a divinity degree and a doctorate in psychology, Strickland had worked as both a Methodist minister and licensed psychologist. Talk about a perfect combination for a politician! Sometimes I wondered if he had perfected the Jedi mind trick, like Obi-Wan Kenobi in Star Wars:

"What about the bad economy, governor?" you might ask.

"The economy is good, there is nothing to see here," Strickland would say, waving his hand to aid in the persuasion.

"The economy is good, there is nothing to see here," you would repeat back.

Alas, despite his fine personality and likability, Strickland could not control the dismal economic conditions brought on by the national recession.

Ohio had lost nearly 400,000 jobs during Strickland's term. The unemployment rate was hovering around 11 percent, the highest since 1983, and 640,000 Ohioans were out of work. State income tax collections, which fueled about a third of the general fund, dropped 18 percent in just twenty-four months.

Worse yet was the looming $8 billion hole the next governor and lawmakers would have to fill as federal stimulus dollars, which had propped up the current budget, ran out.

Strickland had proposed a $1 billion solution to allow slot machines at horse racing tracks. But GOP lawmakers blocked that idea. He also cut the number of people on the state payroll by about 5,000, but putting people out of work at a time jobs were scarce wasn't helping.

"Ohioans are rightfully angry and upset and frustrated," Strickland told me in a 2010 interview. "People who have worked hard, done everything right, tried to provide for their families, been good citizens, paid their taxes, hundreds of thousands of such people in our state have found themselves unemployed, without healthcare, or anxious about the future. So I understand that frustration."

In a year that was clearly favoring Republicans, Strickland came up with a brilliant strategy: acknowledge the bad economy, but focus blame on Wall Street, and specifically, John Kasich and his work at Lehman Brothers.

It kept what could have been a runaway election close to the very end.

Kasich officially announced his challenge to Strickland in mid-2009. On January 15th, 2010, he picked state auditor Mary Taylor as his running mate. The campaign, hoping to show that Kasich was as in touch with modern technology as the Obama campaign had been two years earlier, announced the news on Twitter.

After the official announcement in Columbus, I sat down with both Kasich and Taylor and started my interview by taking a picture of them on my phone and immediately posting it online.

"This is the new technology for campaigns isn't it?" I asked Kasich.

"I think Mary and I were the first candidates in American history to announce what we're doing on Twitter," Kasich answered. "Frankly, there is no surprise here. Obama got it. Guess what? We get it too. My goal is to get a lot of grandmas to learn how to tweet."

The truth is, Kasich rarely used a computer and had never sent an email, let alone used Facebook or Twitter. This would become the first disconnect I discovered between Kasich's rhetoric and reality. Despite appearing to be hip in his campaign, Kasich just wasn't technologically savvy or that interested in the world of social media.

The day he announced Taylor as his running mate in January, Kasich told the crowd, "I think I was in the Tea Party before there was a Tea Party!" But by the time I traveled with him on board his campaign bus in June, he was telling workers in Heath that he walked in the political middle: "I think you all know, you've watched me for many years, I'm a pretty independent guy, I've never gone party line."

In fact, the former Fox News regular was well known in D.C. circles but not as much by Ohioans. It had been nearly a decade since he had been on the ballot. So I asked him why he was seeking the governorship and not a U.S. Senate seat, which he had thought about in 1992 and 1994:

"Jack Bauer couldn't get me back to the legislature again," Kasich told me. "This is the job because to be an executive and be able to take my political experience, my business experience, put them together and know how people make decisions about how to create jobs is really what it's all about."

Throughout the fall, Strickland hammered away at Kasich for his work at Lehman Brothers. In 2008, as I mentioned earlier, the Wall Street titan had declared bankruptcy, triggering the worst economic situation since the Great Depression. If there was one thing as unpopular as the bad economy, it was the voters' view of Wall Street, which had to be bailed out by taxpayers during the Bush administration.

"The choice is between Ohio values," Strickland roared to a crowd of thousands with President Obama at Ohio State before the election, "and Wall Street values!"

"This problem, this recession, didn't start in Ohio, but it did start on Wall Street and the decisions that were made there that drove this economy near the cliff," Strickland told me the day he announced Yvette McGee Brown as his running mate. Strickland's current Lieutenant Governor Lee Fisher was seeking the U.S. Senate seat against Rob Portman.

Kasich, seeing internal polls showing him ahead but not by a safe margin, pushed back. "It's a good thing Ted Strickland had a ditch to drive the state into because if the ditch wasn't there, we would have gone over a cliff," he told me in late fall.

Kasich would talk up his Lehman experience in front of business groups, while downplaying it when asked by reporters. "I ran a two-man office in Columbus in a company that had 30,000 employees," Kasich told me during a campaign stop. "To blame me for the collapse of Wall Street would be like blaming a car dealer in Zanesville for the collapse of GM."

While the race stayed tight, Strickland also benefited by having the strong backing of pro-gun groups. "Governor Strickland, even going back through his time as a congressman, has a 100 percent voting record on gun rights and he's been there every time we've asked for help," Ken Hanson from the Buckeyes Firearms Foundation told me. "John Kasich, from his time in Congress, has about nine or ten votes that were contrary to the stated pro-gun position."

As a congressman, Kasich had backed a ban on assault weapons and said at the time an overwhelming number of calls to his office were against the ban but he ignored them because he knew "the gun lobby" pays people to call." After the crime bill passed, Kasich said, "If somebody wants to accuse me of not being an ideologue, I suppose that's correct." Strickland, also in Congress, voted with the NRA.

By fall, the candidates agreed to two live televised debates. The first in September in Columbus, followed a new poll by Quinnipiac University showing Kasich opening up a lead. Neither candidate committed a gaffe during the debate and both played it safe.

"Kasich is running a rope-a-dope campaign, he doesn't want to make a mistake" longtime political writer Bill Hershey said on *Capitol Square* following the debate. "The erratic John Kasich hasn't shown up. The rude John Kasich hasn't shown up. Governor Strickland needed to make a breakthrough, and if he did we haven't picked up on it yet."

But we picked up on it soon enough. The night of the next, and final, debate in Toledo, a new Suffolk University poll showed the race within the margin of error. Reporting live prior to the debate I told viewers, "Both of the campaigns tell me their candidates are prepared to take the gloves off. Putting aside all those ads, this could be the last make-or-break opportunity of the year."

The candidates did not disappoint.

"You actually have been asleep at the wheel," Kasich charged. "If you had come out of the box when you were elected governor and did what you promised, which was turn Ohio around, you would have created a government that is more effective."

"While we have been working here in Ohio to create jobs, you were working on Wall Street to outsource our jobs," Strickland countered. "I think the people of Ohio can tell the difference between the two of us."

"I call him a Wall Street congressman," Strickland said at another point. "Thousands of Ohioans lost their life savings because of Lehman's bankruptcy."

"We have these 11th-hour promises you made in this campaign," Kasich responded. "You have raised taxes and increased government. We are not competitive."

After both debates Strickland, always fearless of the press, joined me live to analyze his performance. "I don't think either of us hit a home run," he told me in Toledo. Kasich, clearly irritated during the debates, refused to take questions and quickly left both venues.

Heading into the stretch, despite the polls showing the race close, I said on election eve: "We're seeing the trends nationally, this big Republican wave is coming. The Kasich campaign has thought all along that the wave would be big enough to include him in the state of Ohio."

On election night, shortly before midnight on ONN, I announced, "John Kasich is the governor-elect of the state of Ohio. Republicans have run the table. For Governor Strickland it was a valiant effort in this bad economy, but it was too much to overcome."

Kasich narrowly defeated Strickland 49 to 47 percent in a big Republican year. He was entering office with no mandate, having won with less than 50 percent of the vote.

"I'm going to be governor of Ohio!" an excited Kasich told supporters on election night while pumping his fists. To this long-time politician, a win was a win and that meant, in his view, he had a mandate.

Two days after his election, Kasich told a group of lobbyists, many allied with the GOP, "Please leave the cynicism and the political maneuvering at the door, because we need you on the bus, and if you're not on the bus, we will run over you with the bus. And I'm not kidding."

Kasich would place a miniature bronzed bus in his office after being inaugurated and it would come to symbolize his combativeness.

Although he had served many years as a state and national lawmaker, Kasich had never been an executive. And it showed. His first year as governor may have been arguably one of the worst for Ohio in modern memory.

Shortly after his inauguration, Kasich issued a resolution mistaking

Martin Luther King, Jr.'s birthday in January for Saint Patrick's Day in March. With a correction issued but no apology, the Southern Christian Leadership Conference in Cleveland rescinded its invitation for a member of Kasich's staff to attend the annual Martin Luther King Jr. gala.

A week later, the media started to report all of Kasich's cabinet picks and senior staff members were mostly male and white. In a state where 1.6 million citizens are African American, that didn't sit well with members of the legislative black caucus.

State Senator Nina Turner, an African American from Cleveland, said Kasich had told her in a meeting, "I don't need your people" when she complained about the lack of diversity in his administration. "Through his actions and deeds, Governor Kasich has declared that Ohio is open for business, but if you are African American, you need not apply," she said.

Kasich's staff claimed the comment was about Democrats, not race. Kasich told me in an interview, "We pick people on the basis of who's qualified. We don't pick them on the basis of quotas. I mean, I think quotas are yesterday."

Still, the lack of sensitivity from Kasich in a state so diverse was a clear sign of his naiveté in executive leadership.

Then there was this: twelve days after his inauguration, during a speech to Ohio EPA workers, Kasich repeatedly referred to a police officer who ticketed him for a driving violation as an "idiot."

Kasich had been ticketed in early January 2008, for "approaching a public safety vehicle with lights displayed." He paid an $85 fine.

In the speech, which went viral, Kasich said, "Have you ever been stopped by a police officer that's an idiot? I had this idiot pull me over on 315... He goes back to the car, comes back, gives me a ticket and says, 'you must report to court, if you don't report to court we're putting a warrant out for your arrest'... He's an idiot!"

The Ohio Fraternal Order of Police President Jay McDonald immediately responded, "Ohio police officers already do difficult and dangerous work, so it doesn't help when the governor calls an officer doing his job and protecting the public an 'idiot.'"

Kasich's public liaison Michael Hartley was bombarded with phone calls from angry cops all around Ohio and immediately arranged for Kasich to speak personally with the officer and apologize. Still, for months Kasich's office—later blaming it on a glitch—linked the "idiot speech" video to his official state-operated website.

In a bit of irony, Kasich once attacked tennis bad-boy John McEnroe for "throwing his tennis racket and ranting and raving at fans and officials, and soon enough there are thousands of John McEnroe wannabes, throwing their tennis rackets that in my day would have earned a licking." One could argue Kasich at times exhibits political bad-boy behavior, setting an example for his wannabes, many of whom would have received a licking for calling a policeman an idiot.

Kasich then created a controversial agency, JobsOhio, which used $100 million a year from the lease of state wholesale liquor profits to operate. Kasich insisted it was a private, not government, entity designed to help keep jobs and lure jobs to the state. There were immediate questions about its lack of transparency.

One of those doing the questioning was Kasich's fellow Republican state Auditor Dave Yost, who said it was a quasi-private public entity at best. He demanded to see the JobsOhio books, and when the Kasich administration refused, Yost hit them with a subpoena. After months of intense battling, Kasich agreed to hand over the books to Yost, but within weeks, his GOP allies in the legislature—including Speaker Bill Batchelder, who called Yost "erratic"—passed a law in record time declaring JobsOhio a private entity and not subject to any future state audits.

"JobsOhio suffers from poor public records access, little disclosure of financial interests, and conflict-of-interest policies," Catherine Turcer from Ohio Common Cause told me. Her colleague Sam Gresham added, "it's a scandal waiting to happen."

But those incidents were minor missteps compared to the catastrophe on which Kasich and his team were about to embark.

It was called Senate Bill 5.

The Republican-pushed bill, which started running parallel through the legislature with Kasich's own proposals, limited collective bargaining rights for public employees and stopped mandatory union dues. A state full of teachers, nurses, firefighters, police, highway patrol, and sympathetic union supporters immediately thought they were being run over by the Kasich bus.

During his first State of the State address a month after taking office, over 3,000 protesters filled the Ohio statehouse, chanting "No, No, No" and "Kasich's Got To Go!" When the governor mentioned collective bargaining in his speech, "Frankly, folks, the provisions of collective bargaining reform are examples of what we wanted to do…" a few protesters in the House gallery booed, rattling Kasich who looked up and watched as state troopers removed the protesters and then closed the House chamber doors for the first time.

Between the thousands of people chanting "recall Kasich" inside and outside the statehouse, along with those protesters interrupting his speech inside, Kasich decided never again would he hold his State of the State speech in Columbus.

In April, as polls showed public support for the collective bargaining reform bill low, I interviewed Kasich again from his 30th floor office across the street from the statehouse. Four months on the job and there were still unpacked boxes all around. No one could really explain why.

Kasich walked in and pointed out his new haircut, featuring a hard-part on the side. "They want me to look like Harrison Ford in the *Air Force One* movie," he laughed. The style didn't last, soon his infamous 'flowbee' type haircut returned.

As we started the interview, it didn't take long for the topic of SB5 to turn testy. I wondered to myself, *is there anyone in his inner-circle who ever dares question his decision-making?* Had anyone on Kasich's staff or in his cabinet played devil's advocate and suggested the legislation was mistimed or just bad?

Well, I was going to. It was my job.

"Governor, should public workers in Ohio—the police, firefighters, nurses, and teachers—feel directly targeted by your administration?"

"We don't target anybody and we're not going after anybody," Kasich told me. "This effort is part of a comprehensive reform effort to save our state."

I pointed to an interview that I had the previous day with the wife of a firefighter who said, "It's a shame my husband would put his life on the line to save Kasich in a fire, and then he turns around and does this to us."

"How would you respond to her?" I asked.

"I respect, deeply, the efforts made by law enforcement—by our police, our firefighters, our highway patrol, and you know I'm sensitive to that. But I think that the bill that we have is very fair and balanced to the needs of the taxpayers."

I followed up, "A Republican strategist told me yesterday 'we can take on teachers, we can take on state government employees, but we shouldn't have taken on police and firefighters...'"

"Wait a minute, wait a minute," Kasich interrupted. "Somehow the language is wrong, we're not taking anybody on."

"But Governor," I continued, "the politics of this, we've been around politics a long time..."

"I don't..." Kasich attempted to interrupt.

"You know what is said," I continued. "Unions have spent hundreds of millions of dollars over many election cycles trying to defeat Republican candidates. Their point now is Republicans have control and they're going for the jugular. If Republicans can significantly weaken unions then the amount of money that comes into general election cycles against Republicans is lessened. That is a political factor?"

"Jim, Jim, Jim," Kasich said, clearly irritated. "These people must be Machiavellian. They must be thinking about power. In my inaugural, I said I was the servant of the public and a servant of the Lord. This is not a political game for me. This is a dedication to saving my beloved state of Ohio."

The Lord aside, I pressed on, "When firefighters say you're taking away their binding arbitration, when unions say you take away collective bargaining, would you say Ohio was better off before the current law went into effect?"

"Well, the current collective bargaining law was put into effect along a straight party line vote, okay?" Kasich responded.

"Some would say this new law of yours will be put into effect on a straight party line vote, what would be the difference?" I asked.

"Jim, again, this is part of an overall plan, okay? I know you want to keep getting into this and I think I've answered all these questions," Kasich abruptly stopped.

But I wasn't finished.

"There are 350,000 public employees, nurses, teachers, firefighters, police that are watching you on this program across Ohio. What do you say to them directly? Some have chanted, 'recall Kasich' at these rallies. What do you want to say to them?"

"A leader sits back and tries to figure what in the long run will serve the public," Kasich replied. "And change is hard for anybody. Change is difficult. But I think public employees realize there needs to be balance."

The Kasich team was unhappy with the interview, but maybe it was the only time the governor heard the reality of what many Ohioans thought about his position.

It took opponents only weeks to collect, and then submit, over a million signatures on petitions to get SB5 on the November ballot. In late October, while campaigning in Cincinnati, Mitt Romney visited a state GOP phone bank, but refused to take a position on SB5. His spokeswoman Andrea Saul told reporters, "citizens of states should be able to make decisions about important matters on their own." Kasich was furious. He phoned Romney to demand he publicly clarify his support of SB5, and then demanded he fire whoever was briefing him. "Kasich wanted blood. A public, human sacrifice," a source in the Romney camp told me. The following day, Romney changed course and said he backed Kasich and "fully supported Question 2" (it was actually Issue 2 on the ballot) but no one in the campaign was let go.

The public disconnect between Romney and Kasich was blamed, at least privately, on the giant rift between the Chairman of the Ohio Republican Party Kevin DeWine and Kasich. DeWine was close to Romney and he had been advising him privately that internal GOP polls showed SB5 going down—big. DeWine may have thought his advice would help Romney stay clear of the controversial issue, but instead it raised the flip-flop criticism from 2008 all over again.

After a bitter and negative fight that split the state for almost a year, voters went to the polls two weeks later and handed Kasich a stunning defeat. Sixty two percent rejected SB5, forcing its repeal, and handing Kasich an embarrassing loss. A stunned governor told reporters on election night, "It's clear the people have spoken. I heard their voices. I understand their decision. And frankly, I respect what the people have to say in an effort like this. And as a result of that, it requires me to take a deep breath and to spend some time to reflect on what happened here."

Kasich quickly dropped collective bargaining reform from his agenda and told GOP lawmakers to stay away from a ballot initiative, backed by the tea party, to make Ohio a 'Right to Work' state.

Early on, statehouse reporters heard often from Kasich how his decision-making was never based on anything but doing what he felt was right. "This isn't about politics to me," is a line he repeated many times during press conferences. But Kevin DeWine, the state GOP leader who had advised Romney about SB5, was about to blow the lid off that unreality.

DeWine was a former lawmaker and popular party leader. In fact, the sixty-six-member Ohio GOP central committee had unanimously reelected him after the party virtually swept the 2010 statewide elections. But despite the support of every member of the hierarchy of the Ohio Republican Party, DeWine had a serious enemy. John Kasich didn't like him and wanted him gone.

During the 2010 election cycle, DeWine had allocated more party money to the campaigns of Jon Husted (running for Secretary of State) and Mike DeWine (a second cousin and candidate for Attorney General), and that left the Kasich team, which had barely squeaked by Strickland, steaming mad. Having control of the GOP in his reelection year would mean for Kasich bigger contributions, funding for a variety of things from yard signs, to travel, to staff payroll, to TV ads, and, if my gut intuition was correct, help with a future presidential campaign.

After his election, Kasich privately asked DeWine to resign. DeWine refused. Behind the scenes, the Kasich team began the process of strangling DeWine's support on the central committee. They had hoped to keep the effort private, allowing Kasich to continue the "nothing is about politics to me" narrative, but then DeWine made an appearance on *Capitol Square,* blowing the rift wide open.

"There are folks who are close to the governor, agents and allies and lobbyists and political consultants who are trying to take over the party for the benefit of holding all the levers of power as it relates to the politics of the Republican Party," DeWine told me. He also suggested members of Kasich's staff may have been doing some political work on taxpayer time. State law bars political activity by government employees during their workday and it was a serious charge. (A later investigation found no wrong-doing.)

The DeWine interview made the front page of the *Columbus Dispatch* and the rift in the state GOP went public. For months, Kasich refused to take questions about it, and DeWine insisted he would not resign. After all, he had just been unanimously reelected. But, finally, under intense pressure by the governor of Ohio, he finally bowed out. Kasich's hand-picked team would be in control of the state GOP's treasury in time for his reelection bid.

Turns out John Kasich, executing a very ugly public root canal of his own state party chairman, was a politician after all. It wasn't a huge surprise. Conservative columnist Robert Novak wrote about Kasich in 1994, "he's a professional politician first."

At one point during his first term, Kasich was the most unpopular governor in the country. There was every reason to believe if Democrats fielded a strong challenger—perhaps a Strickland rematch—he would be vulnerable in 2014.

Then the national economic picture began to improve, and so did Ohio's. The $8 billion budget shortfall Kasich inherited became a surplus. With the budget balanced, $2 billion was put in the rainy day fund. Kasich cut the state income tax, although his plan to eliminate it altogether was rejected after he proposed paying for it by increasing the state sales tax. The unemployment rate fell, and 240,000 jobs were created from the 400,000 jobs lost during the Strickland years.

As the economic picture improved, Kasich exhibited a maverick streak. He strongly defended Common Core, as an example, citing the need for better educational standards while putting him at odds with many conservatives. He has twice proposed higher taxes on the oil and gas industry in Ohio, which could make the Koch brothers think twice about him in 2016. He has also been a strong proponent of raising sales taxes— on everything from haircuts to movie tickets to rock concerts—to offset deep cuts in income tax rates. And, to plenty of criticism from the tea party and conservative lawmakers, he expanded Medicaid under the Affordable Care Act.

The decision to expand Medicaid showed particular leadership skills by Kasich, who was forced to do an end-run around his own Republican lawmakers. He turned to a little-known state board, comprised of only seven members including two Democrats, to push it through.

His decision guaranteed $13 billion in federal money to Ohio over seven years to cover an estimated 275,000 low-income Ohioans. Among those were 26,000 veterans and 55,000 people suffering from mental illness. Over a dozen other Republican governors, however, reached the opposite decision as Kasich and refused the federal Medicaid money. Louisiana Governor Bobby Jindal said, "We should design our policies so that more people are pulling the cart than riding in the cart."

When Kasich took heat from conservatives, including Jindal and South Carolina governor Nikki Haley, he brought the religion card into the mix. "Now, when you die and get to the meeting with St. Peter, he's probably not going to ask you much about what you did about keeping government small. But he is going to ask you what you did for the poor. You better have a good answer."

Like or dislike his decision to expand Medicaid, the decision to endure the wrath of his own party heading into an election year says a lot about Kasich's leadership ability. It took guts.

Kasich very well could emerge as the John McCain-type "maverick" presidential candidate of 2016 (minus the military experience and connection to veterans which proved vital to McCain's nomination in 2008). In Congress, he voted for the ban on assault-weapons, enduring the wrath of the NRA and Second Amendment groups (although as governor he spent a lot of time making it up to them). He also worked with Democrats in Congress to try to kill the B-2 stealth bomber, putting him at odds with Defense Secretary Dick Cheney. On the decision to invade Iraq, sounding very Ron Paul-like, Kasich said in 2015, "I would never have gone in there... the Iraq thing was bungled from the beginning." Yet another jab at Cheney and the neo-conservatives.

Where Kasich shows no signs of being a maverick, however, is on his conservative views on social issues. For instance, during his first five years as governor, Kasich signed some of the most restrictive abortion laws in the country. One bans all abortions after a fetus is deemed viable outside the womb. Another requires women to undergo an ultrasound and listen to the fetal heartbeat before an abortion. Kasich's anti-abortion position even extends to the controversial "Heartbeat bill", which he has called "reasonable" even though Ohio Right to Life—the official anti-abortion organization in the state—didn't endorse it, worried about its constitutionality. An attempt by Kasich and his Republican allies at the statehouse to squeeze all abortion clinics in Ohio out of existence is working at a record pace, the number falling by half, from sixteen to eight, since 2011.

As we discussed earlier, when a federal court ordered Ohio to recognize Jim Obergefell as John Arthur's surviving spouse on a death certificate, Kasich responded with little sympathy, "people of the state, including me, voted to say marriage should be between a man and a woman." He instructed Attorney General Mike DeWine to aggressively fight the decision all the way to the U.S. Supreme Court. Despite polls showing growing support in Ohio and across the country, and the endorsement from fellow Ohio Republicans Senator Rob Portman and former Attorney General Jim Petro, Kasich remained steadfast in his view. When Ohio lost the case before the Supreme Court, resulting in marriage equality across the country, Kasich responded, "I'm obviously very disappointed." Despite his longtime opposition, Kasich did attend a same-sex wedding following the decision in 2015.

Kasich also says he's "troubled" by a shift in America's "cultural signposts." In his book *Stand for Something* Kasich tells a story of once pulling his car over to throw a hip-hop CD in the trash. He has condemned a variety of celebrities and sports stars who, in his judgement, failed to "use their powers for good." He attacked the Enron scandal which "wiped out the pension accounts of thousands" but while he speaks often about the "greed" on Wall Street he never mentions the millions he made there and the fact the collapse of Lehman Brothers resulted in billions of tax dollars needed to rescue the economy. Kasich has also held up comedian Bill Cosby as a role model, for offering criticism of his fellow African Americans for "not doing enough to right their own situation." For his "courage" Kasich wrote, "Cosby has been ridiculed and attacked for his comments but I think it showed tremendous character." Since Kasich's book was published, over thirty women have come forward claiming they were sexually assaulted by Cosby. My guess is Kasich will never again say publicly Cosby is "standing up and being heard."

In 2014, with the economy improving and unemployment in Ohio below the national average, Strickland announced he wasn't interested in a rematch with Kasich (he would challenge Rob Portman for his U.S. Senate seat in 2016). While state Democrats could have turned to former state attorney general Richard Cordray, whose family remained in Columbus while he was in Washington, D.C. having difficulty being confirmed by the U.S. Senate to lead the Consumer Financial Protection Bureau, they instead recruited little known Cuyahoga County Executive Ed FitzGerald to lead the Democratic ticket.

FitzGerald, who emphasized his FBI career which had lasted only three years, turned out to be one of the biggest political disasters in Ohio history. He first picked a running mate who later quit the ticket after it was revealed he owed nearly a million dollars in back taxes. Then the press learned FitzGerald had been caught in a car by police in an abandoned parking lot at 4 a.m. with a woman who wasn't his wife. Then, FitzGerald was forced to admit he hadn't had a valid Ohio driver's license in over a decade.

Voters may forgive the running mate or something a little fishy in a parked car, but few could shake the idea of FitzGerald believing he was above the law when it came to a simple driver's license.

Donations stopped coming into the FitzGerald campaign. The polls showed him way behind and sinking the rest of the statewide Democratic ticket. And Cordray (a five-time undefeated *Jeopardy!* champion, who told me in 2010 he had every intention of running for governor of Ohio) was finally confirmed by the Senate, leaving him unscathed for a future campaign.

Several months before the election, Kasich's lieutenant governor Mary Taylor fired her longtime chief of staff, and another staffer, after officials discovered they were often not at the office during the hours reported on their time sheets. Taylor refused to take press questions, and Kasich dismissed it with a simple, "You have 55,000 employees, you're going to have problems."

What could have been a legitimate issue come fall about who was minding the store wasn't because the FitzGerald campaign was toast. Along with questions about JobsOhio, unions, charter schools, fracking, abortion restrictions, the botched executions in Ohio, and how much time Kasich planned to be away from the state if he announced a presidential bid. All went unanswered in the nation's seventh largest state due to a lack of a viable alternative.

Kasich coasted to a landslide reelection. Democrats were humiliated, losing every statewide executive office. The chairman of the Ohio Democratic Party was forced to resign. Ohio voters, not having a true race for the state's top political job, were the biggest losers in the whole debacle.

Kasich had refused to debate FitzGerald during the campaign—he prepped for debates but personally pulled the plug after news of FitzGerald's driver's license surfaced—and he also refused to take questions on many political shows, including mine. His campaign strategists told me privately twenty minutes of tough questions about his record was too big of a risk with the polls signaling a blowout.

Kasich now points to his landslide reelection win—64 percent to 33 percent, carrying even highly Democratic Cuyahoga County—as an example of his popularity in Ohio. But it could be argued, after he avoided the press and never gave his opponent a chance to challenge his record, that he simply coasted across the finish line.

Besides the two debates with Strickland in 2010, where he was clearly uncomfortable, Kasich has rarely been in high-pressure, stress-filled television moments. One-on-one with an opponent who challenges everything he says and the stress of a worldwide television audience in a battle for national office? That would be fascinating to watch.

From my experience covering him Kasich has shown real leadership skills on budgeting matters, and a willingness to take on his own party—and special interest groups like Big Oil—when he feels it necessary. In addition, he exhibits a compassion for the poor and a desire to build the Republican Party tent. But where Kasich severely lacks is in the personality and leadership traits—the "warmth" and "ability to relate" factors—where leaders like Reagan and Clinton excelled.

With reelection behind him, the presidential rumors quickly grew. But that was old news to me. Considering Kasich has been active in politics since his teenage years, I thought from the start of his 2010 campaign he had an eye on the White House. After all, he had run before and he soon would be governing Ohio, a state Republicans always need in presidential elections.

"If you do well in Ohio, the rumor and speculation is already out about another presidential bid," I asked him after his election and prior to his inauguration in 2011. "If you turn Ohio around, could that be in the future?"

"No, listen, I like being able to sleep in my home okay?" Kasich said laughing. "If my wife even got a hint of that, I'd be sleeping outside. No, no, no I've been there, done that."

Two years later in another interview, holding a "Kasich 2000" campaign button, I tried again:

"Governor, every time your staff tells me you're not interested in running for president, this button is a reminder that you've been there before. If you're reelected, what is the likelihood this will be a 2016 button?"

"I would suggest that you not flash that near my wife, okay?" Kasich told me. "You would have to hire a bodyguard, Jim. I don't think about that, are you kidding me?"

Following the interview, Jai Chabria, a senior advisor to Kasich who has spent his career with him, stopped me before we left. "Jim, just to be clear, John has never discussed running for president. I've never heard him mention it." Photographer Trey Beck asked me on the drive back to the station whether I believed Kasich's answer. "Absolutely not!" was my reply.

In mid-2015, apparently all of a sudden and out of the blue, Kasich announced, at The Ohio State University where he started his political career at the age of eighteen, he wanted to be President of the United States after all.

OFF AND RUNNING

Mitt Romney made his first appearance in Ohio in July 2011, addressing workers at a factory in Pataskala. Unlike South Carolina, where there were only a handful of political reporters at any given event, Ohio was the big leagues with a much bigger media crowd. Even a year and a half before the election, there were already about twenty of us from newspapers, television stations, and radio.

From the beginning of the primary campaign, candidates are more cautious and guarded in Ohio. In fact, on this day Romney was taking no press questions—not even a gaggle (that's where members of the press all form a circle around an official and ask questions).

"I couldn't even get a good picture of him," my 10TV colleague Kurt Ludlow laughed. "His back was to us most of the time."

Joe Hallett from the *Columbus Dispatch,* the dean of Ohio political reporters, resorted like the rest of us to chasing Romney around the building.

"Jim, we have another year and a half of this, and I'm not sure I can take it," Hallett told me.

"He's not even close to the nomination yet," I replied.

"But this is so typical," Joe said. "Leads us around, promises an interview, and leaves us at the altar. It doesn't matter if they're Republican or Democrat, they're all the same."

A few minutes later, Romney was introduced with the song "Hang On Sloopy" playing in the background, which made Joe and I laugh. The song, closely associated with The Ohio State University, was a strange choice to introduce the man from Michigan, and Romney's facial expression gave away the fact he didn't care for it much.

"Always good to be back in Woody Hayes country," Romney quipped.

"I bet we never hear that song again at any of his rallies," Joe whispered. And we never did.

Covering events with Hallett always reminded me of this quote by journalist-turned-professor Dick Stout: "Hell, political reporters. Shit, they're

185

like sportswriters. The job's a lot the same. It's fun to do and the quality isn't very high. Anybody can be a political reporter and a sportswriter. But you have to be exceptional to do it well. It really takes something to be a good one."

Ask any political reporter in Ohio and they would tell you Hallett is exceptional and a good one. He retired way too soon.

By the way, I have spoken often with my friend Beau Bishop, an expert on everything sports, about the similarities of covering sports and politics. Think of the months leading up to the first primaries as preseason, the conventions as the All Star break, the presidential debates and late campaigning as the postseason. Then election night as the Super Bowl! There really is a lot of crossover between the two, but we'll save that topic for another book.

Let's get back to the circus.

Specifically, Donald Trump. What role does he play under our big tent? Ringleader, fire breather, knife thrower—or worse—buffoon, clown, or the freak show? Maybe a bit of all of the aforementioned?

Many are surprised to learn Trump, the son of wealthy New York real estate developer Fred Trump, started his business career in Ohio. In 1962 Fred Trump flew into Cincinnati and paid $5.7 million for a property in Bond Hill. The twenty-five-year-old Donald—still in business school—was put in charge of managing the property called Swifton Village.

In his book, *Trump: The Art of the Deal,* Trump calls himself the "Cincinnati kid" and takes credit for turning the 1,200-unit apartment complex around. "In college, while my friends were reading the comics and the sports pages of newspapers, I was reading the listings of FHA foreclosures," Trump wrote. "That's how I found out about Swifton Village. It was a job that I bought with my father, while I was in college, and it was my first big deal."

Trump said after the grounds at the property were landscaped, and some ads were placed in the local paper, "Within a year the buildings were one hundred percent rented." That's true according to Roy Knight, a longtime employee. But Knight said it was Fred Trump, not his son, who was responsible for turning the property around. "Donald wasn't skilled, but helped with the landscaping and other menial duties around the complex," Knight told the *Cincinnati Enquirer*. A former secretary at Swifton Village, Eileen Schumaker, told *Cincinnati Magazine,* "Contrary to what he says in the book, he did not run this place. His father did. Now he acts like he bought the place. He was just a kid!" The Trumps sold the property for $6.75 million in 1972.

Trump, who has been married three times, does not suffer from a lack of a healthy ego, and he has bragged about—some might say embellished—his resume throughout his career. Although he inherited a golden spoon from his father, he talks often about "building" a successful empire. While he freely talks about a net personal wealth in the billions, companies that bear his name have declared bankruptcy four times—including Trump Hotels and Casino Resorts which was almost $1.8 billion in the red.

His political views are all over the map. He opposed the Iraq war, has been on both sides of the abortion issue, and he has been a registered Democrat, Independent, and Republican. In 2000, he even launched a brief campaign for the Reform Party presidential nomination saying, "If the Reform Party nominated me, I would probably win." In fact, he allowed his name to be considered in order to block former Connecticut Governor Lowell Weicker—who once called Trump a "dirt bag" and blocked his casino from being built in Bridgeport—from being nominated.

As George W. Bush sought reelection in 2004 Trump said, "In many cases, I probably identify more as Democrat. It just seems that the economy does better under the Democrats than the Republicans." He also said Bush was "not up to par." Four years later he backed John McCain for president saying, "He's a great guy, a great man. He's just a very strong guy, a very strong leader, and he's very, very smart." On Hillary Clinton he offered this praise; "I think she is a terrific woman. I am biased because I have known her for years. I really like her and her husband both a lot." He has donated over $100,000 to the Clinton Foundation, and tens of thousands of dollars to Democratic campaign committees.

At some point after Obama was elected, Trump made a sharp turn to the right and embraced the tea party. He became friends with McCain's running mate Sarah Palin, saying she "is somebody that people respect and admire. I don't even think she knows how important she is and maybe that's part of the beauty of Sarah Palin." Trump also became the most recognized face of the "birther" crowd—those who believed Obama was actually born in Kenya, not Hawaii. At one point, Trump went on a media blitz demanding Obama show his birth certificate (which Obama finally did, saying later he "just wanted to end silly conversations" and the "side circus that sometimes happens.")

You just can't make all of this up.

Throughout most of 2011, Trump—who owns resorts, golf clubs and business properties around the world—was rumored to be "seriously interested" in seeking the GOP nomination. Trump's vast wealth made the Romneys, Bushes and Kennedys look like paupers. Polls had Trump leading all of his potential rivals; one had him up by eleven points over Romney.

There wasn't too much concern, however. Many believed "the Donald" was simply using a potential run to generate publicity for his reality TV show *The Apprentice*. Sure enough, in May 2011 Trump bowed out stating, "I maintain the strong conviction that if I were to run, I would be able to win the primary and, ultimately, the general election."

For months the GOP candidates tripped over each other hoping for a Trump endorsement. Rick Perry, Mike Huckabee, Newt Gingrich, Michele Bachmann, Herman Cain, and Romney all courted the billionaire. The only endorsement more coveted by conservatives came from the less public, but infinitely wealthier, Koch brothers. Finally, in early 2012, Trump announced he was backing Romney, despite having said about him earlier, "He'd buy companies. He'd close companies. He'd get rid of jobs. I've built a great company. My net worth is many many times Mitt Romney." The endorsement, held at Trump's hotel in Las Vegas, lasted only six minutes. Romney, with his wife Ann by his side—both with uncomfortable forced smiles, holding hands in a death grip—offered this memorable soundbite, "There are some things that you just can't imagine happening in your life. This is one of them."

Only Ron Paul refused to step into Trump's sideshow. "I don't think he has that much credibility. I'm the only candidate that didn't kiss his ring.

I don't understand why people pay any attention to him." Later, Paul called Trump a "dangerous authoritarian on a power trip."

That about sums it up.

For the record, the title of my book—*Front Row Seat at the Circus*—was chosen prior to Trump throwing his hat in the ring for the 2016 Republican nomination. Still, he probably represents the circus-like atmosphere of today's politics better than anyone else I can think of.

In the late fall of 2011 photographer Theo Burskey and I traveled to Dayton to cover Herman Cain. For a short time, the former CEO of Godfather's Pizza, the candidate with the 9-9-9 plan, had led in the polls for the GOP nomination.

That was before a number of sexual harassment accusations and an alleged longtime affair.

Now the campaign was on life-support with GOP strategists predicting—down to the hour—his presumed exit. But Theo could have told you something was wrong after we arrived at the venue.

"Where is the riser to set up the camera?" he asked with his voice rising. "And where is the mult-box!?"

We searched but didn't find them. Typically, presidential campaigns set up a row of risers in the back of the room so that cameras can record the candidates above the heads of the crowd. In addition, they provide what's called a "mult-box" for sound that allows many cameras to plug in to a single box directly connected to the microphone in front of the candidate.

At this point, the Cain campaign was operating on fumes. I suppose they figured the press wasn't going to report anything positive anyway, so they were willing to risk the crappy video and awful sound.

Cain was introduced without fanfare and told supporters, "They want you to believe that with another character assassination on me that I will drop out!" Most of the people we interviewed afterwards said they expected him to do just that.

"No riser or mult-box, that campaign is bush-league," Theo complained as we drove back to Columbus. "That campaign is dead," I responded. And a month later, it was.

I appeared on the *CBS Early Show* the day after Public Policy Polling, a Democratic-leaning polling firm, concluded, "If Barack Obama had to stand for reelection today he would likely lose Ohio." The poll found Obama's approval rating in the state at 43 percent. Worse for the president, his popularity with critical Independents was at an anemic 39 percent. On CBS, I described how "the mood and excitement of Obama supporters is more subdued than four years ago." When asked about Obama's chances of carrying the state in 2012, I answered: "The economy is always going to be key in Ohio. If the voters don't sense the economy is improving, it would be difficult for any incumbent, regardless of party, to win in swing state Ohio."

In late October, the Franklin County Republican Party held its first Swing State Straw Poll on the campus of Ohio State. Congressman Ron Paul won by a huge margin of the 400 or so participants, easily outdistancing Cain, Romney, and Newt Gingrich.

"This crowd was charged-up even more than we thought it was going to be," said Doug Preisse, the Franklin County GOP chairman who later backed Gingrich. Paul supporters hoped the straw poll was a sign their candidate would be competitive on Super Tuesday, but campaign insiders didn't see it that way. With limited financial resources, Paul stayed out of media-market expensive Ohio and concentrated instead on campaigning in smaller states.

Two months later, Paul and his enthusiastic volunteers had hoped to win the first mega political event of 2012—the Iowa Caucus. On January 3rd, the night of the caucus, I was vacationing in Arizona when my boss Greg Fisher called and asked if I could go on the air via phone to add analysis of the stunning news that former U.S. Senator Rick Santorum had pulled off an upset win.

"Who would have thought Santorum?" I said on air. The ultra-conservative had lost his last campaign for reelection in Pennsylvania by the widest margin of any incumbent in 2006—41 percent to his challenger Bob Casey's 59 percent. "This is sending shockwaves not just through the Romney camp," I told anchors Mike Kallmeyer and Sandra Cole, "but the entire Republican establishment."

Santorum ended up beating Romney by just thirty-four votes in Iowa;

29,839 to 29,805, both ending with 25 percent total. Paul placed third with 21 percent. But in the weird and wacky Iowa way, Paul would later earn twenty-two delegates to Romney's six and Santorum's zero. (Thanks for voting Iowans, but we have our own way so never mind.)

When I returned to Columbus, Greg told me I would be doing live analysis on the Ohio News Network each night of a major caucus and primary. There would also be a new weekly political show in prime time called *Campaign 2012 with Jim Heath* leading up to Ohio's primary on Super Tuesday.

That was pretty awesome.

As Republicans tried to figure out what had happened in Iowa, the candidates moved on to New Hampshire and its first-in-the-nation primary on January 10th. Romney, a favorite son from next door, was never seriously challenged and won easily. He received 39 percent of the vote to Ron Paul's 23 percent and Jon Huntsman's 17 percent. Santorum was nowhere to be found, placing fifth behind Newt Gingrich—both with less than 10 percent each.

On air that night covering the New Hampshire results I told viewers, "There needs to be the one solo anti-Romney candidate in order for him to be denied this nomination." I also said it was unlikely to be Ron Paul. As for Jon Huntsman, the former governor of Utah, I said, "I don't see how Huntsman goes on. South Carolina is next in this process where he will do poorly and if Huntsman came in third as a moderate and can't make a stronger case in New Hampshire, his campaign cash will soon dry up. If there's a casualty from tonight, it's Huntsman."

Five days later he dropped out of the race.

On Saturday, January 21st, South Carolina held its first-in-the-south presidential primary. Since 1980, the winner of this primary had gone on to be the Republican Party nominee. But things really went haywire in 2012.

As we discussed earlier in the book, Romney had gone from frontrunner to fourth place in South Carolina in 2008. The Mormon issue was always a factor in the evangelical, voter-rich upstate. And Newt Gingrich was a neighbor, the longtime conservative politician from next-door Georgia.

On air that night as it became clear Gingrich would win by a comfortable margin I said, "This is a big win for Gingrich, but Georgia is to South Carolina what Massachusetts was in New Hampshire. Gingrich was the regional southern candidate. He was backed today by the 65 percent of primary voters who described themselves as born-again evangelicals. Romney is a Mormon and the fact is, in the Bible Belt in a competitive primary, that is an issue."

Gingrich cruised to an easy win with 40 percent of the vote to Romney's 29 percent (up slightly from the 23 percent he won four years earlier.) Santorum was third with 17 percent and Paul ended with 13 percent.

That night, I interviewed one of Romney's top supporters, Jay Hottinger, a pragmatic Republican state representative from a central Ohio district. "Romney can't crack 30 percent in a state that's determined the nominee since 1980," I said to him, "where does that leave the campaign looking ahead to Ohio?"

"It's been a very difficult week and a very difficult election night for the Romney campaign," Hottinger admitted. "But he's steady. We knew from the beginning this wasn't a sprint but a test of endurance. Mitt Romney is not a regional candidate and we knew the South is where he was going to have the most difficulty."

Where Gingrich had plenty of political baggage, including his resignation as House Speaker, it was becoming obvious to politicos that Romney was suffering from a serious "warmth issue."

"Ronald Reagan used to go into a bar and hold up a beer to send a message he could relate to blue collar workers," I said to Hottinger. "Bill Clinton was nicknamed 'Bubba'. How do you warm Romney up to people, and is that part of the reason he's struggling?"

"Mitt is a very personable man but he can't change who he is," Hottinger answered. "He needs to reintroduce himself by the time he gets to Ohio. He's been timid. He's been defensive. When it comes to his taxes, or work at Bain Capital, he's got to go on the offensive on those things."

"This is going to get really interesting in Florida," I concluded that night. The next big battle was in the Sunshine State in ten days.

The following Tuesday, during his State of the Union speech, President Obama spelled out his case for reelection. He mentioned specifically Ohio's improving economy and the comeback of the auto industry. The following day I asked Governor John Kasich—who had still not endorsed a GOP candidate—whether Obama was entitled to take credit for Ohio's economy:

"I could care less who gets the credit, are you kidding me?" said Kasich. "If a family gets a job, I don't care who gets credit for it. I hope he gets all the credit and we get everybody back to work in Ohio. That's what this is about, this isn't some political game where somebody is searching for credit. I'd be happy to say I had nothing to do with it if we get them all working."

Then Kasich told me he wouldn't get involved in the bitter and now toxic primary battle that was brewing between Romney and his former colleague Newt Gingrich.

"Right now I'm not getting in the middle of this, I have other things I have to do."

Giving Obama credit for Ohio's improving jobs picture did not go over well in the Romney camp. The lack of coordination of message between Kasich and the GOP frontrunner, already exposed during the Senate Bill 5 campaign, was once again on full display when the press corps covered Romney at a closed gypsum factory in Lorain, where he highlighted Ohio's struggle to keep good paying manufacturing jobs.

"This factory is empty. Had the president's economic plans worked... it'd be open by now. But it's still empty," Romney told the press while pointing around the huge dusty warehouse.

The negative picture Romney was painting about the Buckeye State was at complete odds with Kasich's positive "morning again in Ohio" narrative. I went on air that night from Lorain and pointed out that Ohio's unemployment rate had gone from 9.2 percent in January 2011 when Kasich was sworn-in to 7.6 percent now. And it was below the national rate of 8.2 percent.

So which one was it? The Kasich view that things were getting better in Ohio, or the Romney version that things were still bad?

It didn't take long for the two sides to reach some agreement. Never again would we cover Romney in an abandoned factory in Ohio. And Romney would begin telling crowds, "You've got a great governor in John Kasich, he's showing the president, if he'd only listen, how to create jobs." Kasich would not get on the Romney bandwagon until it was clear no other candidate, especially his old friend Gingrich, could not win the nomination.

After a bitter ten days following the South Carolina results, Romney beat Gingrich in Florida 46 to 32 percent. Santorum, ending with 13 percent, and Paul with just 7 percent, had stayed clear of the expensive and bitter bloodbath in the Sunshine State between Romney and Gingrich.

"Over 65 percent of primary voters in South Carolina described themselves as born-again evangelicals," I explained on air that night. "About that same number in Florida said today they were not. Also, about a third of today's voters in Florida described themselves as a moderate and they went for Romney."

This was the beginning of the end of Gingrich who was viewed as a regional candidate. The Romney campaign and his Super PAC "Restore Our Future" spent millions for ads in Florida's ten expensive media markets, pounding Gingrich on everything from "supporting China's brutal one-child policy" to "supporting amnesty for illegal immigrants."

With fewer resources, Gingrich and his Super PAC tried to counterattack by releasing a couple ads that promoted a mini-documentary called "Blood Money." In it, Romney's business record at Bain Capital, a private equity firm, and his role as a director at Damon Corp, which was convicted of massive Medicare billing fraud, were questioned.

"The negativity on the airwaves this week between Romney and Gingrich is the worst, frankly, I've ever seen," I told viewers that night. "It drove the negatives of both candidates into the stratosphere. A study showed that 99 percent of Romney's radio and TV ads were negative in Florida, and Gingrich's were about as bad. Will this contest make it to Ohio and Super Tuesday? It's sure looking like it."

The following Saturday, Romney won the Nevada caucus, which caused Ron Paul supporters heartburn for months. Romney received 50 percent of the vote to Gingrich's 21 percent. Paul ended up with 19 percent and

Santorum 10 percent.

Roughly 25 percent of the Nevada caucus-goers were Mormon, which helped Romney easily win. But like the wacky Iowa caucus system, Nevada elected the actual delegates to the national GOP convention months later. In that showdown, Paul won twenty-two delegates to Romney's six. Only 7 percent of Nevada Republicans participated in the 2012 caucus (meaning almost no one) and the Republican National Committee attempted to convince Nevada lawmakers to switch from a caucus to a primary state in 2016. Unfortunately, it failed.

In my view, a primary state—not a caucus one—should be holding the first-in-the-West presidential showdown.

It's Not Okay

With Super Tuesday and the Ohio primary on the horizon, Rick Santorum strolled into the television studio confident he was on the verge of an upset in the Ohio Republican presidential primary now just over two weeks away. The former U.S. senator from Pennsylvania had emerged as the leading conservative alternative to frontrunner Mitt Romney. Santorum was unapologetic in his effort to turn birth control into the top issue in the race—"It's not okay"—when asked about contraception just days before his appearance on my political show.

As Santorum and I got into position on the set, he sipped from a bottle of water and nearly spit it out. "Too warm, can I get cold water?" he said as he handed the plastic bottle back to producer Rochelle Young. We waited a few extra minutes before we started taping as Rochelle went on a station-wide search for a refrigerated bottle of water, which she thankfully found. "Cold water is better for my voice" Santorum said as he took another sip, now seemingly satisfied.

Ohio is well known as a top swing state in general elections, but rarely is it as critical in a presidential primary race as it was in 2012. Romney, returning from his 2008 defeat, was the GOP establishment candidate but was having a difficult time, despite outspending his opponents by millions, in nailing down the nomination.

With three weeks to go until Super Tuesday, Santorum was leading in all the major polls in Ohio—Rasmussen had him up 18, the Ohio Poll had him up 11. Ohio's Attorney General Mike DeWine had retracted his earlier endorsement of Romney and made a very public new endorsement of his old colleague Santorum.

"To be elected president, you have to do more than tear down your opponents," DeWine said while standing with Santorum on the statehouse steps. "Rick Santorum has done that, sadly, Governor Romney has not."

Kasich, who was reportedly overheard at a GOP meeting saying, "It can't be Mitt, he's terrible," refused to get involved in the primary fight in

Ohio, which only helped Santorum.

With conservatives on the verge of dealing Romney a fatal blow, the news suddenly shifted from jobs and the economy to contraception and birth control. The Obama administration laid out new rules mandating religious organizations pay for insurance plans that offered free birth control. The action angered many conservatives, and in response, two Republican senators offered separate but similar bills dealing with the issue just weeks before Super Tuesday.

Florida Senator Marco Rubio proposed allowing religious hospitals, universities, and other organizations that morally opposed contraception to refuse to cover it for their employees. Missouri senator Roy Blunt tacked on a proposal to the Highway Bill allowing employers to stop providing any benefits mandated by the government if they had any moral objection in doing so. Blunt and Rubio supported each other's contraception bills, and some politicos and journalists took to calling them Blunt-Rubio.

As I started my interview with Santorum, which would be airing statewide in our new prime time show, I asked him a series of questions about contraception and abortion. Santorum strongly backed the Blunt-Rubio bills, so I asked him if he would go even further and support overturning Griswold versus Connecticut, the historic 1965 Supreme Court decision that ruled a state's ban on the use of contraceptives violated the right to marital privacy.

"Griswold was the basis for Roe versus Wade, so if you believe Roe versus Wade should be overturned—that the United States Supreme Court can't create a right that's not in the Constitution—then I believe that line of cases should be overturned," Santorum told me. "I believe abortion is a great moral wrong, and Roe versus Wade is a great moral wrong, and the American public should collectively decide whether abortion should be legal or not through a constitutional amendment."

"Is this not bad timing for the Republican Party to be debating social issues?" I asked.

"The media has a preoccupation with these types of issues, and of course they want to paint every Republican who stands up for traditional

197

sexual mores as someone who's out of touch with the American public," Santorum answered.

I interrupted Santorum and asked him point-blank if maybe he was out of touch with the American public.

"When I get out there and talk about teen pregnancies, and the out-of-wedlock birth rate in this country, and the destruction of our young people, especially in the inner-city, someone had better be talking about that," Santorum replied. "We're not going to have limited government, lower taxes, or a strong community if we continue to see the family breakdown in America because of the rampant amount of sexual activity among our teens, particularly in the inner city where you're seeing failure rates in school and poverty rates and crime rates. Somebody had better be talking about that."

Anti-abortion activists in Ohio at the time of our interview were circulating petitions that would have defined human life as beginning with fertilization. The controversial "Personhood Amendment" would have banned all abortions, even in cases of rape and incest, and made some forms of birth control illegal. I pressed Santorum on whether he would go so far as to support that cause.

"I think the Personhood movement is a good idea in the sense that it brings up the issue as to the fact that life begins at conception, it's not a moral belief—it's a fact."

Santorum had also raised eyebrows that month by expressing skepticism at a decision by the Pentagon to open up more military roles for women. He had said their "emotions" could get them in trouble in combat. So I followed up by asking if women should be allowed on the front lines.

"I have no problems with them being on the front lines. The question is, should they be in the infantry in combat? And I don't believe they should be in combat in the infantry, and I don't know too many generals or too many people actively considering that concept. So the question is, what role?"

I followed up by asking whether the sum total of all these issues, abortion, birth control, service in the military may all be adding up to the perception that he, and the Republican Party, were anti-women's rights.

"If you look at the record, there is no problem here, it's just the media trying to characterize that if you're a conservative Republican you must be X. Over time this all will come out."

Santorum was firmly and clearly locked on Romney's right. His campaign was hoping a low turnout in the primary would be dominated by conservative evangelical voters, which would lead to the win.

Meanwhile, Romney's campaign was working to get out the vote in the bigger cities where GOP voters were less likely to be fixated on social issues. In addition, Romney's Super PAC "Restore Our Future" was pummeling Santorum on television over his votes as a senator for earmarks—that clever and hidden way politicians get funding for special projects into bigger bills. It was a charge that angered Santorum.

"If you look at the scurrilous charges he's using, like 'Rick Santorum supported earmarks', Mitt Romney, one of his greatest accomplishments that he talks about is restoring the Salt Lake City games and saving the Olympics," Santorum angrily responded.

"It was a multi-million dollar earmark he asked for, tens of millions of taxpayer dollars that bailed out the Salt Lake City Olympics in an earmark he went to Congress and asked for. He asked for nearly a half-billion dollars in earmarks when he was governor of Massachusetts. For Governor Romney to throw that out, it's just the hypocrisy, I think people are tired of that."

Santorum told me he wasn't paying attention to the polls but clearly understood the impact of winning here.

"Ohio is always going to be critical in a general election, but in this case you're going to be critical, in a way the biggest prize because you are so important in a general election and you have a big delegate haul. It's a good weathervane as to where Republicans are going across the country and that's why we're planting our flag here. The key for us is to show this is really a two-person race now. There's Governor Romney and there's somebody who is the best alternative to beat Barack Obama."

The topic of contraception dominated the discussion on my prime time show that week. "This would be a great election issue, if this were the election of 1912," former Ohio Democratic Party chairman David

Leland told viewers. "It's a loser for anyone who brings it up." Former Ohio Republican State Senator Kevin Coughlin disagreed, "The president is the one who brought it up. The real issue is the government telling businesses and private entities they must provide a product free of charge."

Following our interview, Santorum returned to Michigan—the birth state of Romney—where polls showed the two in a dead heat for the upcoming February 28th primary. Santorum, a Roman Catholic, created a stir when he dismissed John F. Kennedy's famous 1960 speech on the separation of church and state, saying it made him want to "throw up."

Romney, a Mormon, was carefully avoiding getting into a debate over religion even as the Billy Graham Evangelistic Association still included Mormonism on its list of religious cults. Michigan was a mud fest with Romney outspending Santorum on both TV and radio, while Santorum was recruiting Democrats to cross over and vote for him. When the dust settled, Romney held off Santorum by three points statewide even as they tied in the number of delegates awarded. Pew Research found Santorum received his strongest support from evangelicals and from voters who said it matters a "great deal" to them that a candidate shares their religious beliefs.

Watching the Michigan returns at home that night and how close the results were, I thought to myself, *this contraception issue is not going away.* Then I went back to preparing for my interview scheduled for the next morning with Mitt Romney, the candidate who four years earlier I thought I'd never see again.

There was no way of knowing the fallout that would happen when the interview was over.

I'm Not For The Bill

After the Rick Santorum interview aired, we heard from the Romney campaign that he would be available for an exclusive sit-down on February 29th, the day after the Michigan primary.

Romney came to Ohio trying to keep his campaign focused on jobs and the economy, but clearly social issues, with the Blunt Amendment scheduled to be voted on that week, were still front-and-center. We were told the interview could go up to ten minutes and I prepared a series of questions, with help from producer Rochelle Young, as we made the drive from Columbus to Bexley, home of Capital University.

My strategy with such limited time was simple: Cover a lot of ground fast. My hope was to get his answers to questions on everything from the economy to healthcare, contraception, his opponents, Super PACs, his Mormon faith, and why he wasn't viewed as very likable. It was an aggressive set of questions, but doable because unlike others—Obama comes to mind—Romney never attempted to filibuster every question.

We were taken to the room where the interview would happen, and just like six years earlier in Myrtle Beach, the Romney staff was ready with an American flag for the background. The purple color of Capital University was moved up and above where Romney would be framed in his close-up shot. I didn't travel light for this interview—two field producers, two news photographers and a promotions photographer, all for a three-camera shoot. We knew this would be our biggest political interview of the spring.

Romney entered the room and as we sat down, I asked if he had gotten any sleep following the Michigan results the previous night. "Yeah, I did okay, it was the night before that was tougher," he laughed. We then chitchatted about how much campaigning he was likely to do in Ohio if he won the nomination. Presidential candidates love to campaign at Ohio State, I told him, where 30,000 to 40,000 supporters can show up. "They hope," Romney quickly added with a laugh.

It was just after 10 a.m. and photographer Andy Wallace gave me the cue, and I started the interview by asking Romney if it was frustrating how much time and money it took to win his home state of Michigan.

"It was a big upset I think. I came from fifteen points behind, and I think it was the message of the economy and jobs. People want to get good jobs again."

I asked Romney about his message for Ohioans and he steered immediately back to that four letter word, jobs.

"I believe the people in Ohio are concerned about the number one issue Americans in general are concerned about, and that's an economy that creates good jobs. If I focus on the economy and jobs, I'll win Ohio. The other guys are talking about everything but the economy and I'm going to talk about nothing but the economy."

Romney was taking a direct shot at Santorum—that he was spending too much time discussing social issues. But had Romney's healthcare system in Massachusetts created jobs and how, exactly, was it different than what Obamacare was doing?

"When we put our plan into place in our state, we were asked if this was a plan we should have for the entire nation, and we said 'no.' I said 'absolutely not.' Our state was collecting taxes, paying for people who didn't have insurance. We said, that makes no sense whatsoever, particularly when people are able to care for themselves. So what we put into place was good for us, still favored in the state three to one, but imposing that on the nation or anything like it is wrong. I'm going to repeal Obamacare on day one."

I asked Romney if he was surprised the primary process, which was beginning to concern establishment Republicans, was taking so long.

"These new Super PACs have been put in place so billionaires can support Newt Gingrich and Rick Santorum..." he replied.

"Your Super PAC has been doing alright," I interrupted.

"But I don't have a billionaire, one person, supporting the entire effort," he responded. "They have one person supporting eighty or ninety percent of their entire effort. By virtue of those billionaires, they're able to go on without worrying about money and keep a campaign going."

I then brought up the subject of earmarks:

"Rick Santorum mentioned on this show last week the Winter Olympics, and called you a hypocrite for blasting him on earmarks. Is that a fair criticism, especially with the help the Winter Olympics received after 9/11?"

"The Olympics went to do what any organization does, which is explain to the Federal Government what the needs are for that organization. We went before committees and hearings and discussions with a wide array of people. They provided the security, which is always part of the Olympic experience. I would put a ban on earmarks; Rick Santorum is in favor of earmarks. Him throwing around names—if he called me a hypocrite—what an outrageous thing to say. It's just silly for people to resort to that kind of rhetoric."

With Romney now calling Santorum "silly," it was time for me to steer the conversation into the controversial area of birth control. Now five-and-a-half minutes into the interview, I mentioned my earlier conversation with Santorum and asked Romney:

"He has brought contraception into this campaign, the issue of birth control and contraception. Blunt-Rubio is being debated this week that deals with allowing employers to ban female contraception. Have you taken a position on it? He says he's for that, and we'll talk about Personhood in a minute, but have you taken a position?"

Without the slightest hesitation Romney answered:

"I'm not for the bill. But look, the idea of presidential candidates getting into questions about contraception within a relationship between a man and a woman, husband and wife, I'm not going there."

"Are you surprised he went there?" I asked.

"I've made it very clear when I was being interviewed by George Stephanopoulos in a debate a while ago that contraception is working just fine, let's leave it alone."

So what about the Personhood Amendment, which Santorum had at least conceptually endorsed, I followed up.

"We had a provision in my state that said life began at conception, and that's a provision I protected. The legislature passed a bill saying that no longer would life be determined to begin at conception and I vetoed that.

So we can have a provision that describes life beginning, in fact when it begins, while at the same time allowing people to have contraceptives."

And that was that.

The interview continued for another five minutes. I asked Romney why middle class voters had been struggling with his candidacy. He leaned back and crossed his legs, slightly irritated by the question, and said:

"Actually, they haven't been struggling with my candidacy. I know that's the narrative that some in the media like to portray, but let's look at the numbers. I tied in Iowa, got more votes than Ronald Reagan in New Hampshire, won in Florida, won in Nevada, won in Arizona, won in Michigan. So it's gone pretty darn well."

The answer avoided the reality that many conservatives were struggling with Romney's candidacy, thus allowing an underfunded and unknown candidate like Santorum—who had been defeated in his last reelection campaign in Pennsylvania by eighteen points—to emerge as a strong challenger.

So again, "Who is Mitt Romney?" I asked.

"My favorite things? Being with the grandkids. Sports I like to watch: baseball, football. I like water skiing, you know, as a boy in Michigan on the Great Lakes, I was able to get out as a kid and water ski with my dad. My favorite TV show? *Modern Family*. It probably keeps the biggest smile on my face."

I mentioned a recent quote by state representative Jay Hottinger, a Romney supporter, calling his Mormon faith the "elephant in the room" as the reason why the primary process was taking so long.

Romney said we had discussed his faith four years earlier and, "I don't have anything new to add."

We then shook hands for a social media picture and sat and talked so that the photographers could get some cut-away shots to be used in promos. At no time did Romney mention the Blunt-Rubio question for a clarification, nor did his staff, who had stood nearby and listened to every word.

In fact, as we sat there following the interview, we discussed the importance of Ohio to Republican presidential candidates historically, and

Romney seemed to suggest he may have a strategy that would not include the Buckeye state:

"What's interesting to me is that there are all these rules that no one has done this and no one has done that," Romney told me. "For instance, no one has become the Republican nominee without winning South Carolina, but my guess is it's almost certain Newt Gingrich will not become the Republican nominee. It's like these rules are rules until something happens that they're not the rules."

I remember thinking it would be a very dangerous strategy for any Republican to believe they could win the White House without carrying Ohio. As we stood up to say goodbye, one of Romney's staff members came over and asked why I had brought up the Mormon issue. I said it was in context to the overwhelming number of evangelical voters who had supported Santorum the day before in Michigan.

Again, there was no talk of Blunt-Rubio.

People have asked me why I didn't follow up or ask for a clarification to his "I'm not for the bill" response. The truth is it didn't particularly surprise me. It certainly surprised me less than his answer of *Modern Family* to my question about his favorite television show.

Romney had not mentioned the Blunt Amendment in any previous interview, but my thought was that his opposition signaled he was thinking beyond the GOP primary fight and ahead to the tough battle against Obama in Ohio in the fall. His opposition to the Blunt-Rubio provisions would signal to women and Independents that he was just as tired of this contraception issue as they were. And it was no big surprise that Romney was moderating on a social issue, after all he had already changed his positions on everything from abortion to mandated healthcare.

On the drive back to the station I told my colleagues that Romney had certainly made news with us today. The 5 p.m. producer slotted me in the top of the newscast to be on set with the anchors to discuss Romney's big "pivot to the center" on the contraception issue. As we neared the station I started logging the interview and at 12:53 p.m. tweeted out:

"ALERT: Mitt Romney says he would not vote for senate bill which

would allow employers to deny coverage for birth control."

Within seconds there were dozens of re-tweets from national reporters and political operatives. When I arrived back at the station, our web manager Don Taylor came running up to me. "We have nothing for the web to direct the national press to, get me something as soon as possible!" He then turned and rushed away saying he had the BBC on hold. Within minutes Greg Sargent, a reporter with the *Washington Post,* called me for details and put the story up on the Post's website.

At mid-afternoon, I was on the Ohio News Network set discussing how Romney was moderating his message with an eye on November. At about this same time, Romney called into the Howie Carr show on WRKO radio in Boston. Carr, a conservative talk show host, asked him about it and Romney said:

"Of course I support the Blunt Amendment. I thought he was talking about some state law that prevented people from getting contraception. So I talked about contraceptives and so forth. I really misunderstood the question."

By 5 o'clock I was live on the 10TV set discussing how the story I broke had evolved. Romney now supported the Blunt Amendment and claimed he thought I was asking about an Ohio law. The Romney camp and his supporters online went into overdrive placing the blame squarely with me and my "confusing" question, even though Romney himself said he heard Blunt-Rubio and associated it with "some state law."

Our newsroom was buzzing. CBS News called and wanted the exchange for their nightly news. The *Associated Press* put it out on the wire, which is the equivalent of hitting every newsroom computer in America. Laura Bassett with *Huffington Post* had her story up quickly. *Hardball with Chris Matthews* led the show with it. Within an hour it was all over the place.

As I watched this tornado unfold, I sat back and was in awe of how quickly an issue can go viral nationwide. I felt a bit helpless being ground zero on this incident and having absolutely no control over the proliferation of it. The interview, and Romney's retraction of his answer, was now the top story on cable news and websites, small and large, across the country. People were also weighing in on Facebook and Twitter by the groves.

My general manager Tom Griesdorn was ecstatic that the highest-rated station in central Ohio was in the middle of the national discussion. In the coming days, *GQ* would place me on their Top Five political "Power List" and the *Washington Post* awarded me with their "Best Super Tuesday" Twitter ranking. Weeks later, Greisdorn awarded me with "Employee of the Month."

The accolades were great, but privately I was very concerned I had burned a bridge with the Romney campaign. If that were the case I would be ineffective—essentially cut off—covering the presidential race in the fall.

Before the interview aired that night, I called Ohio Republican Party spokesman Chris Maloney and Romney's national spokesman Ryan Williams and made clear it had not been my intent to trip up their candidate. There had been plenty of time for those who had been in the room and heard the question and answer to have requested a clarification.

The interview aired in its entirety on our prime time show that evening and I ended the program with this note:

"I've enjoyed covering politics and politicians for more than a dozen years. I've never played gotcha journalism, I have complete respect for the men and women who enter the political arena, battle it out, put up with a lot, and still manage to get things done. I like Governor Romney. Today was my third sit-down interview with him. I've always found him to be engaging, polite, and honest. Today I asked the governor about a bill, explained it, and asked him about his position on it. His answer was definitive and we moved on. I believe the question was clear, the governor now says it was not, and that's all it is. The interview is now history and you can decide what, if any, importance it has on your vote this Tuesday."

That night, Jon Stewart played the clip from the interview on *The Daily Show* and quipped: "The thing's only a week old and Mitt Romney's already taken two positions on it. And he took the two positions within three-and-a-half hours of each other!" I had missed the show but got a text from my twenty-one-year-old niece Mallory, "Uncle Jim you were just on *THE DAILY SHOW!* Of all the accomplishments in my broadcasting career, *The Daily Show* had finally made me relevant with the youngsters in the family!

The following morning during a live appearance on C-SPAN I told viewers,

"This question came up about halfway through the interview. Governor Romney was very definitive in his response. I knew in the back of my mind we had made news, but honestly here we are in Ohio—no Republican candidate in the history of our nation has won the White House without Ohio—so in the back of my mind, while I thought it was unusual, I thought he was doing a pivot to the center knowing that Republicans are struggling now with women voters."

That same day Rick Santorum, campaigning in Georgia, had a field day with the interview telling supporters:

"We saw an insight into what's in the gut of Governor Romney yesterday. He was asked a question about the Blunt amendment... When Gov. Romney was asked that question, his knee-jerk reaction was, 'Oh, I can't be for it.' Well, then after his consultants talk to him, he said, 'Well, I didn't understand the question.' Well, maybe he did, maybe he didn't. If I was asked that question, my gut reaction would be, 'You stand for the First Amendment; you stand for freedom of religion.'"

The interview became immortalized in the book *Double Down: Game Change 2012* by Mark Halperin and John Heilemann. On page 282 they wrote:

"The next morning, Romney flew to Ohio, where he sat down for a local TV interview... 'Blunt-Rubio is being debated, I believe later this week,' the interviewer asked Romney, confusingly. 'Have you taken a position on it?' Romney had never been asked a question about the Blunt provision publicly before. That he was hearing it now was no accident. All throughout the GOP nomination fight, Lis Smith, the Obama campaign's director of rapid response, had been feeding questions to reporters to pose to Romney, with the aim of inducing him to tack to the right—and that was what had happened here."

No, actually, that is not what happened here. If the authors had contacted me, "the interviewer," for background, they would have learned I had asked Santorum the same series of questions a week earlier. Producer Rochelle Young and I had been compiling questions for Romney for days—this was Ohio after all—and we certainly knew the importance of the birth control debate heading into Super Tuesday. It is not uncommon for campaign operatives like Smith, who had been the spokesperson for the Ted Strickland campaign in 2010 and was now with the Obama campaign, or Williams and Maloney with the Romney campaign, or the press people from both the Democratic National Committee and Republican National Committee to send you background information via email and texts on a daily—sometimes hourly—basis. It can be helpful in clarifying a candidate's position, but mainly it lets a reporter know they're in the loop.

Both the Romney and Obama campaigns had very good operatives who worked the Ohio press corps a lot during 2012, but never once did they script one of my questions.

ABC News political director Rick Klein was a guest on my show the following Sunday and said he didn't find my question to Romney "confusing" at all:

"This question didn't come from out of left field. You set it up, you didn't just throw a name or a number out there at him and ask him to respond and he came out against it. So there was something specific in his mind and clearly he didn't know what it was and/or he got it wrong the first time and it wasn't accurately stating his own position."

Klein and I also discussed how Romney could have heard "Blunt-Rubio" and been so emphatic that he opposed anything associated with two of his biggest supporters.

"He shocked a lot of people with that answer and it questioned a couple things. One is, did he really misunderstand it, or did he just get whacked by folks on the right and have to change his position? If he did just misunderstand the question, was he just not paying attention? Because this Blunt Amendment is no small deal—it's being voted on in the United States Senate—it's a very big deal and very high profile and it's something everyone on the right are intensely focused on."

With the benefit of hindsight, I now believe Romney was on mental cruise control, relaxed talking to me, just another in a long line of TV journalists. He may have been thinking about his next speech, or the Michigan win, or a combination of a million things. Blunt-Rubio went inside his head when I said it, but didn't process in his mind and he missed it.

As Romney worked to turn attention away from the interview, opponents were having a field day with that dreaded flip-flop title he had been working so hard to erase since our first interview back in 2007.

Three months later, Maloney called and told me that despite "some concern" in Boston, I could interview Romney again on board his campaign bus in Newark, Ohio. When we arrived at the location, my photographer Ryan Bradford and I were taken on board and then asked to get off the bus. For a split second, I thought this might be payback for the Blunt-Rubio question.

Several minutes later the door opened again and we stepped back inside and Romney smiled and shook his head. I wished him a happy father's day and we chitchatted a few moments while Ryan mic'd us up. In unsurprising Romney fashion, he instructed a campaign staffer—bringing back memories of our first interview in Myrtle Beach six years earlier—to hold up a portable light for the interview and make sure the "Romney '12" bumper sticker pasted on the window behind him was just off his left shoulder. "Why did they make us use the wrong kind of light and frame him all wonky?" Ryan asked me on the way back to the station. The question made me laugh, thinking back to that first interview. "He's still ever the perfectionist for television," I responded.

I have to give Romney and his team credit here. Many politicians and their staff hold grudges that can last for years. From my experience, Romney is just not a vengeful guy. He had a job to do, and so did I.

WALK AND CHEW GUM

Just a week following my Romney interview, Florida's young senator Marco Rubio—at the heart of the contraception question I had asked—was in Columbus campaigning for State Treasurer Josh Mandel. Like Rubio, Mandel was young and anxious to be elected to high office and set his sights on the progressive incumbent Senator Sherrod Brown.

Mandel had only been in office as treasurer for weeks in 2011 when he started raising money for a U.S. Senate campaign. He alienated voters, and some of his own Republicans who were eyeing the race, with aggressive fundraising—at one point heading to the Bahamas to raise campaign cash. As the state treasurer, Mandel was chairman of the state Board of Deposit—which decided where to deposit Ohio's public money—but he had missed every one of its meetings. He also disliked the press and gave few interviews leaving the coverage of all this negative.

I've learned through the years that having a bad relationship with the press creates a self-fulling prophecy for politicians. The more they dislike reporters, the fewer interviews they give. That means less coverage they receive and more coverage for their opponent. And while this cloud of doubt and mistrust is developing, if and when a politician makes a mistake, it is amplified even more because it's the first voters have heard from them in a long time.

One fact I've learned about public officials and the press over many years: Good politicians like to swing at hardball questions. Great politicians master how to hit them out of the ballpark. I can usually tell you which candidates are ready for the big leagues based on their fear—or fearlessness—of the press. Incidentally, the not-so-good public officials fear the game altogether.

Mandel would face in Brown a scrappy longtime Ohio politician who had this fearlessness with the press I was talking about. Even when things got tough—like when reporters learned he was more than four months delinquent in paying taxes on his Washington, D.C. apartment— Brown was always accessible. It helped that his wife, Connie Schultz, was a

211

longtime respected journalist and reporter for *The Plain Dealer*. Having ease with the media can be taught, but being self-confident comes from within.

In fact, of all the politicians I've known through the years, Brown has the distinct honor of being the one who is easiest to detect telling a lie. Most senators and governors are highly skilled in being able to look you directly in the eye and tell you something you know for a fact is not accurate. John Kasich telling me over and over again he had no interest in running for president in 2016 comes to mind. Brown, on the other hand, will squirm in a chair and start sputtering his sentences, which is a dead giveaway for reporters.

As an example, shortly before the 2014 election when it appeared Democrats were going lose every statewide office in Ohio, I asked Brown whether state Democratic Party chairman Chris Redfern would be replaced. Brown tensed up, shrunk in his seat, and softly gave this reply, "I don't know, I want to see what happens on Election Day."

Most senators would have said something like, "We are a united team, and we still expect great things on Election Day, and I'm not worried about that." But Brown has been incapable of spinning what he knows isn't true. I said to my photographer on the way back to the station, "Brown just told us Redfern's fate."

Shortly before the 2012 election, I asked Brown during a conversation about his relationship with President Obama. If ever there should be political camaraderie in Washington, D.C., you would think it would be between these two. In my mind, I thought Brown would be a loyal progressive soldier for the administration, helping carry their legislative proposals.

"Going into the Oval Office is terrible," Brown told me. I was a bit taken aback by the honesty so close to the election.

"Define terrible for me," I replied.

"Back in the Clinton years, you would go into the Oval Office with Bill and he would ask about your family, and remember things you were working on in your state and district. He truly wanted to talk to you."

"Thus why he was always on Clinton Time," I chuckled.

Brown agreed and continued, "Obama is the opposite. He's a law professor, he sits you down and tells you what he knows and expects you to think the same way. He doesn't relate well to people. The only reason why he's winning this election is because the Republicans nominated someone who is even worse."

Yet another brutally honest assessment from Ohio's senior senator.

During a live debate in the fall, Mandel would famously—and awkwardly—look at the camera and say, "Senator, you're a liar!" Brown calmly responded, "Being called a liar, it's just a pretty remarkable thing for a young man, or a man at any age, to say during a political debate." Mandel's performance was widely ridiculed publicly by Democrats and privately by some top Republicans. Still, Brown only won by six points, much closer than many expected.

While Brown would make an interesting selection as a running mate for a moderate Democratic presidential nominee—like Hillary Clinton—in 2016 (think Ohio, progressive, unions, scrappy campaigner) he has denied repeatedly that he's interested. His prospects for reelection in 2018, however, are less promising considering how poorly Democrats have done statewide recently in non-presidential election years. The U.S. Chamber of Commerce, and the Koch brothers, are sure to make him a top target once again.

The Koch brothers, who have made billions in the oil industry over the decades, have upped their game in Ohio in the last few years, funding a full-time staff for the state chapter of Americans for Prosperity.

Their first target in Ohio wasn't a politician, however, but Jack Hanna, Director Emeritus of the Columbus Zoo and Aquarium. The group opposed a proposed Columbus Zoo levy increase and—as their first salvo in central Ohio—mailed out a blatantly misleading flyer suggesting the levy would double a homeowner's taxes, when in reality it amounted to less than 1 percent.

"I'm completely frustrated and I can't believe it," an emotional "Jungle Jack" Hanna told me before the election. "Do I hurt some? Yes. Some people came in here, obviously. When you're at the top in life, whether it's football or your business, whatever it is, there are always those that might not like that. But those people who oppose this need to understand that there's a lot involved here."

AFP used the zoo levy to test run an aggressive ground and data field operation, including a system that automatically updated information for volunteers who were canvassing Columbus neighborhoods in the weeks leading up to the election.

"Absolutely, it was initiated on the ground for our door-to-door effort where we hit thousands of doors," Eli Miller, AFP's Ohio director told me. "It was then initiated in our offices where we made thousands of phone calls for this. For both our ground game, and on our door-to-door efforts, we used this system and it's working."

The levy failed by a staggering 70 percent of the vote, the first time the Columbus Zoo had been defeated at the polls.

"What's most disturbing to me with that zoo levy is the fact outside oil interests, really only one family spent the kind of dollars they did coming into Columbus and telling people how to vote," Brown told me.

It soon became clear, besides Brown, AFP had another longtime Ohio politician on its radar: Columbus mayor Michael Coleman, a Democrat and gun control advocate. In 2014, Coleman, Columbus' first African-American mayor, and the longest-serving mayor in the city's history, eyeing perhaps his most expensive and negative campaign ever, announced he would not seek reelection.

Think of this for a second: The Koch brothers' political network plans to pump nearly $1 billion into the 2016 presidential race, and they may financially fuel more than one of the GOP candidates. "If we're happy with the policies that these individuals are supporting, we'll finance their campaigns," said David Koch.

One big fan of the Koch brothers trying to earn their financial support is Marco Rubio, who was at the center of the question about contraception I had asked Romney, which caused an uproar prior to Super Tuesday.

"Let me ask you first whether it bothered you that your amendment and Senator Blunt's became known as 'Blunt-Rubio?'" I started the interview.

"No, listen, we both believe in religious freedom," he responded. "I happen to believe in the Constitution of the United States and my objection the whole time has been, I don't think the Federal Government should have the power to require a religious organization to pay for something that the religious organization teaches against."

"But would it not have affected healthcare for some women?" I followed up.

"We're not banning contraception, we're not saying to religious organizations you can't offer contraception, this is really nothing to do with contraception," Rubio replied. "It has to do with whether the Federal Government should have the power to force a religious organization to pay for something that goes against the moral teachings of that church. And if they can, then they have the power to do all sorts of things."

"Republicans keep saying 'jobs, jobs, jobs' is what this election is about, yet this contraception issue is not about that," I replied.

"The Obama administration made this an issue through their ruling and it caused an outrage across the country," Rubio told me. "I would add the Constitution is always relevant. Constitutional protections of religious liberties, they're always relevant. I think we can walk and chew gum at the same time. Maybe not the Senate, but certainly the people of the United States can."

I then turned my attention to illegal immigration, where Rubio was working with Senate Democrats to help pass a comprehensive bill that included a path to citizenship for those in the country illegally. But Rubio strongly opposed the DREAM (Development, Relief and Education for Alien Minors) Act, which would grant legal status to illegal immigrants who came to the U.S. when they were young. The young immigrants would have to meet certain requirements, such as going to school or joining the military. A PEW poll in 2011 showed 91 percent of Latinos supported it.

"There are many young people, through no fault of their own, who grow up here and want to stay. What's wrong with that?" I asked.

"The DREAM Act is badly constructed," said Rubio. "It's a specific law and there are things wrong with it. For example, it allows for chain migration. You're not just helping the kids, those kids will now become citizens and claim their relatives and so you have a chain migration problem."

"So what do we do?" I followed up.

"I do think there's a responsible way to help these children that were brought here at a very young age, against no fault of their own, have grown up here their entire lives, and are now high academic achievers, who want to serve in the armed forces, and there's a way to do it. But the way the DREAM Act is currently written doesn't have the support. I'm hoping to find a bipartisan way—this doesn't have to be a partisan issue."

A Rubio alternative proposal in 2012 went nowhere.

I then asked Rubio about the hydraulic fracturing boom in Ohio and whether he felt the risks—links to earthquakes and concern about water aquifers—was worth it.

"Yeah, I'm in favor of domestic exploration and I think it's very similar to an issue we have in Florida, which is off-shore drilling. In the middle of my campaign we had that horrible incident in the middle of the Gulf, and so obviously you always want to be safe. I mean, who's in favor of an environmental catastrophe? No one is. But at the same time, we have to recognize that at a time when more people are using energy sources than ever before in human history, we live in the most energy rich country in the entire world."

At the time of our interview, there was speculation Rubio was on the top of Mitt Romney's list for running mate. Besides Ohio, Florida is a crucial prize in the GOP strategy to 270 electoral votes.

"First of all, I'm not going to be the vice president, I'm not running for a national office."

"You would say 'no?'" I interrupted.

"Yeah, I've said that every time I've been asked. It's not going to change. I'm not going to be vice president."

While he was vetted by the Romney campaign, his inexperience eliminated him from serious consideration, leaving me to wonder if he would have truly said no.

Mandel, who won reelection as state treasurer in 2014 and publicly opposed Governor John Kasich's decision to expand Medicaid in Ohio, wasted no time in endorsing Rubio—and not his fellow Buckeye—for president in 2016.

SUPER TUESDAY

As Mitt Romney and Rick Santorum continued their slug-fest at campaign events and on the airwaves across Ohio, a third Republican was trying to regain traction. For a time earlier in the cycle Newt Gingrich, the always outspoken former GOP house speaker, was leading the pack. He had won a big victory in the South Carolina primary—the contest that claimed to always pick correctly the eventual GOP nominee—and he seemed poised to do well in upcoming southern primaries.

Romney's Super PAC went to work bombing Gingrich on the Ohio TV airwaves with a particularly lethal attack ad called "Happy."

"You know what makes Barack Obama happy? Newt Gingrich's baggage. Newt has more baggage than the airlines. Freddie Mac helped cause the economic collapse, but Gingrich cashed in. Freddie Mac paid Newt $30,000 per hour—$1.6 million. And Newt is the only speaker in history to be reprimanded. He was fined $300,000 for ethics violations by a Republican Congress."

The ads took their toll on Gingrich first in Florida, the contest immediately following South Carolina. In Ohio, despite having prominent Republicans like Franklin County GOP chairman Doug Priesse supporting him, two Quinnipiac University polls showed his support drop from 36 percent in December to 17 percent in February. Not even his old colleague John Kasich would publicly rescue him.

My interview with Gingrich happened in between my sit-downs with Santorum and Romney, and it was via satellite where he was campaigning in Arizona—a much smaller delegate prize than Ohio. It was an indication of what he thought his chances were in the Buckeye state.

The interview was also going to be a personal challenge for me and would confirm—I hoped—my ability to be a professional interviewer despite having a deep distaste for Gingrich, and the personal risky decisions he made during the Clinton impeachment that I believed could have put our nation in peril.

Yes, as discussed earlier, we journalists have our own opinions. The professionalism is in preventing it from showing in our work.

After more than twenty-five years around politicians I've formulated views about some of them, which I'm sharing with you in this book. This isn't a liberal or conservative thing, at least not for me; this is a good one or bad one thing. And Gingrich, similar to John Edwards, was one of the bad ones.

While the fifty-five-year-old Gingrich was leading the impeachment of President Bill Clinton in 1998, it turned out he had his own hanky-panky going on. If that had come to light during the months of impeachment proceedings, Gingrich's hypocrisy would have made a serious mockery of our system of government.

At the beginning of his political career, Gingrich was the "family values" Republican, regularly assailing Democrats for their lack of morality. "Woody Allen having non-incest with a non-daughter to whom he was a non-father because they were a non-family fits the Democratic platform perfectly," he said in 1992. Two years later, he linked Democrats to Susan Smith, the South Carolina mother who had killed her two children by drowning them in car.

Gingrich had also been responsible for harsher punishment for two of his congressional colleagues accused of sexual misconduct. He then spent more than a year hammering Democratic House Speaker Jim Wright, who he called "the least ethical speaker of the 20th century." The charges involving book royalties eventually forced Wright to resign.

Prior to my broadcasting days, I remember attending two Gingrich speeches in the early 1990s when he was leading GOPAC, a GOP fund-raising political action committee. There he gave recommendations on how to run for office, attack the "liberal welfare state," and make ethics a central campaign issue. As the Bush presidency came to a disappointing end for conservatives in 1992, the new Clinton administration gave Gingrich the enemy he needed to fix blame and orchestrate a remarkable GOP takeover of the House in 1994.

But what goes around comes around.

Gingrich became the House Speaker in January 1995, and nearly as quickly, eighty ethics violations were thrown at him. While most were eventually dismissed, one charge he couldn't deny is the fact he had accepted a $4.5 million advance from HarperCollins, Rupert Murdoch's company, for a two-book deal—even though Murdoch had interests before Congress. Charges of hypocrisy were leveled at Gingrich after he had helped bring down Wright under similar circumstances.

After Republicans shut down the Federal Government at Christmas time in 1995, during a budget battle with President Bill Clinton, Gingrich's popularity sank. Clinton ran against both Bob Dole and Gingrich in the 1996 election and trounced both.

Then, days after Clinton's second inauguration, the House voted 395-28 to reprimand Gingrich and fine him $300,000 for using tax-exempt cash to promote GOP goals and lying to the ethics committee. It was the only vote in the history of the House to impose a sanction against the speaker. Only a handful of Republicans defended Gingrich.

During all of this time, attorney Ken Starr had been leading an investigation into the Clintons—specifically their Whitewater dealings and the death of Clinton friend Vince Foster. Eventually, his investigation grew to include Travel-gate, the alleged misuse of FBI files and Clinton's conduct with Paula Jones, a former Arkansas government employee.

Just when Starr thought his investigation—which had found nothing—was through, a government employee named Linda Tripp gave him taped phone conversations in which her friend Monica Lewinsky, a former White House intern, discussed having oral sex with Clinton.

In a January deposition under oath, Clinton denied ever having a sexual relationship with Lewinsky. In an angry appearance before the press soon after, he insisted, "I did not have sexual relations with that woman, Miss Lewinsky!" In August, before a grand jury, Clinton answered the sexual relations question with his now infamous, "It depends upon what the meaning of 'is' is."

Over time, evidence grew to the point that it was clear Clinton had been lying and Gingrich started beating the impeachment drum saying he would never again make a speech without "commenting on this topic."

But privately, behind his closed office doors, Gingrich, the Speaker of the House and third most powerful man in American government, was having his own extramarital affair with Callista Bisek, a much younger House staffer, on the taxpayers' dime.

Bill Clinton was being impeached for lying about his affair. The only difference is Gingrich hadn't been outed with his yet.

Gingrich had been with his second wife Marianne for eighteen years. She was well known in Republican circles, supporting Gingrich during his rise in power. In an interview with ABC News in 2012, Marianne claimed when Gingrich admitted to his six-year affair, he suggested this solution: "He wanted an open marriage and I refused."

In November 1998, three months after Clinton admitted to the nation he had a sexual affair with Lewinksy, and two months before he would be acquitted by the U.S. Senate in his impeachment trial, Gingrich quit—some say he was forced out—as speaker.

Turns out the "family values" guy was full of hypocrisy, putting his own self-inflated ego ahead of the nation.

Now fourteen years later, sixty-eight years old and married to Bisek, Gingrich was taking one last lap around the national political stage. He was the South Carolina primary winner, but it had become clear by Super Tuesday his campaign was on fumes.

I asked Gingrich first about Romney's "baggage" ad that was already on Ohio airwaves:

"The Romney style is to try to shrink everybody else," Gingrich told me. "He's like somebody trying to try out for basketball and he's 4'8. The goal is to make sure nobody else seems no more than 4'4. I think it's a terrible model. Everywhere he's going, his campaign is so negative it just turns people off. It's sad he has nothing positive to say that's worth his advertising."

I then asked him if anyone should be concerned that Las Vegas casino magnate Sheldon Adelson had dropped $15 million into his campaign seemingly out of nowhere.

"Sheldon Adelson is a very successful casino magnet who has one passion in life," Gingrich answered. "He is terrified the Iranians are going to get a nuclear weapon. He desperately wants to make sure Israel survives."

"But that's a lot of money from a single source," I followed up.

"It goes to a Super PAC; it doesn't go to me or my campaign directly," Gingrich replied. "But the reason why we're on the same side is the threat of Iranian nuclear weapons."

With gas prices rising, Gingrich had proposed a plan to get prices at the pump down to $2.50 per gallon. He took a swipe at Obama—and past presidents—when he said during a debate no president "will ever bow to a Saudi king again."

The problem was, oil is a global commodity and its price determined by global supply and demand (the price for a gallon of gas would drop below $3.00 a gallon during Obama's second term). Experts said Gingrich's idea could set the country up for a supply shortage. So I asked him about it.

"I think it means something to Americans, and every time I've focused on big ideas and big solutions, I've ended up back as the frontrunner nationally. I think the people are looking for somebody who has answers on energy and the price of gasoline in a way that's real."

I then asked whether Gingrich was hurt that his old congressional friend John Kasich had refused to endorse his candidacy.

"I think John is focused on Ohio, and he wants all the candidates to pay attention to Ohio, and he and I have talked about it at length."

While Gingrich told me he was "committed to campaigning in Ohio," it was clear he had no dreams of winning there.

Three days before the primary I was a guest on C-SPAN. Most political junkies love this cable network because you can see everything in its entirety without filter. I would hesitate to admit how many hours I've watched C-SPAN through the years. But it's a lot.

The interview would not be from the comfort of the 10TV studio, but rather from Mills James, an independent production company in Columbus. I walked into a completely empty room with a white wall behind me (a Columbus skyline was chroma-keyed in the background). I sat on a stool, put in my IFB, and was told there was no monitor so I couldn't tell when I was on. "C-SPAN keeps you up during viewers' calls, so always assume you're live" was the advice from a Mills James employee who then promptly left the room.

Sitting there alone on a stool in front of a camera, it dawned on me how terrifying this could be for someone not in the business.

One caller wanted to know why we in the "liberal media" only wanted to talk about contraception.

"We're in a primary process here, and among Republican primary voters, social issues are important," I responded. "There's no big liberal press mothership in the sky where we're all getting orders. Right now in the Republican primary, largely fueled by Rick Santorum and his comments, these social issues are part of the conversation."

Another caller wanted to know why Gingrich was still in the race.

"For every vote Newt Gingrich gets in Ohio, that's likely to hurt the chances of Rick Santorum winning the state," I answered.

I was then asked to make a prediction about Super Tuesday.

"I think there is a sense that Romney is picking up momentum. Ohio is perceived as do-or-die for Santorum. If Romney wins Ohio, I think we can safely say he is the national frontrunner."

On election night, Romney edged Santorum by a single point—38 to 37 percent. Gingrich placed a distant third with 15 percent. Ron Paul ended with 9 percent.

On the air that night, in front of a map of Ohio, I explained to viewers, "It was a strategy for Rick Santorum that almost worked. His strategy was to win in smaller rural and conservative counties across the state. It almost worked except for one problem. The population centers. Romney ran the three C's—Cincinnati, Columbus, and Cleveland and overwhelmed Santorum there."

I also pointed out Romney's map of Ohio against Santorum was nearly identical to Barack Obama's map against John McCain in 2008. Romney employed the traditional Democratic strategy in the state; win in the population centers, while Santorum swept about everything else.

"If I'm the Romney camp tonight, I'm looking at the map wondering how I'm going to flip those rural counties around, because enthusiasm for him is going to be a big issue come fall," I noted.

ENTER THE PRESIDENT

A week after Super Tuesday I was reporting live from outside the University of Dayton Arena where President Obama and British Prime Minister David Cameron were enjoying a first-round game (and some hot dogs) at the NCAA men's basketball tournament. "Man, this is awesome, I can't wait to hopefully meet President Obama," *CBS Sports* broadcaster Steve Kerr told me. "It adds an element of excitement to the building that wouldn't be here otherwise."

Prior to Obama and Cameron arriving at March Madness, photographer Andy Wallace and I decided we needed to shoot a portion of my story with the presidential limousine moving behind me. The problem was not knowing where the official entourage would be entering. There was a large crowd gathering at the entrance of the Dayton Arena to greet the president, and that's where the other television cameras had gathered, but something didn't look right to me. I approached a Secret Service agent we had met earlier in the day and whispered, "I know you can't confirm the travel route, but I really need the car behind me for my report." The agent looked at me, then Andy, and deciding we weren't terrorist material replied, "the motorcade would never slow down to make a hard right turn." And he walked away.

I looked over and noticed that in order for the presidential limousine to enter the front of the facility, where everyone was gathering, it would literally have to stop to make a hard right-hand turn into a driveway. "He's not coming here," I told Andy. "Let's head to the back." Knowing we were risking missing the shot that every other news crew would get if we were wrong, the bold gamble paid off and sure enough, a few minutes later, the motorcade headed our way. I was able to say, "expect this to be one of many trips to Ohio by Obama between now and November" as a smiling president drove by behind me.

One week later Obama was back in the state speaking at The Ohio State University to address rising gas costs. Prices had just hit $4.00 a gallon in Columbus and showed no signs of slowing down. "Nearly 65 percent of Americans blame President Obama for rising gas costs, and the administration knows with an election in November, they have to turn the blame-game around," I told viewers live that night.

Obama started his speech with the traditional, "Hello, Buckeyes!" He laid out his plan for oil and gas production, while proposing developing renewable energy sources. Republicans were already on social media condemning him for not backing the Keystone XL Pipeline, but Obama countered, "We've added enough oil and gas pipeline to circle the entire Earth, and then some." The president, already in campaign mode, left the stage by spelling out O-H-I-O with his arms.

It wasn't just gas prices worrying the Obama campaign. The national economy remained sluggish. Unemployment was at a stubborn 8.1 percent (down from a peak of 10 percent) and the portion of Americans in the work force was at its lowest percentage since 1981. Obama's approval rating was below 50 percent, with nearly half of voters disapproving of the way he was handling his job.

And then there was the Affordable Care Act—"Obamacare" as critics, and the President himself started to call it—which was so unpopular in 2010 it cost Democrats the majority in the House. A Gallup poll in early 2012 found in swing states like Ohio, 53 percent of voters wanted Obamacare repealed and a majority also said it was a "bad thing" it had become law.

Despite the negatives, there was a record of accomplishment for Obama to run on. He had backed the nation off the financial cliff he inherited from George W. Bush. While the economy wasn't great, it certainly was not the crisis it had been in January, 2009. The American auto industry, especially good news in Ohio, was roaring back. And after years of hiding in Pakistan, Osama bin Laden, the terrorist who had directed the 9/11 hijackers, had been found and a team of US Special Forces flew in from Afghanistan and killed him.

How many of the presidential candidates I've previously written about in this book wanted to be the one to bring bin Laden to justice?

Obama did. And for that, history will remember.

After covering the President twice in one week, I soon returned to the studio where I heard, "Jim Heath in Columbus, Ohio—hello!"

Magical words if you hear broadcasting legend Larry King say them in your IFB as he was checking his mic. For a generation of politicos, Larry was the voice on radio and then CNN for all things political.

With the election year picking up, King was on my show to discuss President Obama as he prepared to announce for reelection in Columbus. King had interviewed every major American politician over the decades and had a unique perspective on all of them.

"Of the modern presidents, did Ronald Reagan leave the longest-lasting legacy?" I started.

"I was lucky enough to have lunch with him, be in his home. He was engaging, he told wonderful stories and great jokes, he was a good guy and Americans liked him," King replied. "Reagan did not have guile. He did not have hate. He would share funny stories with Tip O'Neill on the day O'Neill would knock him on the floor verbally. The best way to put it, Jim, was he was just a good guy."

"Would you say Bill Clinton is the most popular living politician today?" I asked.

"I'd go further than that, Jim, and I would say if Bill Clinton ran for office again he would win. He would beat any of the current Republicans, and he could beat Obama. He is a magical politician. There's something special about him. Americans, as you know well in Ohio, gravitate to him. Bill Clinton is the supreme politician of our time."

"So," I followed up, "as President Obama prepares for reelection, have the rifts with the Clintons from the 2008 campaign healed?"

"It's healed between Hillary and Obama," King replied. "Certainly she is very loyal to him as Secretary of State and from all I've learned inside the administration, they get along extraordinarily well. I think Bill is less forgiving. Bill did not like things that happened in that campaign and I think he wears his wounds more. He will publicly support the President when he has to, but Obama is not his favorite person."

And Bill Clinton was not Obama's favorite person, as we discussed earlier in the book. But Clinton would go a long way in helping Obama win reelection.

These are some of the nuances in politics that make covering the circus so interesting.

Forty-four days after his speech on energy, President Obama was back on the campus of The Ohio State University to officially launch his reelection bid. The President chose the first Saturday in May, hoping college-age voters would fill the 20,000-seat Schottenstein Center on campus. This had not been an issue in 2008 when Obama was part-politician and part-rock star, filling up every arena.

But as I stood there that day looking around I remember thinking, "this is a bit underwhelming." About 14,000 supporters were there, including John Glenn, former governor Ted Strickland, Senator Sherrod Brown and First Lady Michelle Obama, but thousands of seats in the upper deck were empty.

Noticeably empty.

It didn't take long for Romney's campaign spokesman Ryan Williams to tweet out a picture of the upper deck. What made it worse for the Obama camp was the buildup leading up to the announcement and the suggestion it may be an overflow crowd. "Not the overflow crowd he promised," Williams tweeted.

It was in such sharp contrast to an Obama-Strickland campaign rally on the Oval at Ohio State, which I had covered two years earlier that drew over 35,000 people. Still, Democrats were quick to point out, 14,000 was a lot more than any Republican candidate had been drawing at that point in Ohio.

Glenn welcomed the crowd, "We're honored this is really the kickoff event of the 2012 campaign, and we're glad the president has come to Ohio. You know, Ohio really is representative of this whole country. We are so diverse, we have everything there is in this country except palm trees I guess!"

The palm trees were in Florida, where Glenn's successor, Senator George Voinovich, had retired in early 2011 after leaving office. Voinovich made news during the 2012 campaign when he told author Michael Grunwald that shortly before Obama's Inauguration in January, 2009 senate minority leader Mitch McConnell made it clear to GOP members of the senate, "If Obama was for it, we had to be against it." Voinovich, a popular former governor and mayor of Cleveland, said, "all McConnell cared about was making sure Obama could never have a clean victory."

As Michelle was introducing her husband, Obama was behind the curtain recording a video for social media. "Hello, everybody, this is Barack and we're about to kick off the 2012 campaign here in Columbus, Ohio!"

After taking the stage, to the familiar song "City of Blinding Lights" by U2, a smiling Obama began his speech, "It is good to be back in Ohio! You know, right before I came out someone handed me a Buckeye for good luck! Later in his speech he added, "Ohio, four years ago, you and I began a journey together. We are making progress and now we face a choice. Ohio, I tell you what: This is a make-or-break moment for the middle class, and we've been through too much to turn back now."

As Mitt Romney slugged his way through a long primary season, the Obama campaign was loaded with cash—$104 million compared with a little over $10 million for Romney—and he started to spend it on Ohio television. Keep in mind it was only May. That's how important the state is to win for both parties. While the Romney camp went off TV, Ohioans were seeing a TV ad called "Succeed," highlighting how Obama had guided the resurgence of the American auto industry.

The weeks of unanswered attack ads in Ohio helped define an image of Romney he was ultimately unable to shake.

As Obama's campaign revved up, Congresswoman Debbie Wasserman-Schultz, chair of the Democratic National Committee, and Reince Priebus, chair of the Republican National Committee, were guests on my show.

"We can probably agree that the candidate who wins both Ohio and Florida will be in the White House?" I asked first to Wasserman-Schultz, who represents a Florida district in Congress.

"I can certainly agree with that; both Ohio and Florida are incredibly important, they're both battlegrounds, bellwether states, and they're both going to be critical in this presidential election."

"What's different about 2012 from 2008 regarding the ground game?" I followed up.

"We've got offices open across the state, tens of thousands of volunteers, thousands and thousands of door knocks and phone calls and house parties have already occurred. We're building the most significant grassroots dynamic presidential campaign in history that really Ohio has ever seen."

I asked Priebus if there was any state more important in Romney's electoral strategy than Ohio.

"I think Ohio is just the total epicenter and ground zero for the map in this country to get to 270 electoral votes," said Pribus. "It's a must-win for us, it's a must-win for Obama. You all are very sophisticated and used to the ground effort, the political mechanisms in place to move the electorate. So Ohio will be front-and-center this year and we need to do well there."

"What did you learn from losing here in 2008 that will be different in 2012?" I asked.

"When you consider all of the money that gets raised, and all the resources that come with that, all for about twelve states and the ground operation, it is unbelievable. That's why when you have movies like *So Goes The Nation* about Ohio, it really is a technical, detailed effort to get out the vote. It's not just throwing things up at the sky and seeing what happens. It's literally micro-targeting, lists figuring out what neighborhoods, what homes, it really is something I think both sides have perfected but it's high stakes and important to this country."

I asked Wasserman-Schultz what the president's narrative would be in Ohio through the fall.

"Look at where Ohio, and the country, was when President Obama took office," she replied.

"From the ashes of an economy left in the wake of Bush's presidency, the worst economic crisis that we've faced since the Great Depression, the economy was bleeding 750,000 jobs a month. Now, three years later, we've had nationally twenty-five straight months of job growth in the private sector. A resurgence in manufacturing, which is huge for Ohio. The American automobile industry rescued by President Obama which would have been left for dead, and allowed to die, if it were left up to Mitt Romney."

While the rhetoric was heating up between the campaigns, the lack of access to Obama and the lack of transparency in his administration was becoming a real issue for the press.

Obama would end his first term by having held the fewest press conferences in history. He would rarely sit down with reporters for in-depth interviews, instead flying-in local news anchors from key battleground states and cities for four-minute chitchats on whatever issue he was working on that the campaign believed played well back home.

Remember how poorly my interview ended in 2007 when I took a few extra minutes with candidate Obama? Now as president, Obama's ability to filibuster short interviews was becoming legendary.

While Republicans grumble that Obama and the press are too tight, in reality, he doesn't think any more highly of reporters than most conservatives do. For our part, journalists and transparency advocates are not huge fans of his White House, which curbs routine disclosure of information and attempts to avoid any scrutiny.

In fact, in 2015 the *Associated Press* concluded the Obama administration "more often than ever" censored government files or outright denied access to them under the U.S. Freedom of Information Act.

"What we discovered reaffirmed what we have seen all too frequently in recent years," said Gary Pruitt, AP's chief executive. "The systems created to give citizens information about their government are badly broken and getting worse all the time."

More concerning is the prosecution of whistleblowers during Obama's presidency and increased electronic surveillance programs to track down government employees who speak to the press. Robert Greenwald, director of the film *War on Whistleblowers* told me:

"Journalists more and more are being targeted, are being threatened, pressure is being put on them. The Obama administration is literally punishing the whistleblowers, trying to pass laws that make it harder for whistleblowers, and the danger is the only way we find out about the national security state is by these people coming forward."

Government transparency is not likely a word that future historians will attach to the Obama legacy, and that's a shame considering the previous administration was no hero in that department either. Transparency answers what government officials are doing with taxpayer money. Transparency informs Americans what decisions our officials are making on our behalf.

It's this simple: Transparency keeps politicians out of trouble and the rest of us free.

On race (the topic I had spent so much time discussing with Obama during our interview in 2007) a CNN poll six years into his presidency found four in ten Americans believed race relations had actually worsened. More revealing, only twenty percent of Democrats believed race relations had improved. In 2015, Obama, clearly disappointed hate crimes were still happening, shocked many people by using the "N" word during an interview: "Racism, we are not cured of it. And it's not just a matter of it not being polite to say nigger in public. That's not the measure of whether racism still exists or not. It's not just a matter of overt discrimination. Societies don't, overnight, completely erase everything that happened 200 to 300 years prior."

One thing is becoming clear as Obama nears the end of his presidency: Despite electing our first African American president, the deep divisions on race remain, and will continue to be an issue for the next administration and beyond.

I do believe, however, as the dust settles, and future Americans look back at the Obama years, they will see a very historic period. Our first African-American president, who faced unprecedented partisan opposition, yet won a second term. Love it or hate it, he was the first president to achieve a large-scale healthcare law. On his watch we finally captured and ended the reign of terrorist Osama bin Laden. His economic policies backed our nation's economy off the cliff it was dangling over when he was sworn in as president. The jobless rate fell to just above five percent in mid-2015 (although the number of severely unemployed Americans, nearly 30 million, remained stubbornly high). And he kept a promise, as we had discussed in my 2007 interview, to open dialog with Cuba. His administration re-established diplomatic relations with that nation situated 90 miles off the coast of Florida, and in 2015, the United States opened an embassy in Havana.

A growing appreciation by the American people for his record as he nears the end of his presidency is the only way the Democratic nominee in 2016 has a chance of winning. Al Gore couldn't do it in 2000 (although he got more popular votes than Bush) after eight years of Clinton. McCain couldn't do it in 2008 after eight years of Bush.

In fact, only once in my lifetime, as I mentioned before, has the same party won a third term. It's a hard feat to pull off.

PART THREE:
THE BIG BALLYHOO

THE CONVENTIONS

The national political party conventions are the biggest circus on earth! It's the ultimate big top where celebrities replace the clowns, the media replaces the tigers, the delegates act as jugglers, and the politicians provide the freak show. Everything under this massively expensive big tent is designed for television. The lighting, seating, teleprompters, broadcast booths, balloons, confetti, retractable stage, and those "homemade" looking signs held by the carefully cued cheering supporters. Even the American flag can go from red, white and blue to salmon, azure, and eggshell to look a little sharper on TV. All of the events are timed down to the second for the optimum prime time coverage.

While the relevance of modern conventions is debatable, they still provide some unique, and unforgettable, moments. Grab some popcorn, and let me share with you some highlights.

TAMPA

We arrived in Tampa to cover the Republican National Convention and immediately headed over to the Tampa Bay Times Forum. It was Sunday, but the producers wanted my colleague Tracy Townsend to be live on the 11 p.m. news to report on how Hurricane Isaac was affecting the start of the convention.

We found the seats for the Ohio delegation front and center on the convention floor. These were VIP seats, no other way to describe them. Not surprising considering Republicans must win Ohio or lose the White House. On one chair there was a copy of the *Tampa Bay Times,* which featured the headline:

ISAAC INTRUDES; DAY 1 CANCELED

This was a rough start for the Republicans. With a hurricane—and its eighty mile-per-hour winds and torrential rain falling—roaring through

Tampa, there were few people actually in the huge facility. The first day of the convention had already been canceled. A Republican National Committee spokesman told us convention officials were working with the Secret Service on a plan if the 50,000 elected officials, reporters, and delegates needed to be evacuated.

This was serious stuff.

Isaac forced Louisiana Governor Bobby Jindal to remain in his state and miss the convention. Jindal was trying to rehabilitate his image after a disastrous response he had delivered to President Obama's State of the Union in 2009. In Columbus earlier in the year, I asked Jindal if he would like a do-over: "Absolutely, I think the substance of the speech still stands, but the delivery could have been vastly better. I shouldn't try to read a teleprompter, the president is very good at that, I'm not, I'm better speaking off the cuff and in front of live groups."

Jindal at the time was jockeying to be Romney's running mate—as he had with John McCain four years earlier—and I was struck by his unapologetic, some may call it creepy, ambition. Fast-talking and restless, it surprised no one when Jindal entered the 2016 presidential race.

Back in Tampa it was only 9 p.m., and my analysis of the convention wouldn't start until the following day, so while Tracy, photographer Steve Maguire, and special events producer Rochelle Young prepared for the live shot on the floor, photographer Andy Wallace and I decided to do a little sightseeing in the facility.

That's right, we were a five-person crew covering the political conventions. That kind of entourage for a local news team at political conventions is almost unheard of today. Our bosses Tom Griesdorn and Elbert Tucker had decided to spare no expense in making sure central Ohio's news leader had the dominant political coverage at both conventions. This wasn't just a promo slogan for them; they wanted to prove it with our content. In a year when the candidates and the Super PACs would be spending so much money on the Ohio airwaves, our company believed voters deserved some actual news and analysis beyond the thirty-second campaign ads.

With practically nobody in the building (or so we thought), Andy and

I found a random service elevator and decided to do a little scout work to figure out where various events would be happening throughout the week in case we had to cover them.

Our first stop was on a floor where we found about 100 beautiful hand-crafted wooden captain's chairs, with personal brass plaques (complete with Mitt Romney's autograph) still covered in plastic. The chairs were for the "Founding Partners"—each member committed to raising at least a million dollars for the Romney campaign.

Another level featured "The Lounge," a private bar with big leather seats and a fantastic view where the special VIPs (and by that I mean large corporate supporters) could watch the proceedings at all hours. I'd be willing to bet it was only full on the final night for the acceptance speeches. Contributing a lot of cash to a presidential campaign didn't mean desiring to watch the political sausage being made.

It was back to the service elevator and on up to the third level. As the doors opened, there was my friend Steve Scully from C-SPAN, standing there like something out of a movie.

"Steve!" I said.

"Jim!" he responded. "Are you here for the party?"

The party? *What is he talking about?*

I looked at Steve. Then looked at Andy. And back at Steve.

"Of course we are!" I answered.

Steve, who was also president of the White House Correspondents' Association, led us down the hallway to where a private party was being held. It was like one of those famous Washington cocktail parties except this one was in Tampa.

There was Chuck Todd from NBC. Jake Tapper from ABC was nearby. Norah O'Donnell from CBS was chatting to a small group. Wolf Blitzer from CNN, beard and all, was keeping court too.

And who was there mingling with the press? The five Romney sons: Tagg, Matt, Josh, Ben, and Craig, a group looking a lot like a Republican boy band. None were drinking, but all were seemingly enjoying their time with the national press corps.

Steve showed us around and then left Andy and I to "help ourselves," so we ordered up a couple beers and joined in the conversation. "That hurricane could shut this party down" was a popular topic. "Can Romney carry Ohio?" was the most popular question to us.

After spending about an hour in our own version of the "Party Crashers," we headed back to the service elevator for the ride back down to the convention floor. There we saw CNN's Piers Morgan by himself (and we let him stay that way) and Candy Crowley (who I tracked down and spoke to like a stalker). Knowing our colleagues were still busy working, Andy and I agreed we would skip telling the others about the private party until much later.

After Tracy's live shot at 11, we had to walk about a mile out of the security zone in the torrential rain. I had anchored hurricane coverage while in Myrtle Beach, but never tried to walk around in one. When we finally made it back to our hotel, we had serious questions on whether the Republicans would have to shut down the convention altogether.

The following day in the CBS News booth Bob Schieffer, the long-time newsman and moderator of *Face the Nation*, told me, "This is a very difficult path for Republicans. If this storm barrels into New Orleans—and don't forget this is the seventh anniversary this week of Hurricane Katrina—if it barrels into New Orleans with great force, the people here can't be seen partying and dancing and having a big time."

Isaac moved east and the Republicans started their convention on Tuesday.

That morning at their hotel, Ohio's GOP delegates were treated to briefings by strategist Karl Rove, former secretary of state Condoleezza Rice, and two of Romney's sons. The campaign was loading up the Ohio activists with insight and inspirational speeches, knowing enthusiasm back home was critical. "Winning Ohio is never easy, and we've got a lot of hard work to do," Jo Ann Davidson, former speaker of the Ohio House of Representatives told me.

Several Ohioans—John Boehner, John Kasich, and Rob Portman—would be prominent at the GOP lectern during prime time. On Tuesday, a few hours before his speech, Kasich met with Ohio reporters to give us a sample of what he would be telling the delegates:

"If you're not the presidential or vice presidential nominee, people are moving around on the floor and there's lots of noise. So, I was thinking yesterday maybe I'll just yell 'HEY! Quiet down!' and see how that goes over!" Kasich told us while laughing. "I have sort of a little outline, sort of the way I deliver the State of the States. They've loaded some stuff, kind of the outline, into the teleprompter. I probably won't use that."

For Ohio statehouse reporters, listening to Kasich wing a speech was nothing new. He had gone off-the-cuff during his prior State of the State speeches, all remembered for being long and wordy. "This could be entertaining," I whispered to Tracy.

From our broadcast location, above the convention floor, we could look down to our right and watch the speakers, and to our left we could see the giant teleprompter on the wall in front of them. They could read off the teleprompter and appear to be looking directly into the camera positioned just above.

There was a long, rectangular red light above the teleprompter. When it was off, the speech was running on time. When it turned solid red, it meant time was up. When it started blinking, it meant the speaker was seriously putting the prime time schedule at risk.

From the moment he started his speech Kasich ignored the teleprompter, instead looking down at his index cards and notes. The version of his speech approved by the Romney camp, no longer lined up with what Kasich was saying.

"The poor person running the teleprompter, trying to figure out what Kasich is doing," I said to our producer Rochelle as we watched from our broadcast perch above. Soon Kasich's script on the giant teleprompter was running backwards as Romney staffers behind the stage were frantically trying to figure out what was happening.

About five minutes into Kasich's speech the red light went on. "When you get into public service you must lead and do what's necessary, and I want to tell you the good news of where we are today in Ohio..." Kasich said with no signs of wrapping up.

He was, in fact, just getting started.

At about the seven-minute mark, Kasich mentioned he had been the

House Budget Committee Chairman and paused and pointed to a giant debt clock that was running above the convention floor. "I look at horror up at that clock," Kasich ad-libbed, putting his hand in his pocket, "that's the sword of Damocles hanging over our children's head!"

At this point the red light started blinking.

It took eight minutes, but Kasich finally shifted from his own accomplishments and said, "I am for Mitt Romney for President of the United States!"

The crowd applauded, but he wasn't finished. And the red light kept blinking.

"He fixed the Olympics and every American is proud of what he did in Salt Lake City..."

Blinking red light at nine minutes.

"Joseph Biden told me that he was a good golfer. And I played golf with Joseph Biden, I can tell you that's not true..."

Blinking red light at ten minutes.

Kasich had saved his kudos for Romney until nearly the very end. What the Romney camp had apparently taken out of his speech—the laundry list of accomplishments about himself—Kasich had reinserted.

The speech played well in the hall, and that night on the news I said, "The honorable mention for tonight goes to Governor John Kasich, who delivered his speech without a teleprompter. In fact, at one point, the teleprompter on the floor was going backwards. It was a gutsy move in this era of carefully choreographed conventions."

Republicans would let someone else go on without a teleprompter later in the week to more disastrous results.

During our coverage that night, Kasich joined us and said he was pleased with his speech, especially compared to those offered by Governors Scott Walker and Chris Christie which fell flat with the delegates:

"It went very well, I've spoken to a couple others and it didn't go so well. I called home and my daughter Reese answered and said, 'Daddy, you were awesome.' That's all I needed to hear."

Kasich also said national conventions should be cut back to three days and made this prediction: "We're going to get to the point these conven-

239

tions are brokered. It's going to happen one day, and there will be big fights on the floor and that will get everyone tuning in then."

The following morning, Rick Santorum spoke to members of the Ohio delegation at their hotel. Afterwards, I asked him whether he had "warmed up" to Mitt Romney since their brutal slug-fest in the primaries. "I really like Paul Ryan," he told me smiling.

Don't let it ever be said Republicans don't have their share of celebrities. While in Tampa we saw actor John Voight, country singer Trace Adkins, *Two and a Half Men* star Angus T. Jones, the Oak Ridge Boys, and Kid Rock, who provided the Romney camp with their official theme song, "Born Free."

What you should realize about our coverage during these conventions, or any breaking news story for that matter, is the tremendous effort it takes to collect information before it airs. Those sound bites with officials and video from events don't just magically appear during the newscast. In fact, we would start collecting it each day at breakfast while covering the Ohio delegation. But the focus of our coverage changes many times during the day and at some point we have to write, edit, and beam back everything we have to the station before it can "magically" appear on the news. Plus, you need a few minutes to apply makeup so you don't look like a sweaty mess on air. Yes, real men wear makeup (at least until one minute after the TV lights go off).

So it was about 4:30 p.m., at our deadline to feed all the video and sound, and thirty minutes before the 5 p.m. news, when we were cramming at our work area. I looked up and saw my idol, Tom Brokaw, enter the area.

"Tracy, look up!" I whispered. "Jim, don't do it!" she replied. There is a journalistic ethic that you don't approach network people like a groupie. I had watched Brian Williams, Scott Pelley, Charlie Rose, and other network types walk by without being phased.

But this was Brokaw.

"If he walks by this table I can't be held responsible," I whispered back. Sure enough, Brokaw passed right by and I leaped up so hard the metal chair collapsed in a loud clunk behind me.

"Mr. Brokaw, I know this is completely unacceptable, but you're the reason I'm in this business," I stopped him in his tracks. "You really are a broadcasting god to me!"

Brokaw paused, looked at me, and laughed, "I am no god, but thank you." By this point Andy had his camera out and was taking a picture. Let me state for the record this was the only time—ever—I played fan in my profession.

But, hey, it was Brokaw! C'mon!

That night Rob Portman spoke shortly before Paul Ryan, who had surprised many by being chosen as Romney's running mate. Portman started his speech by making reference to it: "My name is Rob Portman, and they say I was on Governor Romney's short list of vice presidential candidates. Apparently, it wasn't short enough." I watched his speech on the floor with the Ohio delegation and reported that night, "Many Ohio delegates are disappointed Portman is not on this ticket because it would have made life a lot easier for them to help carry the state in the fall."

For his part, I told viewers Paul Ryan "knocked it out of the park" after his speech, raising the enthusiasm level at the convention which had been severely lacking on the first night. "I'm the newcomer to the campaign, so let me share a first impression," Ryan told delegates. "I have never seen opponents so silent about their record, and so desperate to keep their power! They've run out of ideas. Their moment came and went. Fear and division are all they've got left."

The next day I ran into GOP pollster Frank Luntz who shared with me his latest polling from Ohio, which showed Obama maintaining a stubborn six-point lead. Luntz credited all those TV ads the Obama campaign had aired in the state during the summer, when Romney was cash-strapped and off the air, and said in his view those six points "will be very difficult to make up." The fact Luntz seemed so nervous about Ohio for Republicans is something that stuck with me the rest of the fall.

After interviews with Rudy Giuliani and Matt Romney on the floor of the convention, former RNC chairman Ed Gillespie told me about Ohio: "Richard Nixon said in 1960, you have to plant the flag in Ohio, and build out from there. So it's always been a vital state."

On the final night of the convention Mitt Romney delivered his acceptance speech, mixing the personal:

"Mom and dad were married sixty-four years. And if you wondered what their secret was, you could have asked the local florist because every day dad gave mom a rose, which he put on her bedside table. That's how she found out what happened on the day my father died. She went looking for him because that morning, there was no rose."

with the political:

"I wish President Obama had succeeded because I want America to succeed. But his promises gave way to disappointment and division. This isn't something we have to accept. Now is the moment when we can do something. With your help we will do something."

"He did everything he was supposed to do tonight," I told viewers after his speech. "He pointed out the high unemployment and low consumer confidence while giving us his vision to improve the economy and create jobs. He also spoke personally about his parents and family, warming himself up to the American people. But there's a good chance he won't be the only headline tomorrow."

Indeed he wasn't.

The headlines belonged to Hollywood legend Clint Eastwood, who addressed the delegates shortly before Romney's speech. He had refused to use the teleprompter, and the Romney camp had agreed to let him because, well, he was Clint Eastwood.

When he appeared at the lectern, to a cheering crowd, there was an empty chair by his side, a proxy for President Obama.

"So I, so I've got Mr. Obama sitting here, and he's, I was going to ask him a couple of questions." Eastwood said to the delegates and the millions watching on television around the country. "Do you just...you know...I know...people were wondering...you don't handle that? Okay," he mumbled looking at the empty chair. A moment later his imaginary conversation turned surreal, "What do you want me to tell Romney? I can't tell him to do that. I can't tell him to do that to himself. You're crazy, you're absolutely crazy!"

Immediately social media went into overdrive. "I'd feel better if I knew for sure that Clint doesn't see anyone in the chair," tweeted Larry Sabato, director of the University of Virginia's Center for Politics. Actress Mia Farrow wrote she thought Senator Marco Rubio, who introduced Romney following Eastwood's speech, was "rude to ignore invisible Obama sitting right there."

The Twitter handle @InvisibleObama had over twenty thousand followers within the hour. Tweeps (yes, that's a word) across the world started posting photos of themselves pointing at empty chairs with the hashtag "Eastwooding." One widely circulated post was of a Star Wars juxtaposition of a Princess Leia hologram standing on the chair. Despite the hilarity, this was not how the Romney camp had envisioned the final night of their convention. "It was campaign malpractice that the Romney managers sent out a dithering, clueless Clint Eastwood," Sabato wrote on his popular "Crystal Ball" blog.

I was watching with our crew from our vantage point above, and thought to myself *the crowd reaction has gone from excited and happy to confused and nervous.* The red light above the teleprompter began to blink frantically. Eastwood was running long and endangering pushing Romney's speech out of prime time on the East Coast.

"I've been watching these political conventions it seems like all of my life, and I've never seen a moment quite like that," I said on air that night. Eastwood later said, "the chair idea, that just came out of the air." No kidding.

Yes, it still makes my day.

CHARLOTTE

The weather was perfect when we arrived in Charlotte to cover the Democratic National Convention. No hurricane to worry about, but just two days after we left Tampa, the crew was dragging a bit.

"Tracy, have you ever had Bojangles' before?" I asked my colleague when we arrived at the press venue. "Never, is it good?" she responded. The fast food chain was one of my favorites in South Carolina and they were one of the few allowed in our press area. "This is going to be awesome for you!" I replied. And it was. There is nothing like a warm Bojangles' biscuit with honey poured all over it! Properly fed, we were ready to see the sights and sounds of this major North Carolina city.

As we walked around downtown Charlotte, I ran into my old friend Brad Dean from the Myrtle Beach Area Convention and Visitors Bureau, along with Mayor John Rhodes, who were outside the Blackfinn Saloon keeping watch over a fifteen-ton sand sculpture of President Obama. The sand sculptures four years earlier at the presidential debates in Myrtle Beach were so successful the city decided to take the South Carolina sand on the road.

"You know we're a bipartisan beach, Jim," Brad laughed. In truth, over a million people in Charlotte alone traveled to the Grand Strand each year, so having a presence at the largest political event in the world was perfect marketing strategy. Incidentally, Brad has a good Ohio connection. He played high school hoops, and is good friends, with Thad Matta, longtime head coach of the Buckeyes men's basketball team. It is indeed a small world after all.

While we were getting situated in Charlotte, President Obama was—where else?—in Ohio. He had already visited the state more than any other battleground. In Toledo, speaking on Labor Day, he told supporters at a rally, "We're on our way to our convention in Charlotte this week. But I wanted to stop here in Toledo to spend this day with you!"

On the first morning of the convention, Maryland governor Martin O'Malley spoke to the Ohio delegates. "Being Irish-American, I have my differences with the British, but I thought they ran the Olympics just fine, don't you?" O'Malley laughed, taking a jab at Romney who had, in London, questioned the city's readiness to host the Summer Olympics. O'Malley was aggressively courting several state delegations, clearly eying his own White House run in 2016.

Throughout the summer, I had reported on the lack of enthusiasm for the Obama reelection effort by labor, college students, and Independents compared to 2008. Joe Rugola, a longtime state labor leader, acknowledged to me, "It's inevitable that it will be a different election than it was four years ago, but that doesn't mean Democrats or Labor in general are less enthused or committed, not at all."

The Ohio delegation was led by former governor Ted Strickland, who was just itching to give a response to the address delivered by John Kasich a week earlier. "Well, I thought he said things that absolutely were not true," Strickland told me. "Ohio was not 38th in job creation when he took over, Ohio was sixth in the nation and number one in the Midwest." Strickland then credited Obama, not Kasich, for Ohio's recovering economy.

Hours before Strickland was scheduled to give his prime time address, Andy and I ran into him walking feverishly outside the convention building. "We are stuck in here," Strickland said, clearly irritated the security guards were not letting him outside the barriers to give a scheduled speech elsewhere in Charlotte. "It's like a maze inside these fenced areas, and after 45 minutes we've ended up right back where we started from," Strickland's wife Frances explained. For a time we walked with them, in the hot and muggy weather, hoping to find a magical person who could resolve the issue facing Ohio's former governor. We finally parted ways and I said to Andy, "Sure hope he makes it back inside for his speech."

Strickland delivered such a memorable speech that night, he was the top trending topic worldwide on Twitter. In a perfect warm-up act for First Lady Michelle Obama, Strickland offered this memorable one-liner: "If Mitt was Santa Claus, he would fire the reindeer and outsource the elves!" He then told the delegates, "The auto industry is standing today. The middle class is standing today. Ohio is standing today... President Barack Obama stood up for us, and now by God, we will stand up for him!" as the crowd roared approval.

Strickland's speech was "the best of his career," I said on the late news. Tracy added, "The governor sure was fired up. I said for a Methodist minister, he sure sounded like a Baptist minister!"

"One thing all Ohioans can agree on is that they were well-represented by both the Kasich and Strickland speeches at these conventions," I added.

The next day, Strickland was put in charge of digging the Democrats out of a hole. By a voice vote from the floor, delegates had removed God from the official party platform. President Obama was reportedly furious and demanded it be changed. Strickland, the minister, went to the floor and said, "I am here to attest and affirm that our faith and belief in God is central to the American story and informs the values we've expressed in our party's platform." God was back in the platform, but Democrats took a beating from Republicans on social media for the rest of the day.

Reporting live from these conventions is a logistical challenge. We were perched high above the floor (which provided an amazing backdrop) but we were scrunched together in a tight row on cheap plywood with a small handrail behind to prevent us from tumbling over into the abyss. Imagine standing there live as a producer back in Columbus is screaming in your IFB to standby while a dozen other reporters are talking as loudly as possible during their live shots, under the extremely bright television lights, with a crowd watching and complaining you're blocking their view.

In Charlotte, Tracy and I worked beside Azteca America reporters Roberto Ruiz and Armando Guzman. They were providing endless analysis for their Spanish network viewers, but it meant every time we went live we had two Spanish speakers next to us in addition to everything else going on. It took every bit of concentration to keep it mentally together but, hey, we're pros right?

Shortly after our 6 p.m. live shot on the third day, Andy and I decided to secure the camera and take a tour of the Charlotte Convention Center as we had in Tampa. We noticed on the fourth floor a lot of security when the elevator doors opened. There was no getting through without the proper credentials.

This was obviously the floor we needed to check out.

Andy mentioned a stairwell he had seen on the first floor. If we entered there, and walked up to the fourth floor, maybe we could get in. "What kind of security would that be?" I laughed, not believing it could work. Sure enough, when we reached the fourth floor, the door opened and we were in a hallway past the vision of all that security at the elevator.

Note to security at future conventions!

As we started to walk away from the elevators I said to Andy, "Let's appear as if we're too busy to be asked what the hell we're doing here." Sure enough, we were getting plenty of stares, but with the other credentials around our necks, who had time to stop us?

As we rounded a corner, we saw a suite marked for actor Kal Penn, who was speaking at the convention. Soon it became clear this floor was a VIP area for top Democratic contributors: movie stars, recording artists and... the Obama family.

Wait? The Obama family? That can only mean...

"Gentleman, where are you headed?" said the first Secret Service agent. I looked at Andy. We both were thinking the same thing—we were about to be arrested and would likely miss our 11 p.m. live shot, resulting in our immediate termination.

The two agents guarding a section at the end of the floor where Michelle Obama would be watching the proceedings with her daughters, waited for an answer. "We're reporters looking for the CBS booth," I stuttered. "We're lost," is all Andy could offer. The agents looked us over and one calmly said, "Gentlemen, I suggest you turn around and get off this floor."

"Whew—that was close," we both mumbled under our breath.

As we were walking back around toward the elevators, anxious to get off the fourth floor, a young man darted out of one of the VIP suites and frantically asked us, "are you here to interview will.i.am?"

Wait, what, interview will.i.am?

No lie, I'm a huge fan of the Black Eyed Peas—and I'm talking a fan way beyond "I've Got a Feeling." Not just a singer and rapper, will.i.am is a songwriter, producer, actor, and activist. In fact, he had written a song for Obama in 2008.

Even though we only had our cell phone cameras on us, I told the young man, "sure." Soon a few more news crews showed up and will.i.am appeared. As he started discussing some of the issues of the day, I whispered to Andy, "back up, I'm taking a selfie with will.i.am!" The resulting picture is one of my favorites from the conventions.

Democrats had star power at this convention. At one point we saw Jon Hamm and Jennifer Westfeldt on the floor. Then there were actresses Scarlett Johansson, Eva Longoria, and Jessica Alba. The Foo Fighters performed, as did Mary J. Blige, James Tayor, John Legend, and Tony Bennett.

Before one of my live shots, I walked into a CBS broadcast booth and bumped into Biff Henderson from the *Late Night with David Letterman* show. I had literally grown up watching Dave and his crew, and asked Biff if we could take a quick selfie. "I don't know why anyone wants their picture with me," Biff said smiling. "Because you work on one of the greatest talk shows in history," was my reply.

On Wednesday night, former president Bill Clinton was set to speak at the convention. At 6 p.m. I told viewers, "I honestly believe Clinton's speech is the most important thing for Barack Obama that will happen in Charlotte. Only he can get through to the white, male, business community in Ohio and convince them they should stick with this president's economic agenda."

My colleague Joe Hallett, also in Charlotte, agreed and told viewers, "Clinton's popularity cuts across all groups. He is a guy who worked with John Kasich to balance the federal budget. He gives Obama credibility, coming here with a 66 percent approval rating."

Looking at all the speeches from both conventions, Bill Clinton's was—by far—the best in my view.

"Since 1961, for fifty-two years now, the Republicans have held the White House twenty-eight years, the Democrats, twenty-four," Clinton said. "In those fifty-two years, our private economy has produced sixty-six million private sector jobs. So what's the job score? Republicans, twenty-four million; Democrats, forty-two million," as the crowd roared.

Clinton spoke for forty-eight minutes and said 5,895 words. His prepared text, which we were trying to read along with him in the booth, was only 3,136 words. That means Clinton ad-libbed a significant portion of his speech.

"In Tampa, did y'all watch their convention? I did," Clinton laughed. "In Tampa, the Republican argument against the president's reelection was actually pretty simple—pretty snappy. It went something like this: We left him a total mess. He hasn't cleaned it up fast enough. So fire him and put us back in!"

"Clinton was dynamite," Hallett told our viewers the next day. "He raised the bar for Obama tonight and it will be interesting to see if Obama can sell himself as well as Clinton did for him."

Before Obama's speech on the final night of the convention, I spoke once again to Bob Schieffer who told me, "I don't see how Romney wins if he loses Ohio. I think it probably comes down to Ohio."

Vice President Joe Biden delivered an energetic, personal speech, which may have been the best of his career. He landed a few body blows on Romney,

"I don't think he understood that saving the automobile worker, saving the industry, what it meant to all of America, not just autoworkers. I think he saw it the Bain way. Now, I mean this sincerely. I think he saw it in terms of balance sheets and write-offs." and praised his boss for bringing a terrorist to justice, "Barack understood that the search for bin Laden was about a lot more than taking a monstrous leader off the battlefield. It was about righting an unspeakable wrong. It was about healing an unbearable wound, a nearly unbearable wound in America's heart."

Where Biden scored points, Obama's speech fell flat, especially compared to Bill Clinton's and some of the others earlier in the week.

"Our friends down in Tampa," Obama told the audience watching, "want your vote, but they don't want you to know their plan. And that's because all they have to offer is the same prescriptions they've had for the last thirty years. Have a surplus? Try a tax cut. Deficit too high, try another. Feel a cold coming on? Take two tax cuts, roll back some regulations, and call us in the morning."

"I thought it was a very effective speech, and it was wise to surround himself with his allies in this fight; his wife Michelle, and Bill Clinton," I said on-air that night about Obama's acceptance speech. "He went right after Mitt Romney painting him as a champion of the rich. He pointed out his record, ending the war in Iraq, killing bin Laden, and saving the auto industry, but he failed to offer a lot of specifics about his plans to lower the debt, put people back to work, and restore consumer confidence."

As we wrapped up our coverage I told viewers, "The bottom line for

Ohioans at the conclusion of both of these conventions? Reset the clock. We are back at square one! Everything is even. This presidential campaign is now a mad sprint to the finish line."

A QUESTION OF BIAS

After the conventions, and shortly before the election, I was speaking to a civic group in Columbus about the news business when someone asked me, "What do you know about politics, you're just another liberal journalist?"

The statement—and it's not the first time it's been said and certainly won't be the last—made me chuckle. Broadcasting is what I had wanted to do all my life, but it was not my first professional career and I entered the business late—in my early thirties. I share this part of my story with you here so that we can transition into an honest and educated conversation about "bias" in the media.

The fact is, I know a great deal about campaigns, political parties, and behind-the-scenes polling and fundraising because I've been there.

In the trenches. For nearly a decade.

As a teenager growing up in the 80s, I was a dedicated "teenage Republican" inspired by the idealistic Ronald Reagan. My first vote for president was the year he won forty-nine of fifty states. Talk about a unified country.

I went on to be elected the youngest Republican county chairman in the country, chosen the Arizona GOP "Man of the Year" in 1990, and elected a Bush Delegate to the Republican National Convention in 1992.

Add a run for statewide office to my resume at the age of twenty-eight (unsuccessful but no regrets), and a five-year stint as congressional press secretary to my conservative friend J.D. Hayworth, and you have a pretty good understanding of how grassroots politics works.

Am I still a Republican today? Nope. I re-registered as an Independent when I signed my first contract in the news business. For over fifteen years I have done my best to officiate the political fights fairly and most of my work is available today on YouTube for the world to judge.

People have asked how I could turn off my personal political views so quickly. It was actually quite easy having never been particularly ideological. I have always preferred to be seated at a round table with multiple points of view rather than a rectangle one with everyone agreeing and saying the same thing.

I'm sure that's true for the others in this unique journalism fraternity of former politicos who have turned into broadcasters. ABC News anchor Diane Sawyer was a press assistant in the Nixon administration and helped the former president write his memoirs after he resigned. CNN anchor and former ABC White House correspondent Jake Tapper served as the press secretary for Congresswoman Marjorie Margolies-Mezvinsky. And my hero Tim Russert, NBC News Washington Bureau Chief and the late, great moderator of *Meet the Press* (and still dearly missed) was a political strategist and operative who was once Chief of Staff to senator Daniel Moynihan, and a counselor to New York governor Mario Cuomo.

"I was a little skeptical to learn that Mr. Russert would be moving to the news business," said Adam Nagourney, political reporter for the *New York Times*. "But after watching him over the course of four presidential campaigns, it was an adjustment that he made completely and easily."

Russert, who moderated *Meet the Press* for nearly seventeen years, said he followed this advice from Lawrence Spivak, the show's founder: "The job of the host is to learn as much as you can about your guest's positions and take the other side. And to do that in a persistent and civil way."

In my view, each one of the above has established an impeccable record of fairness while offering an expertise—something insiders respect in the reality of the political process.

So it is from the knowledge of all these political experiences I have incorporated into my reporting and analysis. My television work through nearly two decades has earned various industry awards, but the most rewarding accolades to me have come from political activists— on both sides—who have respected and acknowledged the effort I've made to be balanced in my government and campaign reporting.

In fact, when I left WBNS 10TV in Columbus at the end of 2014, three members of Congress, Democrat Joyce Beatty and Republicans Steve Stivers and Pat Tiberi, each stopped by the newsroom to see me off. Both of Ohio's U.S. Senators—Democrat Sherrod Brown and Republican Rob Portman—called to wish me well, as did the state Republican Party chairman Matt Borges and his Democratic counterpart David Pepper. Political strategists from all sides—as was the case when I left South Carolina—attended my farewell party in Columbus. That bipartisan sendoff made me feel great.

No one really loves the referee, but coaches and players admire those who call the games fairly. That's all I've tried to do.

So with this background in both politics and journalism, let me try to get the facts separated from the fiction on this question of media bias. I don't intend this chapter to be a definitive and final word on media bias. It's simply my take after decades in and around politics and the press. Let it spur debate and get people thinking about it from a new perspective.

To answer this question—and it's important especially in battleground states like Ohio where the presidency is often decided—you must first understand what it is we in the media do. A political reporter's job is to challenge an elected official, make them explain policy decisions, hold them accountable for mistakes, and explore what it is, exactly, they want to do for the future.

None of that is bias. It's journalism. And both sides complain regularly about it.

I wouldn't be doing my job properly if I didn't have regular "discussions"—sometimes heated—with people from all sides of the political aisle. My job isn't to write a newsletter with your point of view. My job isn't to make a politician look good, although it is never my intent to make them look bad. It's to get answers to the tough questions of the day. There is no big invisible liberal or conservative mothership hovering in the sky beaming down what to say or ask.

To understand the television news business, you must first know the business structure of a TV station. First, an ownership group hires a general manager, who spends a great deal of their time worrying about sales. If you don't have ads on the station, you can't pay salaries. Now consider: If your station is "too biased" on anything, you run the risk of losing accounts. And a GM never looks to lose accounts!

Within the newsroom at that TV station, you have a news director who leads the other managers (assistant news director, senior executive producer, managing editor) along with the producers and assistant producers (of which there are usually over a dozen depending on what sized market and how many shows), reporters, photographers, editors, and anchors.

In many speeches I've given to various groups through the years, I've always stated the most important person in the newsroom each day—in my view—is the producer. Like an artist with a blank canvas, this person picks the lead story for the newscast, what other stories will make it (and those that don't), the length of time each story receives along with where reporters will be fronting the information out live. Most producers are writing most of the scripts for anchors too (although anchors can modify the script to put in their own words so it sounds more natural).

Most newsrooms, regardless of size, are driven by four major "sweeps" periods each year in February, May, July, and November. The results of those ratings numbers help out the sales department and determine how much a station can charge for those thirty-second commercials.

Viewer research has shown through the years that political and government stories generally rate low on their list of "favorites." Shootings, fires, burglaries, accidents, shootings (yes I said that twice) and of course weather top the list. Thus, a producer each night generally tries to find stories related to what viewers want most. Trust me, from all the producers I've worked with through the years, biased political coverage is the least of their goals.

In fact, my experience with political bias in the newsroom isn't based on liberal or conservative, it's whether I can get ninety seconds instead of just one minute from a producer to tell my story (some producers like politics, most tolerate it, some hate it). And that's based on ratings, not ideology.

In order for there to be daily political bias in television news—as is so commonly alleged—there would have to be pressure from the GM, to the news director, to the producer, to the reporter. Sorry conspiracy lovers, but politics just isn't that big of a concern inside most newsrooms, and research shows it doesn't drive the ratings.

That's not to say it never happens. In fact, I believe media bias in some places is real, obvious, and growing every day. You may be surprised where it is.

When I was growing up in the 1970s, there were three television networks and the evening news anchor had enormous influence. Walter Cronkite was at the top of that list. In 1968, Cronkite flew to Vietnam to report on the war effort first-hand and, according to historian David Brinkley, was "sickened" by what he found, and felt "conned" by Democratic president Lyndon Johnson. When he returned from his trip, he editorialized at the end of a broadcast that the Vietnam War was "at a stalemate" and Johnson reportedly reacted, "If I've lost Cronkite, I've lost the country." A month later, LBJ told the nation he would not seek reelection.

Then a few years later came the coverage of Watergate during the presidency of Republican Richard Nixon. Led by reporters Carl Bernstein and Bob Woodward of the *Washington Post,* the TV networks closely followed the developments of the scandal that would lead to Nixon's resignation—the only time in American history that's happened. As details about Watergate emerged, Nixon and his top aides introduced the notion of a "liberal media bias"—as if CBS, NBC, and ABC were responsible for making him cover up a crime. Supporters who loved Nixon, who had overwhelmingly been reelected in 1972, picked up the rhetoric and blamed the press for all his troubles. Thus the era of "liberal media bias" was born and has been repeated without much question for over a generation.

But does the claim still make sense in the vast media world forty years after Nixon's departure from office? Let's take a quick look.

LOCAL NEWS

When it comes to local news, Sinclair Broadcast Group has spent nearly $3 billion over the past few years and now owns 162 television stations in seventy-nine markets. That's about 40 percent of all local television stations across America, including some in key presidential battleground states.

Think of that for a second. One ownership group now runs four in ten local news stations, including some key markets in swing states where the presidency is decided.

Sinclair is run by the Smith family, who have donated tens of thousands of dollars to Republican candidates and conservative causes through the years. And their obvious lean to the right shows up in local news products.

Before the 2012 election, Sinclair stations in Ohio and other battlegrounds aired a corporate-produced "news special" featuring partisan criticism against President Obama. The "news special" preempted *World News with Diane Sawyer* in Columbus during a critical ratings period. Main anchor Yolanda Harris later tweeted "I had no choice" and "I need my job" in answering criticism for reading copy written by Sinclair executives.

Before the tightly contested 2004 presidential election, Sinclair executives had considered airing a documentary attacking John Kerry's military record. They backed down only after threats of an advertiser's boycott.

Sinclair's affiliates across the country have broadcast regular "town hall" infomercials produced by conservative strategist Armstrong Williams and featuring Dr. Ben Carson, a conservative who officially announced his 2016 presidential bid on Sinclair stations.

Sinclair also provides a Washington, D.C.-based conservative commentator for their local affiliates to use in their regular newscasts. Former CBS reporter Sharyl Attkisson, who I'll discuss later, hosts a Sunday morning "mini-Fox News" investigative political show for Sinclair-owned affiliates.

Charles Lewis, the founder of the investigative Center for Public Integrity, said about Sinclair employees, "They are stuck with an idiosyncratic owner with its own political views and agenda. It's a nightmarish scenario for journalists."

So the right-leaning Sinclair is now a dominant player in local news. What about cable?

CABLE NEWS

When it comes to cable television, Fox News dominates in the ratings. The president of Fox News is Roger Ailes, an Ohioan, who was a media consultant for three Republican presidents. Former Republican National Committee chairman Lee Atwater, who we discussed earlier, called Ailes a "soul brother." They worked closely together in the 1988 Bush campaign, which featured the Willie Horton ads.

In fact, Ailes is responsible for one of the most memorable moments in political television history. In January 1988, he insisted an interview between Bush and Dan Rather about the Iran-Contra scandal be conducted live during the *CBS Evening News*. Ailes sat off-camera during the interview using cue cards to prompt the vice president. When he felt Rather was too aggressive in his questioning, Ailes held up a card which said, "WALKED OFF THE AIR." It was a reminder of Rather storming off the CBS News set several months earlier after his newscast had been preempted by women's tennis.

Bush saw the card and said, "It's not fair to judge my whole career by a rehash on Iran. How would you like it if I judged your career by those seven minutes when you walked off the set in New York?" The stunned Rather, speechless for a few seconds, continued on but the showdown made headlines and helped Bush secure the GOP nomination.

Ailes is the man who now runs Fox News.

Fox News producers—and I'm talking newscasts, not the commentary shows like Bill O'Reilly—stack their rundowns to the political right. I watched Fox News and CNN for months side-to-side, and noted whenever there was positive economic news (like a lower unemployment number), Fox featured "experts" who pointed out what was still wrong with the economy. When there was bad economic news, it would be repeated throughout the day. Anything that could hurt Republican congressional leadership was minimized. As the 2016 campaign heats up, Fox News has consistently targeted Hillary Clinton in stories, while little to no attention has been paid to the flaws of the many GOP candidates. It's not just the repeated coverage of Benghazi, or donations to the Clinton presidential library, or those deleted emails, but actual thirty-minute specials, one called "The Tangled Clinton Web."

It's not just in political coverage where we see this rightward slant. In early 2015, there were numerous stories before the Oscars about the movie *American Sniper* (a patriotic military film directed by Clint Eastwood, who gave that memorable speech at the 2012 Republican National Convention) but little mention of the other nominees. In fact, after the movie lost for Best Picture, the discussion in various segments on Fox News was, "why didn't *American Sniper* win, is Hollywood too liberal?" instead of an examination of *Birdman,* the movie that did.

Fox News is the star-spangled, red, white, and blue anti-Obama and anti-Clinton network.

There is nothing wrong with the Republican Party having its own news channel. In fact, in the 19th century, American newspapers made clear their bias—think the *Arizona Republican* or *Arkansas Democrat.* But let's be honest here and call it like it is: Fox News broadcasts from the right-field of American politics, it's biased, and it dominates in the ratings.

Yes, MSNBC is out in left field and also has biased prime time commentary shows in an effort to compete with (or copy) Fox News. The difference is they will always—always—fail because their news division is so intertwined with NBC News, which is not produced with a deliberate political bent. Fox News producers know they're located in right field and their rundowns reflect it from sunup to sundown. Unless MSNBC's mothership becomes blatantly leftist—which it is not—it will never enjoy anywhere near the freedom or success.

As for CNN, the days of left-leaning Ted Turner are over, replaced by the pragmatic Jeff Zucker. "CNN will be the only news channel that doesn't take a side," Zucker told advertisers in 2014.

Of the three big cable news stations, CNN is the only one producing more news than commentary. The network is trying to play center field, between the other two stations, but is getting killed by Fox News in the ratings.

In the old days, CNN featured the political show *Crossfire,* which allowed a liberal and conservative strategist to go after each other and their guests. It was mandatory viewing for us political geeks when I was in college. But that concept seems antiquated now compared to the constant shouting on both Fox News and MSNBC.

True, many Republicans hate CNN. Former House majority leader Tom DeLay called it both the "Clinton News Network" and the "Communist News Network." Liberals have been angry too, some claiming CNN was biased in support of George W. Bush following the 9/11 attacks and first year of the Iraq War.

But, let's be honest here: CNN's endless coverage of the Malaysian Airlines plane disappearance in 2014 had nothing to do with politics, left or right. It was driven by ratings. "Breaking News" has become CNN's specialty, and that isn't driven by political ideology.

CNN today is trying to cover news from around the whole world. It should be important for Americans—citizens of earth's remaining superpower—to have a better understanding of the people, cultures, religions, and events around the planet. When Fox News is on yet another segment questioning Hillary Clinton's role in Benghazi, CNN is live in Nepal where an earthquake just killed thousands of people. That doesn't make CNN "liberal," it makes them a true news organization.

Pew Research found in 2014 that the ideological makeup of CNN viewers is 32 percent conservative, 30 percent moderate, and 30 percent liberal. Compare that to the 60 percent of Fox News viewers who describe themselves as conservative, 23 percent moderate, and 10 percent liberal.

CNN is trying to occupy the cable news center in an era where politicos on both sides would rather tune-in and hear their own opinions. Unfortunately that doesn't make it a ratings winner—at least not yet.

So right-leaning Sinclair is a dominant player in local news, and Fox News is a dominant force on cable. What about radio?

TALK RADIO

When you turn off Fox News and turn on your radio, there is a good probability you'll hear Rush Limbaugh. He has been the king of talk radio for decades. And if you don't hear Rush, you'll probably find other conservatives like Sean Hannity, Mark Levine, or Glenn Beck somewhere on the dial.

Progressives and liberals tried to compete on the radio with conservatives some years back with *Air America,* but it was nothing short of a mismanaged ratings and financial disaster. Yes, *National Public Radio* is available and House Republicans have tried continually to defund it. But surveys have found most Americans do not believe NPR, with in-depth daily reporting on both *Morning Edition* and *All Things Considered,* is biased.

iHeartMedia, formerly *Clear Channel,* owns or programs most of the nation's strongest, 50,000-watt AM radio stations—859 total radio stations in over 150 markets if you're counting—and it's there you'll find your favorite conservative voices.

Like Sinclair in local news and Fox News on cable, Rush Limbaugh and other conservative voices dominate the radio airwaves. What about newspapers?

PRINT MEDIA

Newspaper readership is on the decline—a steady and serious drop each year as younger generations get their news elsewhere. Daily newspaper circulation is down by more than seven million readers over the past decade according to the Newspaper Association of America. Most people under the age of thirty do not subscribe to a daily paper and never will.

The influence on elections from the editorial page has never been historically great. Yes, the editorial page of the *New York Times* is liberal. Has that ever won a Democratic presidential candidate the electoral votes in Florida or Ohio? No. Did the endorsement of George W. Bush from the conservative editorial board of the *Columbus Dispatch* help him win Ohio in 2004? Yes.

But you can't claim media bias from editorial pages—that's where you expect different viewpoints—you have to examine the reporting. And whether it's the *New York Times* or the *Columbus Dispatch,* the political reporters I've met and worked with are interested in finding—and scooping their colleagues on—good stories. I couldn't tell you much about their political ideology.

Sure, if conservatives want their own national newspaper with an editorial bent, there is always the *Wall Street Journal* to counter the *New York Times.* Daily newspapers also feature more conservative syndicated columnists (think George Will) than liberals on their editorial pages. And when it comes to choices on the Internet, either news or commentary like *Newsmax,* conservatives have plenty of choices there too.

There is also this fact: In 2012, Mitt Romney received a majority of newspaper endorsements in critical swing states—the states that actually determine the winner. Romney received twenty-four editorial endorsements to Obama's fifteen—that's a landslide. In Ohio, Romney was endorsed by the *Cincinnati Enquirer* and the *Columbus Dispatch,* yet still lost the state.

As for *TIME, Newsweek* and the other formerly influential weeklies, they are largely forgotten in political land. Once a week news is now too old and too stale for readers who have access to the web. *U.S. News & World Report* is gone altogether. Like dinosaurs, they once ruled the land but now find themselves primarily in museums.

Incidentally, the *Associated Press,* where many local papers get their national and world news, is not immune to regular criticism from both the political left and right. After reading wire copy for years, my belief is the AP is a lot like C-SPAN. They put up hundreds of stories every day with just the facts, usually updated several times, if not more, as new information becomes available. Newspapers can take the AP copy and write their own headline, and radio and television can cut and paste information for their newscasts. But no news agency has fought harder on behalf of the U.S. Freedom of Information Act, and reported on the lack of transparency in both the Bush and Obama administrations, than the AP.

So right-leaning Sinclair is a dominant player in local news, Fox News is a dominant force on cable, conservative voices rule radio, and most newspapers have professional reporters independent of the editorial page, but what about network news?

NETWORK NEWS

As for the "big three" network newscasts in today's world, let me paint the picture. Walter Cronkite is no longer around. David Muir is the new generation of network anchor. His newscast features lots and lots of him. Every story he does, he's in it, the center of everything. The newscast also features a growing number of feature stories. And weather—national and regional. Anything viewers like during sweeps that helps the ratings go up and sell the ads. Muir, unlike Cronkite, is never going to sway the public with his commentary, nor is he ever going to command a high percentage of viewers because there are now too many choices.

Furthermore, do network producers go into work each day, look at a blank rundown, and think, "How do I get liberal political news in here?" No. They think, "I need a lead that people across the country will relate to in the first thirty seconds of the newscast or they'll change channels." And I'm willing to bet all network producers today check the weather map to see if they can lead with a big storm. Viewers love the weather, even though I usually cringe when I see it in a national newscast (big storms like hurricanes of course, but leave regional weather to local stations who can do it so much better).

True, right before the 2004 election, Dan Rather and CBS News botched a fifteen-minute *60 Minutes* report on President Bush's Texas Air National Guard service. Its claims were explosive, too rushed, and built on unverifiable documents. The controversy created by the sloppiness of the story forced Rather out of his anchor chair two months later along with a half-dozen other CBS News employees.

But if CBS News is so biased and liberal, why would Dan Rather, the face of the network, or anyone else for that matter, be shown the door for airing an inaccurate story about George W. Bush?

Four years later, when Katie Couric asked Governor Sarah Palin this hard-hitting question, "What newspapers and magazines did you regularly read before you were tapped for this to stay informed and to understand the world?" Palin answered, "I've read most of them, again with a great appreciation for the press, for the media. Um, all of them, any of them that have been in front of me all these years."

Conservatives pointed to this question as yet another example of "liberal media bias." The fact that a nominee for Vice President of the United States and a sitting governor could not name one newspaper or magazine she reads does not make Couric, or the network news, "liberal."

More recently, the issues for *Good Morning America* anchor and *This Week* moderator George Stephanopoulos relate more to his own stupidity and less about media bias.

In 1991, Stephanopoulos was among the first senior staffers to join Governor Bill Clinton's struggling campaign. After Clinton beat President George Bush in 1992, he became a key White House adviser. After four years in the West Wing, Stephanopoulos left and wrote a tell-all book about the Clintons. He called Bill Clinton, among other things, "an overgrown boy" and said both Clintons had a temper: "When Hillary was angry, you didn't always know it right away—a calculated chill would descend over time. Bill's anger was a more impersonal physical force, like a tornado. The tantrum would form in an instant and exhaust itself in a violent rush." And he wrote a lot more.

The Clintons, still in the White House, were livid. The *Washington Post* quoted one veteran Clinton aide saying about the book, "This is such a betrayal, George was family, he was that close." A close friend also told the paper, "The Clintons can't stand him."

Republicans weren't complaining at all about it.

After Stephanopoulos joined ABC News he refused to offer disclaimers about his White House days before interviews, which was a mistake. When Tim Russert interviewed Governor Mario Cuomo or Senator Patrick Monahan on *Meet the Press,* as an example, he would always offer the "full disclosure" that he had once worked for them. Then he would interview them in the same way as everybody else. In 2015, Stephanopoulos failed to disclose he had donated $75,000 to the Clinton Global Initiative before interviewing guests related to the topic.

Frankly, I was stunned by this poor decision-making, and would have avoided making those contributions due to the appearance of a conflict of interest. I am not alone in that assessment. Former ABC News reporter Ann Compton said, "It is an egregious, egregious failing, and George knows it."

Stephanopoulos admitted his mistake, apologized, and is working to restore his credibility. He will not moderate any GOP presidential debates in 2016, and I'd be shocked if he's asked to do any for the general election. The irony here is if Stephanopoulos were biased for the Clintons, he would have never written such a scathing book about them. Still, his poor judgement in failing to disclose large financial contributions to the Clinton Foundation has correctly damaged his reputation, at least through 2016.

Are there network reporters who have a differing view about media bias? Yes. Two come to my mind, and both Sharyl Attkisson and Bernard Goldberg have become quite wealthy becoming regulars on conservative media.

Attkisson, an award winning broadcast journalist, left CBS News after twenty years, citing frustrations with the network's liberal bias and a lack of investigative reporting. CBS claimed her coverage of the Obama administration had become agenda-driven, and executives questioned the impartiality of her reporting. Months after leaving CBS, Attkisson filed a $35 million dollar lawsuit against the Federal Government claiming the Obama administration had hacked her computers while she was doing stories on Benghazi, Fast and Furious, and Obamacare. CBS News confirmed her office laptop had been breached in 2013, but did not identify the party or parties behind it. In early 2015, an investigation by the Justice Department's Office of the Inspector General found no evidence that her personal computer was hacked, as she claimed in her book *Stonewalled: My Fight for Truth Against the Forces of Obstruction, Intimidation and Harassment in Obama's Washington.*

There is a lot going on here. We don't know what was happening inside the CBS newsroom as Attkisson's dismay with her colleagues was growing. But what I can say, from experience in a newsroom environment, is that personality, and relationships, can go a long way. Reporters and producers don't have to be best friends, but over time, there must develop a level of mutual respect. If that doesn't happen, a reporter has an increasingly difficult time selling their story ideas to producers. I've seen it happen numerous times in my career. I'm not sure about Attkisson's relationship with her newsroom colleagues, but as she pushed to get more of her stories about the Obama administration on the air, if her reputation among producers had become strained, she would have had difficulty making her case. Poor working newsroom relationships don't necessarily have anything to do with a "liberal" bias. A third, fourth, or fifth story on Benghazi, with little new information, can also be viewed by a producer as a potential ratings killer, having nothing to do with ideology, as we discussed earlier.

Goldberg left CBS News after nearly thirty years and wrote a best-selling book about media bias. Leading up to his exit from the network, he had become increasingly angry with his colleagues, especially Rather, and wrote: "If CBS News were a prison instead of a journalistic enterprise, three-quarters of the producers and 100 percent of the vice presidents would be Dan's bitches." Because so much of Goldberg's book is dedicated to attacking Rather, with few other specific examples of actual bias ("There is no vast liberal media conspiracy, but it is group-think" he writes) it comes off more as an angry reporter who had reached a dead-end after thirty years in the same newsroom.

There was also this: While he was still working for CBS News, Goldberg wrote a scathing op-ed in the *Wall Street Journal* attacking his colleagues. It didn't go over real well. This goes back to what I said earlier; poor working newsroom relationships, and being on the outs with producers, can be the root cause of the problem, not bias.

Both Attkisson and Goldberg have their views, which have been widely embraced by the political right. Attkisson, as I wrote earlier, has her own political show on Sinclair, and Goldberg is a regular on Fox News. While they are two voices who have made quite a living from their opinions, I would point out there are thousands of other network news employees through the decades who have not voiced the same concerns.

STATISTICS

Some conservatives also point to the 2013 study of the media conducted by Indiana University journalism professors Lars Willnat and David Weaver. It found 50 percent of journalists are Independents, 28 percent Democrats, and 7 percent Republicans.

True, that's over a twenty-point spread between the R's and D's.

But let me add an important point here: The survey of over 1,000 journalists did not specify "government" or "statehouse" reporters. Most surveys regarding the media do not. That's critical because a food critic, concert reviewer, home repair expert, meteorologist, sports writer, or advice columnist may have no ethical reason to express a party identification because they will never report on areas having anything to do with politics. Journalism is a big arena, so be careful painting everybody with the same broad brush.

From another perspective, in my lifetime, Republican presidents have been in the White House 56 percent of the time (rounding forward to the end of Obama's second term). In addition, I've witnessed Republicans take back the majority in the House for the first time in forty years in 1994—a body they've now controlled for eighteen of the last twenty-two years. Today there are thirty-one Republican governors across the nation to eighteen for Democrats (one Independent). As of 2015, Republicans have a majority in sixty-eight out of ninety-eight state legislative chambers, the highest number in the history of the GOP. In fact, Republicans now control both the governor's office and the legislatures in twenty-four states, Democrats in only seven.

If the network news, and the media in general, has a "liberal" bias, they sure are doing a lousy job at influencing federal and state elections.

It has always been the job of the press to challenge those in elected office. Considering a vast majority of Republicans are serving in offices at every level all across the country, many conservatives may interpret constant tough questions from the media as bias. But it's not.

Frankly, if I had walked into journalism and discovered a vast liberal media conspiracy, with my background, I would be reporting it to you in this book. Others believe they did encounter it, and some of them are now employed by Fox News and Sinclair. I did not.

As a former delegate to the Republican National Convention—who wore a *"Rather Biased"* sticker on my Bush/Quayle shirt in Houston—I hope you will trust me when I say: The era of the Nixon-created "liberal media" is over and the era of unapologetic biased "conservative media" has begun. Many on the right know this to be true. Gone are the days of complaining about the media; now there is a concerted effort—key word "patience"—to turn it around.

Those on the left who remain quiet when it comes to this media bias argument remind me of the story of the frog placed in a pot of cold water on the stove as the temperature is slowly raised. Will it be too late when they finally notice they are boiling?

THE FALL IN OHIO

The day after his first televised debate with Vice President Richard Nixon in 1960, Senator John F. Kennedy was campaigning in Canton, Ohio. During the fall he made stops in Cincinnati, Dayton, Toledo, Elyria, Youngstown, Lorain, and Cleveland where crowds often numbered over 20,000. Yet, on election night it was Nixon, not Kennedy, who carried the Buckeye State.

JFK is the last person to lose Ohio and still win the presidency, and he never really got over it. "There is no city in the United States where I get a warmer welcome and less votes than Columbus, Ohio," JFK told an audience to laughter and applause in 1962.

That was a long time ago. Only about a third of America's current population was alive when Kennedy moved into the White House. Thus why all modern presidential candidates have spent more time in Ohio than any other state.

It's foolish to think you're going to be president without it.

In late fall, former secretary of state Colin Powell, a Republican who had served in the Reagan and both Bush administrations, endorsed Barack Obama for reelection. The next day he was scheduled to be at an event in Columbus.

"Absolutely no press" is the word our assignment desk got from The Ohio State University officials when an interview was requested. "Let me take care of that, put it in the rundown" is what I told the producers in the morning meeting. I had no idea how, but I left the station determined to speak to him.

Powell was on the OSU campus to address thousands of people at the Young Scholars Program. After we arrived, photographer Dave Schulte and I were escorted to the back of Mershon Auditorium and told we could record the first three minutes of his speech—but nothing else. As I peered at the stage, I thought Powell could have been speaking from Mars, and it would have seemed as close.

Powell had made the endorsement on the *CBS Morning Show* the previous day. "I think we ought to keep on the track that we are on, I voted for Obama in 2008 and I plan to stick with him in 2012."

So here he was now in the biggest battleground state, and I stared at the stage perplexed on how to get him to talk to me. Sensing my frustration, Schulte whispered to me, "I know where he has to exit."

One thing I learned early on in this business is that a good story requires a reporter and photographer working together. Teamwork. And Schulte had my back. I smiled at him, said "let's go," and we drove around to the back of the building where Powell's car and driver were parked in front of a barely visible door.

Schulte got out and chatted with the driver who said Powell didn't want to do interviews. Then an official from OSU came outside to inform us Powell would be walking from the door straight into the back of the SUV. "Would it be okay if we just stand here and maybe he'll change his mind if he sees us?" I asked. We were told, "okay, but it won't do any good, he is not talking."

About twenty minutes later, Powell emerged from the back door. Every minute that had ticked by seemed like a million years to me because it was so cold standing outside. "I am not leaving here without something," I muttered to myself.

"Mr. Secretary, do you have a minute to talk about Ohio?" I shouted at him, doing my best impression of Sam Donaldson. Powell, who had already opened his door, stepped back, paused, looked over and said, "sure."

Dave and I walked up to the SUV and I asked Powell, based on his endorsement the previous day, what message he wanted to send to Ohioans before the election:

"My advice for the wonderful people of Ohio is to take a look at the status of your state, how do you think it's doing, and vote accordingly."

Powell didn't mention Obama directly, but seemed to direct his message to the handful of undecided Ohio voters remaining that the economy was improving and while Obama had not been the perfect president, many in 2008 had hoped he was still the better alternative.

"We are the super-people," he told me. "There are no super-men or women who are coming. We the people are the ones who have to decide how best we're going to be governed."

When I asked him whether he was worried about the amount of money Super PACs for both presidential candidates were spending, Powell said, "if we reach a point where we prefer to destroy a person than debate a person, we'll no longer recognize America."

THE CASH

The proliferation of fundraising on presidential campaigns could be leading us to destruction. The U.S. Supreme Court blew the lid off any cash limitations in their Citizens United v FEC decision in 2010, and the campaign of 2012 gave us a glimpse of what's happening.

The controversial 5-4 ruling allows business and labor treasuries to raise and spend what they want for individual candidates each election cycle. (They have to do it, the law says, without "coordinating" with the candidates they support- wink, wink.)

In 2008, Citizens United, a conservative group, produced a negative documentary using corporate donations about Hillary Clinton called, *Hillary: The Movie* which they planned to air on television. The FEC said it violated campaign finance laws. Citizens United took the FEC to court, claiming a free speech violation, and the High Court agreed.

The decision invalidated a campaign finance law known as McCain-Feingold, named after two senators—John McCain, a Republican, and Russ Feingold, a Democrat—which regulated the financing of campaigns and reduced the influence of special interest money.

After the Citizens United decision, McCain ripped the five supportive justices on the Supreme Court, calling it "the most misguided, naive, uninformed, egregious decision of the United States Supreme Court I think in the 21st century. To somehow view money as not having an effect on elections, a corrupting effect on elections, flies in the face of reality."

For her part, Clinton has told voters if she wins the presidency in 2016, "I will do everything I can to appoint Supreme Court justices who protect the right to vote and do not protect the right of billionaires to buy elections."

But in reality, Clinton has benefited—a lot—from the ruling. Her "Ready for Hillary" PAC in 2014 alone raised $13 million. She has also promoted two huge Democratic Super PACs, "Priorities USA" and "Correct the Record," which combined are likely to raise hundreds of millions of dollars for her campaign in 2016.

An even worse lower court decision following the Citizens United ruling—SpeechNow.org v FEC—determined any limits on contributions to "groups" that make independent expenditures are unconstitutional. That means the limit of a maximum $5,200 donation to a candidate is meaningless. And that's where the Super Political Action Committees (Super PACs) have spawned.

Now individuals can make unlimited contributions to a Super PAC, which in turn, like a hired gun, does the dirty work for the candidates (without any coordination—wink, wink.) What's worse than Super PACs is Dark Money Groups—where wealthy contributors give anonymously to non-profits that keep their donations secret.

All of it legal, but incredibly shady.

The non-partisan Brennan Center found in the three federal elections held since Citizens United in 2010, there has been more than $1 billion in Super PAC spending. Just 195 individuals and their spouses gave almost 60 percent of that money—more than $600 million.

Let's think about that for a second. Less than two hundred Americans are spending over $600 million to influence elections.

Who are these people?

One is Sheldon Adelson, owner of the Las Vegas Sands casino. He was the top Romney contributor in 2012, giving $34.2 million. Another Romney backer was Harold Simmons, owner of Contran Corporation who gave $16 million. And Bob Perry, head of a Houston real estate empire, gave Romney $15.3 million.

Obama's top individual contributors were not as generous. Hollywood film producer Jeffrey Katzenberg donated $2.6 million. Irwin Jacobs, founder of Qualcomm, gave $2.1 million. Fred Eychaner, founder of

Newsweb Corp., and Jon Stryker, a philanthropist, both gave $2 million apiece.

In total, outside groups for Mitt Romney in 2012 outspent Barack Obama by $260 million and still lost. But the amount of money being poured into campaigns on both sides—from the U.S. Chamber of Commerce on the right to the labor unions on the left—gives transparency advocates cause for concern.

I'm all for the First Amendment and Free Speech—my job depends on it—but that doesn't mean everyone can yell "fire" in a crowded theater. We need common sense to prevail here. There is way too much political money in the stream, with laughable restrictions (wink, wink) on coordination between campaigns and Super PACs and those dark money groups.

I'm willing to put it in writing here in this book—there are some serious scandals just waiting to happen. The question isn't if, but when.

THE ADS

Two things are a certainty during the fall of every presidential election year in Ohio. First, on any given Saturday, most of the television sets in homes, bars, and restaurants across the state will be tuned in to the Buckeyes. Second, political ads will run back-to-back during every single commercial break during the game, news, prime time, and beyond.

Appearing on C-SPAN the week before the election, my friend Steve Scully, in amazement, asked me about the number of television ads running every hour. "Just this morning on your station, channel 10, there was a six minute commercial break, and in that six minutes, six different political ads aired," Steve said. "At what point is there a law of diminishing returns from all these ads?"

I responded,

"If your campaign has the money, you can't go silent if the other campaign is running ads. We now have early voting going on in Ohio. The vote in Ohio is today, it's this week. These candidates have even restructured their ads, talking directly into the camera, talking directly to Ohioans, knowing there are voters who will head to the polls today. This is probably just one of five states where this is happening, but keep in mind Ohio is key to both campaigns' strategy to 270 electoral votes."

The Obama and Romney campaigns spent about $150 million on television commercials in Ohio—more than in any other state (to answer where a lot of that campaign cash goes). Six of the top ten stations airing political ads in the country were in the Buckeye State. Ohioans saw a total of 219,414 political ads during the 2012 campaign—100,674 for Obama, 41,162 for Romney.

Whew.

If you're not from Ohio, or any of the other few battleground states, you have no idea why, come fall every four years, viewers can't wait to see the local car dealer ads again!

THE SCHEDULE

It's hard to describe to you the daily grind of covering the massive number of political events in Ohio. I can point to the two pairs of shoes I wore out in 2012, or several suits where the sleeves needed to be patched, or the dozens and dozens of press credentials from campaign events all across the state. But, maybe, it would help to show you part of my schedule from throughout the fall:

8/26-31 - REPUBLICAN CONVENTION, TAMPA
9/2-9/7 - DEMOCRATIC CONVENTION, CHARLOTTE
9/12 - Biden, Dayton
9/13 - Obama, Parma
9/17 - Obama, Columbus
9/24 - Romney, Lima
9/25 - Romney, Dayton
9/26 - Obama, Bowling Green
9/29 - Ryan, Columbus
10/1 - Obama, Mansfield
10/2 - M. Obama, Cincinnati
10/9 - Obama, Ohio State

10/10 - Romney, Sidney
10/10 - Romney, Mount Vernon
10/12 - Romney, Lancaster
10/15 - M. Obama, Delaware
10/17 - Obama, Athens
10/23 - Obama/Biden, Dayton
10/24 - Biden, Marion High School
10/25 - Romney, Columbus
10/29 - Romney, Avon Lake
11/1 - A. Romney, Easton
11/2 - Obama, Hilliard
11/2 - Romney/Ryan, West Chester
11/4 - Romney, Cleveland
11/5 - Obama, Columbus
11/5 - Romney, Columbus

The above list does not include appearances made by Obama and Romney earlier in the year, or those of their surrogates. It also doesn't include the campaign events covered by my colleagues at 10TV.

I'm not complaining at all. If you're going to be covering a presidential campaign you may as well be situated at Ground Zero. But it can be grueling at times. My secret for the endless traveling and hearing the same political speeches over and over again? Energy drinks and Skittles! Lots of them.

Here's a taste of my fall coverage from my live shots across Ohio:

Covering Romney, September 25, Dayton - On board Romney's campaign bus, we waited a few extra minutes to start the interview as Romney made, and then ate, a peanut butter and jelly sandwich. I remember thinking, *this could be the next leader of the free world and he's eating a PB&J!* I left that detail out and reported live at five, "I just finished a one-on-one conversation with Mitt Romney and he is strongly hinting Ohio is the key to his political future. There was a good crowd here today, about twenty-two hundred, and despite being slightly behind in the polls, he believes his economic message will play well here."

"We're going to win Ohio," Romney told me. "This is coming down to a battle for the direction of the country. The president represents higher taxes and bigger government. My message is going to create more jobs and bring manufacturing back to this country. I think that's what the people of Ohio want to see."

Covering Obama, September 26, Bowling Green - "No president with an unemployment rate this high has been reelected since Franklin Roosevelt, but Barack Obama maintains a slight lead in several swing states. His message in Bowling Green today to his supporters—vote early. That could be key to the Democrats' chances in Ohio."

The day I was covering the president in Bowling Green, we started our 6 p.m. newscast with a split box—Romney was live speaking in Toledo, and Obama was live speaking at Kent State. "It's been a dizzying dash across the state, with the candidates crisscrossing each other at one point," said anchor Kristyn Hartman.

Covering Biden, September 27, Columbus - "Beau Biden, Attorney General of the state of Delaware, and son of the Vice President, was working on undecided business voters today. I asked him if the gaffe-prone image of Joe Biden is a fair representation of his father?"

"My dad says what's from his heart and what's in his head," Biden told me. "I think that is why so many people love him, and look, he was the most watched speaker at the Democratic convention and I think that's because Americans relate to him and understand he says exactly what he believes."

Covering Ryan, September 29, Columbus - "Paul Ryan is here on a Saturday to watch the Buckeyes—he did the O-H-I-O—and then headed to Easton to be the speaker at a pro-gun group fundraiser. I was invited to sit down with him":

"Karl Rove says it may be time to write off Ohio," I asked Ryan. "No, we will not do that," he quickly responded. "Ohio is central to this. We really believe we can win Ohio. The president has been outspending us on TV enormously in Ohio. More to the point, the president has cluttered the airwaves with distractions and distortions to get people for focusing on the fact we can't afford four more years on these terrible policies."

Covering Michelle Obama, October 2, Cincinnati - It's the first day of early voting in Ohio—five weeks' worth—and First Lady Michelle Obama is in Hamilton County. Live at five I reported, "On the first day of early voting in Ohio the first lady had a simple message: 'Go vote today!' She told the nearly 7,000 supporters who packed the convention center here in downtown Cincinnati to march to the local election office as soon as she was done speaking."

Covering Obama, October 9, Ohio State - "The 15,000 supporters here at Ohio State make up the largest campaign rally we've seen this fall. The Obama campaign made it clear today they will be challenging Republican secretary of state Jon Husted and his decision to eliminate the weekend before election voting. They want the Supreme Court to overturn it. That final weekend traditionally benefits Democratic candidates and they feel it could be the difference in this election."

Covering Romney, October 10, Sidney - "We are here in the breadbasket of Ohio as Mitt Romney looks to build his support in these heavily Republican counties that were lukewarm for John McCain four years ago. Romney is still basking in the glow of the positive reviews of his performance in the first presidential debate where President Obama struggled. Still, I spoke with Romney spokesman Kevin Madden a few days ago, who tried to draw me a picture of how they could win even without Ohio—including winning Wisconsin. I just don't buy it; they need Ohio's eighteen electoral votes."

Covering Obama, October 17, Athens - "A very enthusiastic crowd for the president here in Athens, these Democrats in a very good mood after the president's performance in the second debate last night. Some told me privately they were a little concerned with his lackadaisical performance in debate one. Polls have shown Mitt Romney slightly ahead in Ohio for the past couple of weeks, but the Obama campaign believes energy is picking up here on college campuses. They're also encouraged there will be weekend before the election voting, that's a stinging defeat for Republicans. They believe that could be the difference between Barack Obama winning or losing the Buckeye State."

Covering Obama, October 23, Dayton - "The president was relaxed the day after his final debate with Mitt Romney. This was the first joint appearance between Obama and Vice President Joe Biden since the Democratic Convention. We heard today about the president's record of cutting taxes for the middle class, bringing the troops home, and the auto industry coming back. He also developed a new phrase for Romney, "Romnesia."

Covering Biden, October 24, Marion - It was at this point, with two weeks to go, that I started to notice a considerable difference in the ground game in Ohio. I met volunteers who were flooding into the state to help the Obama campaign. Josh Albrektson was a young physician from Los Angeles who was taking two weeks off to help volunteer to get out the Obama vote. The fact that an M.D. from LA had made his way to central Ohio, knowing it was the key part of the state and likely to determine the presidency, stuck with me through election day.

In Marion I reported, "The Vice President is here in Marion County, an interesting choice for Democrats. It's a Republican county, but the actual city of Marion can go Democratic. Biden has spent three straight days in Ohio, and the campaign tells me there are volunteers arriving from Virginia and North Carolina. The campaign also tells me they've given up finding undecided voters. They are concentrating on getting out their targeted voters."

Covering Romney, October 25, Columbus - "A confident crowd today, about 3,000 strong. Romney pounded home the message he can create jobs with the unemployment rate remaining high. Scott Jennings from the Romney camp told me today they really don't know who is leading here. They believe, in his words, 'the campaign is dead even.' He believes Romney is outperforming McCain in four key urban areas."

Covering Romney, November 2, West Chester - "This is one of the largest rallies we've seen in the state of Ohio this year—30,000 strong for Mitt Romney. It was a 'who's who of Republicans'—Speaker of the House John Boehner, the 2008 Republican nominee John McCain, and Senator Marco Rubio were here, along with the Romney and Ryan families. I spoke with Rubio, South Carolina senator Lindsay Graham, and McCain who each told me they believe it's all down to Ohio."

"If he wins Ohio, he'll be moving into the White House," said Rubio.

"It's not about Ohio, it's about a handful of counties in Ohio, and Hamilton County went the other way four years ago, and it's why we're here tonight," Graham told me. "You and I both know Jim, we've been around long enough to know, that it's all coming down to turnout," McCain said. "We'll be up late waiting for Ohio, but I do sense momentum."

Covering Romney, Election Eve, Columbus - "Here we are on election eve, and the Romneys decide to spend it in Columbus, Ohio. Both campaigns believe Central Ohio will be the key to winning the state. The Romneys had a little difficulty tonight. After being introduced, their campaign plane attempted to pull into the hanger. It missed the mark, not once or twice, but three times, backing in and out while the song *Common Man* was blaring in the background. There is also a huge poster of Ohio, paid for by the Republican National Committee, hanging in here with Ohio painted in blue. Some supporters say they hope it's not an ominous sign for tomorrow."

Covering Obama, Election Eve, Columbus - "This has been by all accounts a political heavyweight fight. Barack Obama and Mitt Romney giving it everything they can in Ohio. Both campaigns tell me privately it's now all about turnout, forget the undecided voters."

"This state is important to us, we know that our message of fighting for working families is working with people here in Ohio," Jen Psaki, the Obama campaign spokeswoman told me. "So we'd much rather be us than the Romney campaign."

THE DEBATES

I was in the studio for the three presidential, and one vice presidential, debates offering live analysis on the 11 o'clock news. Working with executive producer Michael Gant, I picked three of the best soundbites from each event to highlight. "How will you know which to pick?" Michael asked before the first debate. "I know it when I hear it," I responded. The newsroom trusted my judgement, and that only comes after years of working with producers and earning mutual respect. (Although our editors weren't huge fans of my strategy of yelling "that's it!" to them when I heard a usable soundbite.)

President Obama faltered in the first debate while Romney had a near-perfect performance, but Obama got it together and finished strong in the third. The second town-hall style debate, with moderator Candy Crowley from CNN, provided this memorable exchange during discussion over the embassy attack in Benghazi, Libya:

Obama: "The day after the attack, Governor, I stood in the Rose Garden and I told the American people that this was an act of terror and I also said that we're going to hunt down those who committed this crime."

Romney: "I think it's interesting the President just said on the day after the attack he went into the Rose Garden and said that this was an act of terror."

Obama: "That's what I said."

Romney: "You said in the Rose Garden the day after the attack, it was an act of terror? It was not a spontaneous demonstration, is that what you're saying?"

Obama: "Please proceed Governor."

Romney: "I want to make sure we get that for the record because it took the president fourteen days before he called the attack in Benghazi an act of terror."

Obama: "Get the transcript."

At this point, Crowley, who was also the moderator of her own Sunday morning political show on CNN, interjected while looking at Romney.

Crowley: "It -- it -- it -- he did in fact, sir. So let me -- let me call it an act of terror."

Obama: "Can you say that a little louder, Candy?"

Crowley: "He did call it an act of terror. It did as well take two weeks or so for the whole idea of there being a riot out there, about this tape to come out. You are correct about that."

Crowley was right, Obama had, in fact, used the word "terror" the day following the attack. But administration officials had gone on television insisting for weeks the act was "spontaneous" and Obama did not use the word terrorism in a speech before the United Nations two weeks later. It would have been better, in my view, if Crowley—as moderator—had left the details to the press to work out after the debate, instead of trying to interject into such a hot issue where there were caveats to the story. This is one of those moments where it was best for the referee to leave it to the instant replay, instead of working it out on the floor.

The traveling to and from the endless rallies across Ohio was becoming a big blur, although I do recall in the closing days of the campaign David Muir's entourage at campaign events was quite the conversation. The heir-apparent to the ABC News anchor chair didn't travel lightly; there were plenty of photographers and producers nearby (and always a mirror). Other reporters would stand shoulder-to-shoulder on the riser waiting for our live shots and just shake our heads. Muir is never going to be confused for Peter Jennings.

Many of the national reporters, including Muir, wore jeans with a sports coat and tie while covering the campaign. I requested to wear the same outfit, but was denied by my producer Rochelle. At one point she ran into Carl Cameron from Fox News who was sporting the look. "Tell her it's acceptable!" I said to him, half-joking. For the next five minutes Rochelle and Carl argued about it. Heatedly. Rochelle never changed her mind.

After months of hearing U2's "City of Blinding Lights" introduce Obama and Kid Rock's "Born Free" introduce Romney at campaign rallies (Kid Rock actually performed the song live in West Chester) reporters were ready to delete them once-and-for all from our playlists. Unfortunately, Chevrolet picked up "Born Free" for their car ads, and every time it plays I suffer flashbacks of the circus of the campaign trail.

I was born free! I was born free. I was born free, born free.

ELECTION NIGHT

Our station had been on air covering the election since 7 p.m., running non-stop on our digital channel along with updates on 10TV. Just after the start of our 11 p.m. news, CBS anchor Scott Pelley interrupted us with this announcement:

"We are now projecting President Obama has been reelected. It is the state of Ohio that has done the trick for the President. CBS News is projecting President Obama has won the state of Ohio and that should be the end of this presidential race."

The networks calling the race while Romney was leading in Ohio led to a lot of viewer confusion and phone calls into the newsroom.

"Get out to the map and tell us why the projection is right!" my boss Elbert Tucker told me with a slap on the back. This was the moment I had waited for since starting my time in Ohio.

"First, the votes are all in, so these projections won't change the outcome in any way," I calmly told our viewers. "Mitt Romney is in the lead with nearly 80 percent of the vote counted, and that's why we haven't heard a concession from him yet, and Republicans have every right to say, 'let's just slow down' and let this play out. But look at the map (the Romney counties were in red, Obama in blue, and when I clicked on them the percentages popped up on screen) the problem here for Romney is that only 12 percent of the vote from Lucas County (Toledo) is in, and it's overwhelming for Obama. And only half the vote is in from Cuyahoga County (Cleveland) where Obama leads right now with 68 percent. So even though Romney has a slight lead, when you factor, as we have, where the remaining votes are coming from, we expect the president to catch up and go into the lead."

I was explaining this to viewers because over on Fox News, Karl Rove, whose Super PAC had spent around $300 million to back Romney—was complaining the networks had blown the call for Obama in Ohio. "I think this is premature," he said on air. "Remember, here is the thing about Ohio, a third of the vote or more is cast early and is won overwhelmingly by the Democrats. It's counted first and the question is, by the time you finish counting the Election Day votes, does it overcome that early advantage the Democrats have built up in early voting?"

It had become clear to me two hours earlier, along with strategists Terry Casey and Sam Gresham, Romney's totals in Republican-rich Clermont and Hancock counties were below the expectations predicted by his campaign. Republicans in Ohio typically have to carry the rural counties by a ratio of 2.5 or better to offset the massive amount of votes for Democrats in the urban population centers and we weren't seeing it happen.

"I have to be honest with you, if I'm in the Romney camp, alarm bells are beginning to go off," I told viewers an hour before the network call. "Look at these counties in coal country that went for John McCain in 2008. Right now they are too close to call. Our bellwether counties, when combined, show the president leading with 51 percent of the vote."

As Rove continued to insist the election wasn't over, I told anchors Jerry Revish and Kristyn Hartman, "we have a blueprint and road map in Ohio we can use to figure this out. Everyone be patient. The networks have it right. Romney had to perform a lot better in some counties where he just isn't."

Casey, a longtime Republican strategist in Ohio, told me off air that Rove was doing some funny math and kept us calm as Romney continued to lead up until midnight.

Then, as expected, the big wave of votes from Democratic areas came in, and Obama took the lead—for good. In the end, Obama received roughly 2.8 million votes in Ohio to 2.6 million for Romney and won 51 to 48 percent.

How did he win? A CBS exit poll showed Obama beating Romney among women voters by a 55 to 43 percent margin. Young voters in Ohio favored him by a 63 to 34 percent margin. And the "cares about me" factor went to Obama 84 to 15 percent.

"It all came down to Ohio, as many of us thought it would," said Bob Schieffer on CBS. "This is a state where the employment picture is better than it was in other parts of the country. Where the bailout of the auto companies had actually worked and yet Mitt Romney was on the wrong side of that. He had said it was better to let these companies go into forced bankruptcies, people took that as just let them go broke. It was the wrong state of all the states to be on the wrong side."

Top Romney supporters I called on election night were stunned he had lost the state. "We honestly didn't see this coming," Romney's state spokesman Chris Maloney told me. They had been confident Independents would break their way, but in reality Obama ended up winning their vote by ten points. Democrats, including Joyce Beatty, who was elected to Congress representing Columbus, had been confident going into election day. Beatty, who was from the "swingiest" part of the swing state, pointed to all the major polls showing Obama ahead by anywhere from one to five points. In fact, the polling average had the president ahead in Ohio by 2.9 percent which was right on the money.

Paul Ryan, as I had predicted when he was chosen, made no impact in Ohio. Just after midnight I said on air, "I can honestly say now at 12:15 in the morning if Senator Rob Portman is on this ticket, he would have been good for two or three percent for Romney's total because the enthusiasm level among GOP activists across the state, to have an Ohioan on the ticket, would have gone for Romney tonight."

We'll never know about Portman's impact. But I did make a bold prediction about John Kasich's future.

"If Governor Kasich is reelected in two years, he'd be a two-term governor of Ohio. No Republican has ever won the White House without Ohio, and he'd be in a good position. My prediction is we'll follow him to Iowa and New Hampshire after the 2014 election. His team tells me he's not interested, but time will tell."

He was interested alright.

Our election night coverage, which had lasted all night in 2004, wrapped up by 1 a.m., much to the delight of a tired 10TV crew. After arriving home I noticed Donald Trump had tweeted out, "Congrats to Karl Rove on blowing $400 million this cycle. Every race Crossroads GPS ran ads in, the Republicans lost. What a waste of money." The outspoken billionaire had backed another losing candidate and he was livid. *Could Trump seriously consider running himself in 2016?* I wondered to myself as the election night wound down. I chuckled out loud and thought, *certainly not, the political circus will never get that weird!*

A few months later, my colleagues Elbert Tucker, Rochelle Young, Tracy Townsend and I headed to Washington, D.C. to accept the *Walter Cronkite Award for Excellence in Television Political Journalism* award for our coverage of Campaign 2012. It was a wonderful and humbling conclusion to covering presidential politics in America's top battleground state.

It's probably no surprise that Ohio was considered to host both major political party conventions in 2016. While Democrats ultimately chose to head to Philadelphia, the Republicans picked Cleveland, an interesting move putting them in the traditionally Democratic part of the state.

"Hosting the Republican National Convention in Cleveland is a big win for Ohio and for our next presidential nominee," said state GOP chairman Matt Borges. "Republicans nationally will be focused on Ohio, the nation's most critical swing state."

Indeed. The presidential candidates keep coming and the circus never ends.

EPILOGUE

"I, Barack Hussein Obama, do solemnly swear..."

With the sun setting behind the U.S. Capitol, I was standing on the roof of the CBS building about to go live from the Inauguration in Washington, D.C., remembering how busy and frantic it was covering the presidential race in Ohio. When the dust finally settled after the election, we learned President Obama had invested more time, more offices, more staff, more technological resources, and more ads in Ohio than anywhere else. The end result was he had received another contract for four more years.

"...that I will faithfully execute the office of President of the United States..."

Obama's ground game in Ohio was far superior to Romney's. Obama had 123 offices up and operational in Ohio, compared to forty for Romney. The president also had more money for staff. That meant more manpower to identify supporters and get them to the polls. The Obama camp had targeted potential voters at barbershops and beauty salons, and "faith captains" were appointed at churches across the state to implement "Souls to the Polls."

The president also had a technological edge not only on social media, but in keeping up-to-date neighborhood information that was utilized on Election Day. Republicans and their special interest supporters, like the Koch brothers, have promised not to allow that disadvantage to happen again.

..."and will to the best of my ability, preserve, protect, and defend the Constitution of the United States..."

As a reporter who loves politics, and respects the people I cover, there is one alarm bell from 2012 which most concerns me: The Federal Election Commission says in 2012 more money was raised and spent on the election than there were people living on planet Earth.

Let your mind wrap around that for a second.

After reviewing about eleven million pages of documents, the FEC concluded about $7 billion was spent by candidates, political parties, and special interest groups. (Incidentally, there were 7.043 billion people on earth in 2012).

Barack Obama and Mitt Romney set records in the most expensive presidential election to date. Obama raised $1.123 billion, Romney $1.019 billion.

There is every indication 2016 will set an even higher record. Until the Citizens United decision is revisited, there will be even more cash flooding into our system, buying more influence, more legislation, and more politicians. We would be wise as Americans to remember democracy is about the debate of ideas, not the purchasing power of a select few.

"So help me God."

ABOUT THE AUTHOR

Jim Heath has logged thousands of hours covering campaigns and state government from Arizona to South Carolina to Ohio. He has also written, produced, and edited several documentaries on presidential elections. A recipient of the Walter Cronkite Award for Excellence in Television Political Journalism, Jim is also a two-time Emmy award winner for his political reporting. During the 2012 campaign, *GQ* Magazine listed Jim on their Top Five political "Power List" and the *Washington Post* named him to their "Best Super Tuesday Twitter List." You can follow Jim on Twitter at "JimHeathTV" or find him on Facebook under "Jim Heath." You can also find many of Jim's interviews and reports on YouTube under "Jim Heath" and "Jim Heath Documentaries."